CARDIGAN OF BALACLAVA

CARDIGAN
OF BALACLAVA

Piers Compton

ROBERT HALE & COMPANY

LONDON

ISBN 0 7091 3104 6

Robert Hale & Company
63 Old Brompton Road
London S.W.7

PRINTED IN GREAT BRITAIN
BY EBENEZER BAYLIS AND SON LIMITED
THE TRINITY PRESS, WORCESTER, AND LONDON

Contents

7

Contents

Illustrations

PICTURE CREDITS

Photographed by Henry Cooper and Son, reproduced by
courtesy of Mr. Edmund Brudenell: 1, 4, 17; *Radio Times*
Hulton Picture Library: 2, 5, 6, 8, 9, 10, 11, 13, 14, 15, 16,
18, 19; The Mansell Collection: 7, 20; City Art Gallery,
Manchester: 12

Acknowledgements

This book seeks to look behind the several features, some of them grossly exaggerated, from which the popular and erroneous image of Lord Cardigan has been compounded; and in doing so it takes on a task that Cardigan never attempted. For while he was always ready to advertise himself, he made not the slightest effort to influence the public.

He was too independent (or, if it be preferred, too haughty) ever to answer the stories propagated by journalists who, naturally enough, echoed the political and social viewpoints of the particular paper they served.

He came of two breeds that are the subjects of much misunderstanding today—being a soldier of the colourful kind that figured as a hero of romance, and, by birth, what our ancestors rightly and unashamedly called 'a gentleman'. On both those counts it is all too easy to fall in with the spirit of our age and tip the scales against him.

The appreciation of 'atmosphere' is an essential part of biography: and in that respect I must convey a special debt of gratitude to Mr. and Mrs. Edmund Brudenell of Deene Park, who more than once have given me access to the place where the leader of the Light Brigade lived for the quieter and more settled years of his life.

I was also greatly helped by Mr. P. I. King and the staff of the Northamptonshire Record Society, at Delapre Abbey, who made available the Brudenell papers.

The Marquess of Anglesey most kindly sent me two typescripts with permission to quote from them—the Crimean chapter from the forthcoming second volume of his *History of the British Cavalry*, and *Little Hodge*, the diary and letters of Colonel Edward

Cooper Hodge written during the Crimean War. This *Diary* is the source of anecdotes relating to Captain and Mrs. Forrest in the Crimea.

I am grateful to Mr. S. G. P. Ward for referring me to the *Memoirs of Prince zu Hohenlohe Ingelfingen*; to Mr. J. F. A. Mason, Fellow and librarian of Christ Church, Oxford; to Mr. F. Higenbottam, City Librarian of Canterbury; Mr. C. H. Shaw, librarian of Harrow School; to Prebendary G. A. Lewis Lloyd, Vicar of Chiswick; to Canon W. E. Watts and Doctor J. Elliott, both of Hambleden, Bucks; to Mr. R. P. McDouall of the Travellers' Club; and to Mrs. Margery Fisher of Ashton Manor, Northampton.

I must also record my debt to the following authors and publishers: Miss Joan Wake and Cassell and Co., for permission to draw upon anecdotes from *The Brudenells of Deene*; and Messrs. Michael Joseph who allowed me to quote from *Henry Clifford, V.C. His Letters and Sketches from the Crimea.*

My thanks are due to the Staffs of the War Office Library, the London Library, the British Museum Reading Rooms at Bloomsbury and at Colindale, and the Kensington Public Library.

P.C.

"We have no doubt the whole British Army has given Lord Hill [Commander-in-Chief] less trouble than the Earl of Cardigan."
The Morning Chronicle, December 1840

"To my mind there is something bordering upon the pathetic in the solitary and friendless figure which this distinguished, but unfortunate, military commander presents in the history of the Crimean War: his memory uncared for by one intimate and loving heart, proudly isolated and apart, with his reputation at the mercy of the verdict of a harsh and pitiless adjudicator."

W. H. Pennington, actor and formerly one of the 11th Hussars who served under Cardigan

PART ONE

From Cornet to Colonel

I

When Charles II, in the year following his proclamation as King (1661) conferred the title of Earl of Cardigan upon Thomas Brudenell, a Northamptonshire gentleman, he was redeeming a promise that his father, Charles I, had made to Brudenell during the Civil War.

Brudenell had been a staunch supporter of the Royalist cause. He was 'on the run' for a time as a fugitive; he was heavily fined and sent to the Tower. He supplied Charles I, when the latter was imprisoned in Carisbrooke Castle, with the sum of £1,000, which Charles promised to repay with the title of an earldom. But Charles was captured and executed before he could honour the pledge, and it was left for his son to elevate the old cavalier—and, incidentally, to sting him for another 'loan' of £1,000 at the same time.

The Brudenells had been settled at Deene, a village off the main road between Kettering and Stamford, since Tudor times. Their rise to prosperity had been quiet, without historical repercussions, and along the generally accepted line of law. The name Deene means 'valley', and the house, rebuilt and added to over the years, was originally a manor which passed into the possession of the Abbot of Westminster. Sir Robert Brudenell, Chief Justice of Common Pleas and a member of Henry VIII's Privy Council, took over the property in 1514.

The family acquired a certain notoriety towards the end of the sixteenth century, when Sir Edmund Brudenell, who married a Lincolnshire heiress, Agnes Bussy of Hougham, laid claim to his wife's ancestral home. The Bussys opposed this, and a long law suit developed that finally found its way to the Star Chamber. Agnes, while this was dragging on, sickened and died, and on the day of her funeral the disputed property, with other Bussy estates, passed to Edmund.

Always a somewhat sinister figure, Edmund was suspected of having poisoned his wife in order to consolidate his claim; and, whatever the truth, the present owner of Deene Park will tell you, in all seriousness, that the ghost of the troubled Edmund long haunted the house until structural alterations apparently caused the visitant to lose his way.

Thomas Brudenell, the first Earl of Cardigan, who inherited from his uncle John Brudenell in 1606, was under a cloud from the first. His wife was Mary, one of the Treshams of Rushton Hall, Northampton, a family not only Catholic at a time when that religion was proscribed, but one that was also suspected of conspiring against the Crown.

Although one of the first baronets created by James I after the founding of the order in 1611, Thomas was convicted of recusancy under the existing penal laws; and his unqualified support of the doomed Royalist cause furthered his ruin. After spending two years in the Tower and incurring a fine of £10,000, at the age of 80 he was again charged as a recusant and imprisoned for a time at Northampton. His belated earldom came in the year following the Restoration.

The second Earl of Cardigan, Robert, is noteworthy only on account of his daughter, Anna Maria, the wife of Lord Shrewsbury. Her behaviour caused comment at what might now be called the 'over permissive' Court of Charles II, and Samuel Pepys wrote of her with admirable frankness: "My Lady Shrewsbury, who is a whore, and is at this time, and hath for a great while been, a whore to the Duke of Buckingham. . . ."

The affair ended in a duel between the Duke and Shrewsbury, at which the latter was run through the body, dying some weeks later. Anna Maria, dressed as a page and holding the Duke's horse, watched the duel, and was not deterred from sleeping that night with her lover, who still wore the shirt that was spattered with her husband's blood.

For the next century the Brudenells, surrounded by their wealth and their acres, never deviated from the unobtrusive, kindly and generally respected pattern of life that was normal to the landed gentry.

George, the third Earl, who was born a Papist but who turned Protestant during the reign of Anne, lived in great state, hunted the fox, became Master of the Queen's Buckhounds, and married the sister of the Earl of Ailesbury, whose seat was in Wiltshire. When he died of a "bleeding of the nose", he left four sons, the youngest of whom, Thomas, was adopted by Ailesbury.

By a series of complicated legal dealings Ailesbury's other title, of Baron Bruce, passed to Thomas, who was later elevated to the peerage as the Earl of Ailesbury when his uncle died. The Bruce's possessions thus passed to a Brudenell; while the fact that Ailesbury controlled two seats in the Commons, Bedwyn and Marlborough (both in Wiltshire) was to have some bearing on the Brudenell story.

For some years the possessors of the Cardigan title remained in the rut of pedestrian dullness that was, however, well within the aura of the throne. George, the fourth Earl, was governor of the sons of George III. He was followed by James, who became Master of the Robes and later the governor of Windsor Castle.

James, who had no children, was succeeded by his nephew Robert, who was handsome, thoroughly staid, and content with a wife who came of a family that was vastly inferior, in terms of wealth, to the privileged Brudenells.

She was Penelope Anne Cooke of Harefield, in Middlesex; and Robert, at 24, had been sufficiently impressed by her pretty face to make the one determined stand in his life in order to marry her. He was reduced to tears by the objections of his relatives, who opposed the match; but Robert and his bride eventually settled at Hambleden, a village in South Buckinghamshire some 3 miles equidistant from Marlow and Henley-on-Thames.

Hambleden then comprised some 970 inhabitants, with 30 farms and 154 cottages. The home of Mr. and Mrs. Brudenell, as they were called, was a brick and flint Elizabethan manor, still standing, a little to the east of the parish church of St. Mary the Virgin.

Both Brudenells entered fully into the spirit of their rustic surroundings. She was obviously one of those women who exercised the privilege, as lady of the manor, of keeping a watchful and charitable eye on the village folk, the church, the children and

2

their schooling. The rector found her "sweet", with a mild and engaging temper. Her husband had some good qualities, though
the rector, without describing them, also noted his failings. They
took over a piece of land close to the village, which they let in lots
at a low rent to a number of the poorest inhabitants.

In course of time the Brudenells availed themselves of the courtly
influence that was open to the family. Robert became equerry to
Queen Charlotte, the wife of George III, and Penelope was
appointed Lady of the Bedchamber. A natural Tory, Robert sat
for the borough of Marlborough. In the Commons his convictions
only ever took shape as a positive "No!" whenever the question
of Catholic emancipation was raised.

A birth at the 'big house' was then an important event in an
English village; and there were several births at Hambleden
Manor to be celebrated. First came a son, who died in infancy,
and then a daughter. She was followed on 16th October 1797 by
James Thomas. Seven girls, of whom six survived, completed the
family. The second eldest girl, Harriet Georgina, was to marry
Richard, Earl Howe, who became Lord Chamberlain to Queen
Adelaide, wife of William IV. The youngest, Anne, married
George Charles, Lord Bingham, later the Earl of Lucan—a
domestic, normal enough happening that was, however, greatly
to influence the conduct and character of the male representative
of the Brudenells, who was the central figure in the christening
party that crossed from the manor to the church in the first week
of November.

The place is still quiet enough to admit the presence of spectres:
the proud mother, the plodding, jejune father; the nurse bearing
her precious burden who was destined—it was 5th November,
Gunpowder Day—to surround the name of Brudenell with
lightning and to shake the family tree to its very roots.

But family upheavals apart, the traditional soil and pastoral
quality of the air in which that tree had been nurtured were
becoming things of the past. Englishmen, looking over the
Channel to France, had seen a sky red with the embers of revolution, where the bodies of a murdered king and queen had been
mixed with clay in the pits of Paris. A young ex-captain of
artillery, Napoleon Bonaparte, at the head of an army of raga-
muffins, had struck into Italy to enlarge the frontiers of revolution.
In the name of that revolution new doctrines were being shaped

that would change the destiny of England, and to counter which the power of the Cardigans, and their like, would be exerted in vain.

Meantime his early years found the young James Thomas, who was to be a symbol of that struggle, surrounded by a bevy of worshipping sisters with their coloured silks, high waists, sashes, ringlets, gentle voices, and their small feet in flat shoes, a predominantly feminine atmosphere that would leave him with a sense of chivalry at a time that was only some few decades away from the age of elegance.

2

No definite date emerges from the school register, but it appears that the heir of the Brudenells went to Harrow in the year 1810 or 1811. He entered with the courtesy title of Lord Brudenell, as his father had by now become the sixth Earl of Cardigan. The family left Hambleden and divided their time between Deene Park and a London mansion in Portman Square to the north of the Oxford Road, an area described by the poet Robert Southey in 1807 as being "approached on one side by a road unlit, unpaved, and inaccessible by carriages".

The head of Harrow was then Doctor George Butler. As a boy of 12 Brudenell would have been placed in the lower remove of the fourth form, which made him liable for fagging. One of his duties was to field when the senior boys were at cricket; and in cold weather, or when some 'great man' entertained, he would be sent to the nearest public house for tumblers of hot rum punch; several inns flourished in the village street where the quiet was only broken by the coming and going of post-boys in their red, blue or yellow jackets, taking some local traveller by chaise to pick up a stage-coach.

Brudenell developed as a hunter, a rider, and a duellist. It is therefore likely that he was one of the dozen or so boys who subscribed to a pack of beagles. These enthusiasts, armed with whip and horn, had permission to leave school before daylight and to cover the farmland and lanes around Harrow in search of hares and rabbits.

Besides football and cricket, rackets were played in the school yard; but there is nothing to say whether Brudenell had much to do with games, though one thing may safely be asserted. His nature would not have allowed him to take part in the then highly fashionable fist-fights, where hearty young bucks, stripped to their shirts, slogged each other without mercy till one was felled or exhausted.

Other questions may turn on whether or not he made good use of his study, one of a row of closets with a fixed table and a small barred window; or whether he knew of another Harrovian, the son of Mad Jack Byron and author of the recently famous *Childe Harold*, who had limped his way to a tomb in the church-yard and there meditated for hours with his eyes on the view stretching away towards Windsor.

Two school customs of the time, that of 'rolling in' and of being 'tossed into the shell', must have been known to Brudenell. The first was observed whenever a boy was promoted from the common breakfast-room to the sixth-form room, where break-fast and tea were taken. The boy would sit in a corner of the hall, with his head covered by his coat-collar and his hands, resting on the table. Those who were to pilot him through the ceremony stood on benches and tables at the other end of the hall. Near them was a large basket of hard-baked rolls; and when the boy to be initiated put a plate against his head it was the signal for his fellows to bombard the plate with the rolls. The plate was soon knocked to pieces, whereupon the boy himself became the target till the ammunition gave out. He could then count himself a member of the hall.

When a boy was moved from the fourth form into the shell, the process was a little more painful. It took place in a low-ceilinged room, after evening prayers. The boy to be tossed stood upright, minus jacket and shoes, on a blanket, which was seized and stretched out by as many as could gather about it. A vigorous tossing up and down caused the victim's head to bump against the ceiling, eventually bringing down laths and plaster till the eyes of all concerned were blinded and smarting beyond endurance.

Brudenell had left Harrow by 1813; and for the next year or two his education did not proceed along normal scholastic lines. Instead he was developing the tastes and qualities of an English landed proprietor and inheriting the traditions that, in his parti-cular case, went with them—those of the Midlands, and of a great horse-riding community.

Deene Park is in the midst of an agricultural county that was studded with the lordly homes of noblemen, squires, and of yeomen who had risen above their kind. The traveller John Norden, writing in 1610, said that Northamptonshire, "a most pleasant" part of the realm, had "allured" large numbers of the wealthy to be "seated in those parts". William Camden later referred to the shire as being "everywhere adorned with noblemen's and gentlemen's homes".

This concentration of wealth allowed for the indulgence of architectural fashions, so that old Gothic flourished alongside Tudor and Jacobean designs, and the neo-classic style that found its way to England from Italy. A combination of these different but not wildly opposing tendencies is reflected in the ornament, detail, and the general character of Deene Park.

With the virtual disappearance of the old English gentry, we are apt to forget how large a part the horse played in their character, make-up, and day-to-day existence. Men took pride in jumping impossible fences, or in seeking to emulate the whip who took horse, chaise and all over a turnpike-gate, with every stitch and buckle left intact. Fox hunting with the hounds out of cover and in full cry; feats in the field, what jumps had been cleared and the qualities of this or that hunter; the echoes of a modulated "Holloa!" and where the scent had lasted perhaps till moonrise, were then perennial topics of conversation.

Such things were not merely recreations, still less amusements. They were the free life of the time as it was known to young Brudenell when he rode with the Pytchley through the wooded stretches of Rockingham Forest and across the grassy uplands of High Leicestershire. Pytchley was said to have the best wooded runs in the world, though according to the diarist Thomas Creevey, members of the Pytchley (where the annual subscription was ten guineas, with a further ten payable on election) were "very second rate to the Quorn or Melton men". Brudenell followed the hounds of all three hunts.

A superb rider and a good jumper, he took his falls with the best. The most serious fall when his hunter, after a tiring run, failed to clear a gate, left him senseless for a day and a night. But his sporting prowess did not extend to swimming. There is the much quoted incident of Brudenell and a male relative, at the end of a long day, galloping hard to see who would be first home.

Coming to the River Welland, both spurred their tired horses into the water and were swept out of their saddles. Brudenell was soon in trouble; but such was his determination not to be beaten at the post that he gasped to his companion, who was making easy work of the Welland, "Don't forget, I was in first."

These interests apart, however, young Brudenell's mind was fixed upon a certain objective that his parents did not at first approve. For instead of following the usual round of sport and travel, and then settling down to a privileged existence on the family estate, he wished to become a soldier. As their only son his parents wished to keep him safely at home, within their compass. The Brudenells were not a military-minded race, and such an aspiration on the part of the heir was a marked deviation from type.

There was much in the news and conversation of the time to encourage his ambition. For during his formative years the map of Europe was being changed by the sword. The "invincible phalanx" that was Napoleon's Army had overrun Spain, and the English had sent a young Lieutenant-General, Sir Arthur Wellesley, to counter the thrusts and strategy of the French marshals on the ridge at Vimeiro, and later on the wide dusty plain of Talavera, overlooked by the rounded hills and the tall sierras. Sir John Moore had been carried to his grave by lantern-light on the field of Corunna, and in the autumn of the same year Wellesley emerged as Lord Wellington, high-nosed and tightly buttoned as ever in his frock coat.

The summer of 1812 brought tidings of Salamanca, where a regiment that Brudenell would one day make famous, the 11th Light Dragoons, took part in a charge that routed the French left. Then had come the misty June morning when, having seen his redcoats triumph at Vittoria, Wellington pointed over the Pyrenees to the open passes that led to the courtyard at Fontainebleau, where Napoleon said farewell to the last of his legions; and so, it was thought, with the signing of the Peace of Paris the long war came to an end.

It had not been uncommon for young men of Brudenell's age to serve in the Peninsula; and he must have looked on the celebrations that marked the 'downfall of the tyrant' as the close of a revolutionary epoch in which his ambition might have been realized.

As it was, he was due to go to Oxford at Michaelmas 1815.

There were quiet days ahead, in which England could develop her Romantic heritage. It was true that fanatics like the poet Shelley, and a handful of political extremists, were trying to beat the tin drum of revolution. But Shelley had been sent down from Oxford, and there was now another and more domestic breed represented by the mature Wordsworth, stamp distributor and lyrical anti-classicist, who was settled at Grasmere. John Keats was walking the wards of Guy's and St. Thomas's. Sir Walter Scott's *Waverley* had set in motion his long pageant of novels. A young woman in a mob cap, who refused to let the noises of a Europe in turmoil penetrate to her parlour, was busy over *Mansfield Park*. The waltz was heard for the first time in London ballrooms, where a smiling bevy of Charlottes and Amelias succumbed to its giddy pleasures; Lord Wellington was elevated to a dukedom; and the mountain of gouty flesh that was Louis XVIII had subsided on the throne of France.

But the quiet was short lived. On a night of full moon in February 1815, Napoleon slipped out of Elba, and four months later Wellington's "infamous army", following the line that the Duke had traced on a map with his thumb-nail on the evening of the Duchess of Richmond's ball, took its stand on the rain-sodden ridge of Waterloo. The young Lord Brudenell knew several of the men, scarcely older than himself, who stood in square to receive the French charges, and who waved their swords to encourage the volley that shattered the Imperial Guard. The battle brought another reminder of the 11th Light Dragoons, who swept over the sunset-reddened field to sabre the last of the French gunners who kept their battery in action.

That year, as it passed into autumn, brought a firmer promise of peace than the one that had preceded it. Wellington had brushed away the tears that sprang to his eyes when he read the casualty returns of Waterloo; the Allies marched into Paris, re-establishing the power of the old régime with their bayonets; and James Thomas Brudenell was admitted to Christ Church, Oxford, on 21st November. Two days later he matriculated as a member of the university.

For some half a century Christ Church (the original Cardinal College founded by Wolsey in 1546) had been the college most favoured by young men of rank and fashion. Christ Church pride, and the privileges that went with it, such as the right to influence academical contests and elections, and even the election of burgesses to Parliament, were very real things. This eminence had been achieved under Dean Cyril Jackson, who was largely responsible for introducing the public examination system which, during Brudenell's time at Oxford, took the place of the college exercises which had hitherto been required for a degree.

But no lasting profit was derived from Jackson's high standards. Under Dean Hall, who was appointed in 1809, discipline relaxed to such an extent that Brudenell entered a community remarkable for the low tone, heartlessness and viciousness of its conversation; given over to "disgraceful irreverences" in chapel; and so vandal-like in its treatment of the library that undergraduates were forbidden to take out books except under supervision.

For one thing the college was overcrowded. Some under-graduates were sleeping in shelving garrets or even in the cellars. Some who could not be fitted into any hole or corner were sent home. But Brudenell, who entered on a privileged footing, and who therefore paid a higher tuition fee, avoided any such extremes of Christ Church austerity.

His tutor was probably the senior censor, or disciplinary officer of the college, William Corne, to whom Brudenell's deposit or 'caution money' was paid. Brudenell wore a silk gown with gold brocade that, according to an ancient statute, was the academical dress proper to the sons of peers. He brought his own servants and horses to the university, and provided his own food. The books he read each term included the *Orations* of Cicero (1815); Herodotus, book one; Livy, book three, and the *Odes* of Horace, book one (1816); Herodotus, book nine, and Virgil's *Eclogues* (1817).

A typical instance of the influence exerted by Christ Church, and in which Brudenell shared, occurred under Dean Hall. A seat in Parliament, previously held by the Speaker, fell vacant, and the question of filling it was referred to the Dean. At a meet-ing of college officers he proposed George Canning, the future Prime Minister; but this nomination was thwarted by Brudenell's tutor, Corne. The name of Robert Peel, whom some remembered arriving at Christ Church in 1805 as a fair-haired, smiling boy, was then put forward, and this was accepted. The Chapter and students of the college were then informed, and after a canvass of Christ Church voters Peel was elected without a contest.

This odd procedure might well have been reckoned on to provoke Radical opposition, especially when established creeds were being challenged by the doctrines of Rousseau, Tom Paine and Jeremy Bentham. Merton and Exeter Colleges were tainted with Whiggery. University College had heard the excruciating voice of Shelley raised in revolt. John Keble, staid author of *The Christian Year* and a coming leader of the Oxford Movement, responded to a temporary touch of the heady fervour by flinging a bottle that damaged a sundial at Corpus Christi. But the conservatism of Oxford in general, and of Christ Church in particular, was never in doubt; and foremost among the opponents of dissent was the young Lord Brudenell.

Trained in command, and in the privilege that implied responsibility towards the structures of States and society, he had already taken his stand as an unflinching defender of the Throne, the Church, and the proven order of established things, in a way that was to make him a target for ostensible reformers all his days.

With politics never a prime interest, and with his mind fixed on soldiering, whatever distinction he gained at Oxford was in sporting rather than in student circles. There was tandem driving, hack riding, and hunting for those who, like Lord Brudenell, could afford it. He was a daring rider, careless of his neck, and ready to mount the most dangerous brute that was saddled and waiting for him outside the Canterbury Gate in Merton Street. As one of the figures who was to attain the super-reality of a legend he can easily be pictured—tall with a narrow waist (his enemies were to invest him with corsets), long supple legs, auburn-tinted hair and whiskers, high-nosed, his blue eyes flashing contempt for many of the precepts by which lesser mortals pretended to be bound; striding, already the incipient cavalryman, through Tom Quad and Peckwater; perhaps rubbing shoulders in the street with a freshman at Trinity, John Henry Newman, with Thomas Arnold, who was destined to give a new tone to public schools, or with a grotesque figure in a clerical collar, Richard Harris ('Ingoldsby') Barham.

Brudenell left Oxford at the end of the Hilary Term 1818. He left his 'caution money' in his account there and so remained on the books of Christ Church. The fact that he did so may argue (as a present member of the college says) that he had some affection for the place.

3

After Oxford, Brudenell took advantage of his Ailesbury connection to enter Parliament. On 18th February he underwent the
formal process of being elected for the pocket borough of
Marlborough, which meant that by the time he was 21 he was
fully launched into public—and London—life.

The London he knew was ringed by suburban villages, market
gardens and fields. Portman Square, where the Cardigans had
their residence, was one of the favoured spots that, together with
Grosvenor, Hanover and Berkeley Squares, and Piccadilly, made
up the town preserves of the leisured classes. Trees flourished in
the West End; coaches, landaus and barouches brought visitors to
the steps of mansions, where they were met by liveried servants,
often coloured, with padded calves and family badges in their
hats. Beyond these quiet squares and courts that, together with
Westminster and the clubs of Pall Mall and St. James's, defined
the London with which Brudenell was acquainted, the busy
tide of everyday life flowed along narrow pavements and
thoroughfares where vehicles of every kind grated over the
cobbles.

An easy walk in any direction brought one to the country of
long grass, brooks and streams, and cattle in pasture. Wild game
rose into the air from marshes when the guns of sportsmen
echoed over the grounds of Buckingham Palace. Fields of hay
stirred in the wind blowing from Paddington Canal. The innova-
tion most noted by men like Brudenell, who had their being in
the shires, was the flickering of gas jets from dark till dawn in the
main streets.

Brudenell took his seat at a time when the landed classes were
letting their age-long control of the reins of legislation slip
through their fingers. They exercised authority as of right, but
carelessly and with consummate ease, regarding the House as a
pleasant centre away from home where they could lounge,
snooze, or sometimes listen to a debate that meant nothing except
to the speakers.

Brudenell never veered from his heritage of strong Tory convictions. But at this stage he lacked the maturity, and probably

the probing intelligence, to be swayed by the warnings of some older men who saw the rise of a new class, created by the wealth of the Industrial Revolution, as a growing political force that would one day overwhelm them.

Their appearance of menace was somewhat blunted by their general lack of breeding, which made them seem too distant, from those of the old school, to be taken quite seriously. Instead of coming from the broad acres, they were backed by machines. They were Radicals mostly from the north who, though richer than many of the lords in government, promoted agitations, such as the demand for universal suffrage, that were echoed by the rising multitude of dissatisfied urban and working populations, whose lot had been worsened by the enclosure of the common lands, the disastrous economic effects of a long war, and the sudden surge of manufacturing power that drove many to forsake the country crafts by which they had lived.

The Radicals were a growing force in the Commons. The reforms they advocated acquired the moral consistency and strength of catchpenny phrases. But the privileged, hereditary, or merely ornamental legislators, unaware that they were already under siege, reposed on their benches, scarcely regarding the intrusive, voluble, active, and badly groomed apostles of change.

Soon after his election to Parliament, Brudenell went on a tour of Europe. On his return he became one of the founder members of the Travellers' Club, which was in the then recently named Waterloo Place, off Pall Mall.

His page in the candidate's book, dated 10th August 1819, records that he qualified according to the club's regulation (still in force) that those elected must have travelled 500 miles from London out of the British Isles: and Brudenell's tour had included visits to Russia, Italy, and Sweden.

It may be assumed that Brudenell, having entered Parliament as a matter of course, regarded the House as little more than a club where he could at least feel that, merely by attending, he discharged some part of his obligation as a future landed proprietor. He also, about this time, took a first step towards the military career that was always the goal of his ambition. There were strong parental objections to his being a soldier, but the Yeomanry, with its uniform and drill, offered a safe part-time occupation for a young man with martial ardour to be expended.

Special forces of foot volunteers and yeomen had been raised, for home defence, during the threat of a French invasion. The Yeomanry troops were mostly recruited from farmers' sons, or men with a stake in the land, who could normally be expected to find their own mounts. In the absence of a regular police force, they were frequently called on to aid the civil power in suppressing riots, with the result that they were far less popular in the big towns than in the counties.

The colonel of the Northamptonshire Yeomanry was Earl Spencer, and the lieutenant-colonel a local squire, William Ralph Cartwright, whose estate was at Aynho. The badge of the corps was the white horse, a tribal sign of the Saxons that had been brought into England by the Hanoverians. It was to Cartwright that Brudenell wrote, with his father's permission, offering to raise a Deene troop. The regiment was never under strength, and there were then eleven troops based on various centres.

Cartwright's reply could hardly be other than favourable, especially as outbreaks of mob violence continued in several parts of the country; and in accepting Brudenell's offer he went on to say that "all loyal subjects ought to feel much indebted to your Lordship for so praiseworthy a step at so critical a moment".

So the 12th (Deene) troop of Northamptonshire Yeomanry was formed. Lord Brudenell, who became its captain, at once revealed himself as a military perfectionist whose demands were sometimes excessive, often not appreciated, but which would one day produce a brigade of unexampled discipline and courage.

It was customary to obtain the services of regular cavalry officers for the training of Yeomanry: but failing that, and touching Brudenell's qualifications for commanding a troop, albeit an irregular one, he must have studied the abridged manual of cavalry regulations which gave instructions on the various roles in which Yeomanry were employed, such as providing escorts, and the precautions to be observed when moving through turbulent districts.

Brudenell was commissioned in the Yeomanry on 14th December 1819. In the same month the privates, non-commissioned officers and the trumpeter of his troop were fitted with gold-laced jackets, overalls and cloaks, paid for out of a county fund to which Lord Brudenell was the largest individual contributor. Officers were responsible for their own clothing and saddlery, supplied by the Northampton firm of Stanton, Dunkley and Walker; privates found their own horse.

There was great excitement at Deene Park, and the Brudenell girls expressed new pride in their brother, when a corporal and three privates, of the 22nd Regiment of Foot, arrived from the Office of Ordnance, Weedon, with arms from the regular store—swords with scabbards, light cavalry belts, buff leather knots and pistols—for the fifty-eight men of the local troop.

There was much drumming of hoofs, shouted words of command in Brudenell's somewhat hoarse voice, and shrilling of trumpets to break the serenity of the park when the Deene tenantry, local farmers and sportsmen put on their uniforms (and some of the Yeomanry were peacock proud) to model themselves as best they could on the squadrons that had thundered over the dusty levels of Spain, with sabres flashing bare, as the Duke raised his hat.

It may be that Brudenell, even in this amateur capacity, was already known as a martinet. For when he tried to obtain the transfer of a certain Robert Sharade, a member of the Oundle squadron, to the Deene troop, with the rank of subaltern, Sharade replied that such a move would weaken the regiment. "I don't mean by this to arrogate anything to myself, but the men have said as long as I remain they would, and if I were to withdraw they would do the same."

One of Lord Brudenell's uncles, on his mother's side, was a soldier, Colonel Sir Henry Frederick Cooke. He served at Waterloo, and later became a private aide-de-camp to the Duke of York, the "rare old Duke" of the rhyme who marched his men up hill then down again. It may be that Colonel Cooke influenced the Earl of Cardigan to think more favourably of the military profession: for in 1824, when James Thomas was 26, there were "certain family reasons" (the words are Brudenell's) that enabled him, at that somewhat advanced age for an ensign or cornet, to enter the army.

Apart from the Duke of York's influence, the way was made easy for him by the system, then in force, of purchasing commissions. The sums involved varied according to the type and standing of the regiment. A fairly modest sum could buy a commission in an ordinary line regiment; but it needed real money to wear an epaulette in the Guards or the Household Cavalry. The system had obvious drawbacks. It was not proof against bribery in high places; bunglers could be hoisted into commands for which they were unfitted, while men of talent who chanced to be poor were often passed over.

But there was nothing in the system to justify its wholesale condemnation by critics who fail to realize that leadership demands special qualities of habit, self-discipline and tradition, standards that cannot be produced by a few years of democratic thought and training. Money could lead to the rapid promotion of inexperienced officers over the heads of those who had seen years of service; but British military records in the Peninsula, for example, show that men who had purchased their commands were not found wanting in the field, while their courage was never in doubt.

Most officers favoured the system, and agreed with Wellington who later was to say: "It is the promotion by purchase which brings into the service men of fortune and education, men who have some connection with the interests and fortunes of the country besides the commissions which they hold. It is this circumstance which excepts the British Army from the character of being a mercenary army, and has rendered its employment for nearly a century and a half not only consistent with the constitutional privileges of the country, but safe and beneficial." Wellington, like Wolfe, had climbed by the ladder of purchase, and both had ridden at the head of regiments while still in their twenties.

Critics of the system also forget that few officers could, at that time, maintain the form that most regiments demanded simply on their pay. It was pointed out by the future Lord Panmure, Secretary for War, that British officers were the hardest worked and the least rewarded of all public servants. The pay of a lieutenant-colonel, when essential deductions had been made, was just over £100 a year. But despite the fact that some separate income was almost a necessity for officers of every grade, promotion from the ranks was more common than is generally believed; though it was known that soldiers less readily deferred to one of their own kind than they did to those whom they recognized as superior in birth and education. Rifleman Harris, who served with the 95th in Sir John Moore's retreat to Corunna, endorsed the views of many of his kind when he wrote in his *Recollections*: "Whatever folks may say upon the matter, I know from experience that in our army the men like best to be officered by gentlemen."

Armed with his father's consent, and a recommendation from Colonel Cooke, Brudenell presented himself to the Duke of York. The Duke promised to take a more than perfunctory interest in the candidate for military glory, saying that if Brudenell applied himself seriously to the service his rapid promotion would be assured.

There was no need to make that proviso. Few budding soldiers can ever have been more eager than James Thomas Brudenell, who, having decided to enter the cavalry, was gazetted cornet in the 8th (King's Royal Irish) Hussars on 6th May 1824.

4

The 8th Hussars, at first red-coated and called Dragoons, were raised in 1693. Drawn mostly from Ulster, they were pledged to support William III, who, five years earlier, had occupied the throne in place of the lawful King James II. Recruits to the regiment, from which Catholics were excluded, were called on to swear "to be true to our Sovereign Lord and Lady King William and Queen Mary". In 1776 they were classified as the 8th Kings's Royal Irish Light Dragoons, but some years later they became Hussars. The word 'hussar' is derived from the Hungarian *husz-ar*, meaning twentieth. It refers to the system employed in the fifteenth century when Hungary was at war, whereby one man out of every twenty was summoned to serve in a body of horsemen against the Turk.

With their new title, the 8th adopted the blue dress and undress jackets common to all hussars; their badge was the harp and crown.

When Brudenell joined, the regiment was quartered at Norwich and later at Ipswich, under Lieutenant-Colonel the Hon. Henry Westenra. He was neither an efficient nor energetic soldier, and discipline suffered accordingly. From the time he first put on uniform Brudenell showed the rigid respect for orders (whether issued by others or himself), the tireless application and the sometimes pedantic attention to detail that distinguished him all his life; and it must have been hard for him to keep silent when observing irregularities, such as men being absent from barracks at unusual hours, that passed without notice.

His expert eye found much to criticize in the horses, which were too young and of varied description. He deprecated too the type of schoolboy ragging indulged by the cornets, younger than himself, and to which, as a newcomer intent on his duties, he probably submitted with a bad grace.

Colonel Westenra soon retired and was succeeded by Lord George William Russell. Some years earlier an official manual had been issued, *Instructions in Military Equitation and in all the elements of Field Movements of Cavalry*, and the new colonel introduced a number of reforms in the regiment. After an inspection at Brighton, in 1826, the horses and the privates were commended as being "reasonably good", while in field exercises the regiment moved with great steadiness, but not, it was added, "with great celerity".

Over the next few years Brudenell sampled quarters at a variety of southern cavalry stations including Christchurch (Hampshire), Dorchester, Canterbury, Hounslow and Hampton Court. Then came a period of service in Dublin, where the Hussars acted as armed peacemakers, coming between rival gatherings of Catholics and Orangemen. They were also more actively engaged in suppressing the threats of a national revolt when the two sides, as not infrequently happened, joined forces and turned on the troops.

Brudenell was now fairly embarked on his chosen career. In January 1825 he was gazetted lieutenant; before another six months were out he was promoted captain, in command of a troop. The Duke of York was proving loyal to his promise, though without his backing Brudenell's zeal was such as to merit advancement. Those who disliked him most could never accuse him of slackness. But together with his dash and devotion to duty he developed a colossal self-confidence, a belief in his own untried powers of co-ordinated command. He watched with an eagle eye for a chance to put them into practice. He felt it could not be long delayed, especially after serving for a time on the Staff at Dublin, where his chief was Major-General Sir Charles Dalbiac, a Peninsular veteran. Russell retired from the regiment and was followed by the Hon. George Berkeley, a young colonel of 28, while Captain Lord Brudenell was nearing 30.

But in spite of, or maybe because of, these changes in command, Brudenell saw that the regiment was not living up to the improved reputation it had earned at Brighton. After inspecting it, General Dalbiac reprimanded the non-commissioned officers, especially the sergeants, for failing to inspire a proper respect in the men. If there was no improvement in their deportment, he warned that it would be his duty "to bring the matter under the special consideration of the General Commanding-in-Chief", Lord Hill. Brudenell agreed that the stricture was deserved.

A little later part of the regiment, with Brudenell at the head of his troop, marched northward to Dundalk, overlooking the bay of that name, in County Louth. There had been another change in command and the colonel was now the Hon. G. B. Molyneux, who was absent at the time of the move. The Major was indisposed, and Captain Brudenell, as senior officer present, grasped his opportunity and took charge.

It was winter, but it might have been summer on the Downs, for he ordered a field day, risking the confusion that resulted from his precipitate will to lead, and leaving the horses in bad condition. When the Colonel returned, he inflicted on Captain Brudenell a reprimand that (as one who was present said) ought of itself to have been a check on his judgment for the rest of his military career.

But Brudenell was not be to deflected from what he felt to be his duty, and in pursuit of which he devoted less and less time to his political obligations. On entering the army, formal procedure demanded that he gave up the Marlborough seat. He was then just as formally re-elected, but he later resigned the seat when a difference developed between him and his patron, Lord Ailesbury.

Conditions in Ireland could in no way be judged by the Anglo-Irish social life that flourished in Dublin. The desire for independence, the bitterness engendered by the obsolete landlord system, found expression in futile but continued attempts at insurrection throughout the counties.

But for Captain Brudenell and others of the foreign (Protestant) garrison, regular military duties were far from arduous—guard mounting at the Bank of Ireland and at the Royal Barracks, reviews in Phoenix Park; while between these there were picnic parties at Powerscourt and the Dargle, balls at the castle and in the candle-lit drawing-rooms of Merrion Square, where uniformed cavaliers and girls in silk or damask gowns moved in the latest dances from Paris and Vienna.

Meanwhile the discipline of which Brudenell was a foremost exponent was having its effect upon the regiment. In the process, courts martial became a frequent occurrence, numbering nearly fifty in the space of fifteen months; and at the end of that time General Dalbiac reversed his earlier judgment and declared the 8th Hussars to be "a most excellent and most efficient corps".

But between the regiment's spells of service in English and Irish garrisons there had been an event in which Lord Brudenell, flooded by the limelight of scandal, made the first of his many appearances upon the public stage.

5

No date can be given, but probably at some time following his travels Lord Brudenell had made the acquaintance of the Tollemache family, then living at Ham House near Richmond, Surrey. The Cardigans owned a house in the vicinity, Cardigan House in Terrace Walk on Richmond Hill, built on the site of a rowdy place of amusement, called Richmond Wells, where dancing and gambling flourished in the time of William III.

The new property, described as having "pendant gardens" that were almost in the river, and where trees were set so thick as almost to shut out the sun, was built for the Cardigans late in the eighteenth century: and the fact that Lord Brudenell and his parents paid more than passing visits to the place is shown by their being listed among the regular pew-holders at the nearby church of St. Peter, in Petersham village.

There were nine Tollemache daughters, and the eldest, Elizabeth, had married in 1817 an old friend of the Brudenells. He was Frederick Christian Johnstone, then a half-pay captain in the 19th Lancers.

Elizabeth's parents were Admiral John Richard Halliday (who assumed the surname of Tollemache), and Lady Elizabeth Stratford, a daughter of the Earl of Aldborough.

Something of the Admiral's perverse and stormy nature

entered into the future Mrs. Johnstone. He once threw a
Frenchman who annoyed him out of the window; he was not
above spanking a pert young woman: and although a convinced
Tory, he fought an election as Radical candidate for Cheshire.

Elizabeth was passionate and unstable. Her finely chiselled
mouth, and big eyes loaded with innocent pleading, were set in
a delicate oval face. But behind the melting expression and the
artless fairy-like charm, was a petulant spirit bent on little else
than its own satisfaction.

Knowing that her father was against the marriage, Elizabeth
was all the more determined to carry it through. But within
twelve weeks it had broken down. Johnstone was the first to
admit it by going to the Admiral and saying that he wanted a
separation. His income was too modest for Elizabeth's needs, and
she showed her resentment of this by making life impossible.

The Admiral attempted to talk his daughter into a better frame
of mind, but only made things worse. Both became angry: her
temper was equal to his: she had finished with Johnstone. Red-
faced and fuming, the Admiral heard the door slam behind her.

When next he heard of Elizabeth she was staying in Paris with
her grandmother, Lady Aldborough, who was a hardened old
fille de joie who used barrack-room language and spoke of her
amorous past without reserve. The gossip Thomas Creevey des-
cribes her as being rouged up to the eyes and wearing huge
diamond ear-rings and an opera hat. She was thoroughly at home
in the Paris of Louis XVIII that was striving hard to forget the
Revolution and to promote, as the Countess of Granville said, "a
return to amusement, hats, and flowers". There were splendid
balls, fashionable parades in the Tuileries, concerts at the Palais
Royal; every hostess of reputation was 'at home' three days in the
week, the approved hours being from nine to midnight;
restaurants, now frequented by ladies for the first time, produced
bills of fare containing upward of two or three hundred dishes.

Elizabeth, piloted by the notorious dowager, entered fully into
the round of gaiety and pleasure from which she had been
debarred ever since marriage. Then came an unfortunate reminder
of her husband. She discovered that she was pregnant, and went
back to England. In a half-hearted attempt to tide things over the
Johnstones settled at the Berkshire village of Englefield Green,
where a daughter was born.

But as soon as she was well enough to quarrel Elizabeth broke out again, and in 1823, while the Captain was visiting friends in the West Country, she repaired to Ham House and told her father that she was again leaving Johnstone, this time for good. The Admiral shouted; Elizabeth, whose spirit belied her frail appearance, shouted back. But neither gave way, and Elizabeth returned to Paris where she met Lord Brudenell, who was passing through France while making a tour of European countries.

Brudenell, chivalrous to the backbone where women were concerned, was a natural knight-errant. There was much in Elizabeth, her plight as a sadly disillusioned woman who had not been appreciated by her husband, her suggestion of tears behind a fragile and gentle exterior, that appealed to him; while Brudenell's gallantry, and his fortune, produced a similar effect upon Elizabeth. They withdrew from Lady Aldborough's hectic circle and showed a mutual contempt for the society to which they would have to return by openly living together at Versailles.

So much was learnt by Johnstone when he went in search of his wife: and as a result he brought against Lord Brudenell an action for damages which was heard at the Sheriff's Court, Red Lion Square, on 23rd June 1824.

Brudenell offered no defence and was represented by counsel who declared that his client was a nobleman of the strictest honour, as shown by his insisting that no reflection was to be made either upon the lady or the plaintiff in the case. He could not be accused, counsel said, of having played the part of a seducer. Reference was made to "Lord Brudenell's violent and irresistible attachment", and to the lady who had become "the partner of his cares"—a lady, as counsel reminded the court, of great personal charm and distinguished beauty.

It was pointed out (at a time when large families were taken for granted) that only one child had been born to the Johnstones after six years of married life—which surely indicated a lack of affection between them. Counsel insisted, more than once, that nothing had occurred between Mrs. Johnstone and Lord Brudenell until the lady had left her husband; but as it was, his client would willingly submit to such damages as the jury might think it proper to award.

Johnstone's counsel invited the jury to consider the painful condition of the Tollemache family. They had lost, by death, three lovely children in as many months; now had come a further catastrophe—the seduction of a fourth daughter . . . the Captain's damages were assessed at £1,000.

About this time Brudenell became involved in his first recorded duel. He had his own sometimes peculiar code of honour, which would certainly have led him to agree with his counsel's dismissal of the charge of seduction against him; and when he heard that one of his sisters had been 'badly treated' (whatever that may mean) by a certain Gill Heathcote, his sense of chivalry and of family pride led him to challenge Heathcote to a duel in which, apparently, neither received a scratch.

Now Heathcote was Elizabeth Johnstone's cousin; and the humour of the situation was seized on by the scandal-loving Lady Derby, who remarked to gossip Creevey that Heathcote should have said, when taking aim: "And now, my Lord, I must beg you to receive my shot for your conduct to my cousin." Creevey agreed that such a declaration would have been "damned fair".

Lady Cardigan died on 2nd February 1826. Her reserved nature, which seems to have avoided, if not shrunk from the common gaze, must have been acutely distressed by her son's flagrant emergence as co-respondent.

The machinery of divorce was then cumbersome, slow moving and very costly. Until 1858 all jurisdiction in matrimonial matters was vested only in the ecclesiastical courts, and it required a special Act of Parliament before a marriage could be dissolved. The Johnstone divorce was not made valid until 1826: and on 19th June that year Lord Brudenell and Elizabeth were married, by licence, in the parish church of St. Nicholas with St. Mary Magdalene, near the iron gate on Chiswick Mall, behind which (as told by Thackeray in the opening pages of *Vanity Fair*) the young ladies of Miss Pinkerton's academy had been shocked and titillated by the bitter comments of Becky Sharp.

Elizabeth was ironically described in the register as being "a spinster of this parish, being now single and unmarried".

It took Brudenell not much longer than it had taken Captain Johnstone to realize that he had made a bad bargain. He and Elizabeth had lived together for some time. He might gently have disengaged himself without much hurt to her feelings or to her reputation, since their moral standards were on much the same level. Brudenell was a highly irritable man: but Elizabeth's flaming

temper, being feminine, was more lasting and deadly; and she
had the small selfish mind that usually goes with an extravagant
nature. Even allowing for the social pleasures of the time, and
for Brudenell's solid income, she could never have settled to
anything resembling a normal domestic round: and she probably
welcomed, more than did Brudenell, the fact that they had no
children.

He was still, however, first and foremost a soldier; secondly, a
lord of the hunting field; while both by privilege and by whatever
right attaches to heredity he was one of the confident, self-
assured, highly indulged but by no means wholly irresponsible
governors of England.

To be genuinely resident in a Midland county was to belong to
one of the great hunts. Brudenell had ridden with the Pytchley
when scarcely more than a boy; and when the mastership fell
vacant about this time his influence secured it for Thomas or
'Gentleman' Smith. The latter had made himself famous among
his kind by successfully clearing a park wall that was 6 feet 2½
inches on the taking-off side, and 8 feet on the landing side. At the
end of one of their coursings together Brudenell, in a fine show of
emotional gratitude, flung his arms about Smith for having
provided such a pleasurable long straight run.

Brudenell also rode with the Quorn under Squire Osbaldeston,
reputed to be the greatest all-round sportsman of his own or
any age—he once rode a distance of 200 miles in forty-eight
hours. Throughout these years stags were ceasing to be regarded
as 'beasts of the chase', and it was only for a time, when living at
Melton Mowbray, that Brudenell kept a pack of staghounds.
Between the frequency of these runs Brudenell shone as a
practically certain 'shot' on the grouse moors.

His social philosophy scarcely admitted the possibility of change.
His naturally insular satisfaction, his several forms of sport, his
brief appearances in Parliament, and his more serious army
commitments, seemed as permanent as the land (so far untouched
by even the shadow of a chimney) that nurtured his being. He was
a stock, self-contained figure; almost unaffected by such cultural
influences as the early Romantic revival that faded with Keats,
Shelley and Byron; very straight and stiff, with strongly marked
features and with whiskers that broke the outline of his high
collar; one in a timeless procession of men and women, all of his

line, whose shadows were reflected in the great rooms and
galleries through which he passed.

6

The difference between Lord Brudenell and his patron, the
Marquess of Ailesbury, developed over the question of Catholic
Emancipation, which had been a prime concern of Parliament
over several years. The old penal laws of Elizabeth's time had
never been rescinded, and as a result Catholics were excluded from
Parliament and from most civil offices, although (as was often
said) they could still fight and die for the power that denied them
political rights.

Bills in favour of Catholic relief had been rejected time and
again. Emancipation was feared as the thin edge of Popery, and
as a threat to the liberties enjoyed under the Protestant supremacy.
Interests connected with the Established Church saw the granting
of civil rights to Catholics as an insult to the royal conscience,
while many held that any furtherance of Catholic claims might
lead to treason.

Robert Peel, when representing Oxford University in the
Commons, had opposed emancipation. His speech rejecting it,
and declaring that "an honest despotic government" was best for
Ireland, had been echoed at the university, and by none more
passionately than by Brudenell when he was at Christ Church. In
1828 he voted against the measure, but he very soon changed his
mind.

It may be that his service in Ireland was mainly responsible.
Perhaps he was influenced by Wellington, who in 1819 had gone
against the grain by reminding the Lords that the Protestant
Church had been established in Ireland "at the point of the sword
and by means of confiscations", so that Catholics were bound to
be inspired by the idea of unmerited suffering. The Duke declared
that he had found the Irish to be loyal subjects—statements
which caused many of the highest Tories to fall away from their
leader.

Meanwhile the menace of civil war was growing in Ireland.
Catholics numbered three-quarters of the population. The
Catholic Association, led by the lawyer and 'liberator' Daniel

O'Connell, claimed the backing of an almost entire people. The attitude of Catholic troops in Ireland became more doubtful as the agitation spread; and by taking advantage of a change in the climate of popular opinion in England, which was affected less by liberalism than by practical promptings, Wellington was able, almost on his own authority, to again bring in the Bill for Catholic Emancipation, this time with promise of success.

George IV, in his speech from the throne in January 1829, announced the measure. "Damn it, you mean to let them into Parliament," he grumbled. The Bill was carried through both Houses with comfortable majorities, and soon became law. Brudenell and Peel were among the many who changed sides and now supported it. Lord Ailesbury was annoyed and Brudenell resigned his seat for Marlborough, which Ailesbury had given him, and sat for the borough of Fowey in Cornwall.

In the same year, 1830, Brudenell purchased his majority in the 8th Hussars, and before the year was out he obtained a lieutenant-colonelcy, and went on half-pay. According to *The Times*, this later rank was purchased at a cost of between £35,000 and £40,000.

George IV died of dropsy on 26th June, and dull, red-nosed William IV, the 'sailor King', was called upon to weather the storms of the Reform Bill.

Men of Brudenell's age had been aware, throughout their lifetime, that the demand for a reform of the electoral machinery of Parliament was gathering strength. The shadow of the French Revolution had never wholly lifted from the social scene; more than one European city was threatened by violence. Radicals everywhere were pressing for their many different versions of reform, a sweeping away of feudal abuses, an end to the traditional system of influence and patronage. In England it turned on the question of parliamentary representation, for an end of government by landowners and country gentleman who, like Brudenell, accepted the exercise of hereditary power as their duty, their responsibility, and their right.

On the whole, allowing for the human tendency to be corrupted by custom, they exercised it well. They could not have done otherwise without failing their caste. Tyranny and cruelty were not among their vices; and below them, on a less exalted level, the middle class contributed in their own solid way to the maintenance of State, society, and the Church.

But with England taking on the character of a vast industrial and commercial centre, a virtually new class, representing the wealth of the great manufacturing towns such as Manchester, Birmingham, Leeds, was making inroads on the established order. They had strong organizing ability. Many were thrusting (so-called progressive) northerners, who had risen above their kind by expert application of the new machinery. They moved in the vanguard of reform, demanding a wider franchise to include some representation of their own commercial class and of the rising towns. Their spokesmen on the popular level were men like Richard Cobden and John Bright. Lord John Russell, a son of the Duke of Bedford, endorsed the view of many reasonable men that the system of representation might well be improved, though not by fomenting class warfare with its imminent attacks on property and the social values.

Brudenell was wholly on the side of Wellington in opposing reform. They saw it as a first step to undermining the Constitution, to subjecting the country to the rule of undisciplined people supported by an irresponsible Press; and their fears appeared to be justified when riotous mobs, in the name of reform, started a reign of violence and destruction in half the counties of England. At the height of the trouble Wellington's government fell and was replaced by a Whig ministry under Lord Grey.

But each time the Reform Bill was carried in the Lower House the Lords were still able to reject it; and each time they did so the agitations increased. Bristol was plundered, great houses were burned to the ground; coaches were attacked, and stones crashed through the windows of Apsley House, where the Duke's lady was lying dead. When the King and Queen drove from Windsor to London a mob surrounded the carriage and pelted it with mud and filth. The escorting Life Guards were encouraged to use the flats of their swords by the purple-faced sailor king, who shouted through the window, "Let the damned lubbers have it!" There was the usual revolutionary talk of barricades going up.

Several of the Lords wavered; their opposition thinned; but Brudenell was not among those who thought of giving way, a fact that was remembered against him; and the last obstacle to reform was overcome when the King (no sailor at heart) was persuaded by Grey to create a sufficient number of new peers, all of them Whigs, to carry the Bill through the Upper House.

Brudenell's place on the opposition benches was empty when, on a summer afternoon in 1832, the Royal Assent enabled the Bill to become law; and that night the great majority of dwellers in the metropolis placed lighted candles or tallow dips in their windows to show their approval of the Bill. There was at least one house in Portman Square that manifested the recalcitrance of the Cardigan family by remaining in darkness.

The Bill swept away some obvious abuses. More than fifty rotten boroughs were abolished. New representatives were allotted to the counties and to the rising towns. The borough franchise was fixed for occupiers of property valued at £10 or over. But Brudenell and his kind, who never believed as did idealists such as Russell and Grey, that the right to cast a vote would inevitably lead to the improvement of man, looked with critical eye at the new Liberal capitalists who were now filling the benches of Reform; and Brudenell would surely have echoed the words of the Duke: "I never saw so many shocking bad hats in all my life."

7

One of the political effects of the Reform Bill was the creation of a new constituency, North Northamptonshire. It was then regarded as a stronghold of the Whigs, and when the 1832 general election came round their cause was represented by Lord Milton, the eldest son of Earl Fitzwilliam of Milton Hall, near Peterborough, and Squire Hanbury of Kelmarsh. The Tories opposing them were Squire Tryon of Bulwick, and Lord Brudenell.

A leading issue was the Corn Laws. The country was divided on the question, though the Whigs, in general, favoured their repeal, while the Tories, pledged to defend agricultural interests, insisted that such a move would be ruinous to farmers. It could only react to the benefit of the new industrial plutocracy which Brudenell consistently opposed. (The Corn Laws were repealed in 1846, fourteen years later.)

Elections then were openly and shamelessly corrupt. There was bribery by both sides, either in form of money or free meals and beer. Hired mobs paraded with music and banners, shouting slogans or abuse. A candidate appearing on the hustings needed to be protected by a bodyguard of toughs, otherwise he was pelted, shouted down or driven off. Agents rounded up voters and drove them to the polls by threats, if necessary. Newspapers whipped up tempers by holding out golden promises or hints of doom. The air was thick with charges of intimidation. The people, inflated by the knowledge that they were now being courted by 'their betters', entered fully into the spirit of what was in every district a local war.

Lord Brudenell was referred to in the Tory papers as "the farmer's friend". The Radicals, it was said, with their manufacturing background, would degrade agricultural interests; but Lord Brudenell, who supported the Throne and "those venerable institutions which have for so long existed", would defend the farmers against the new economic doctrines. His Lordship's heart "was as far from fraud as earth from heaven". He was charged with having threatened tenants with notice to quit if they voted against him; but when he canvassed for votes several farmers were said to have replied: "It is not in our power to vote against Lord Milton. But of this your Lordship may rest assured, that nothing shall induce us to vote against you. Since we are not permitted to assist you, we will not injure you. We will not vote at all."

At the conclusion of his canvass, Lord Brudenell assured the gentlemen, clergy, freeholders and other electors of the division "that he was left in no doubt that he would have the honour of being returned as one of their representatives". But he was not welcomed everywhere.

In the course of the campaign Brudenell and a small party of supporters passed through Wellingborough. They found a narrow part, Cheese Lane, blocked by carts and wheelbarrows. Having dismounted and cleared a way the party entered a main street where a mob pelted them with stones. Brudenell and his friends again dismounted, and nothing daunted by numbers rushed in to attack and seized some of the demonstrators. Brudenell was cut on the head by a stone. The Riot Act was read, and finally some Yeomanry and a detachment of troops from Weedon Barracks restored order.

Nomination day was 15th December. Both sides were confident, the season was mild, and (a propitious sign that was greeted by Radicals and Tories alike) a full-blown double primrose had appeared in the county woodlands. Three hundred special constables had been sworn in, but they were not needed. Soon after daybreak the rain fell in torrents, but Kettering was crowded when the preliminary ceremonies took place at the White Hart Inn.

Suddenly the rain stopped; the flags that decorated the hustings in the Market Place flapped in a drying wind, and, headed by a raucous brass band, Lord Brudenell and Squire Tyron entered to a storm of cheers, boos and hisses. But the whole affair passed off without incident, especially as a body of yeomen, from Brudenell's old Northamptonshire troop, rode in the procession. Each rider carried a small flag of Tory blue, and they formed a half-circle about the hustings. Whenever anything promising to the Tory cause was said or enacted, a large blue flag was hoisted as a sign to those on the outskirts of the throng that things were going well.

The two elected members were Lord Milton, with 1,562 votes, and Brudenell, who came a close second with 1,541. In his speech Lord Milton referred to a certain candidate who would have been more respected, and more English, if he had not gone creeping up the back stairs of every house to explain his objects in private, instead of in public. Lord Brudenell retorted that he had never crept up the back stairs of any elector. "The fact which troubled the noble lord's mind was the backstairs way in which he had got into Parliament last time." There was more cheering and booing; the rival members glared at each other and the people streamed away from the hustings.

Lord Brudenell held the seat until 1837. It was said, by his enemies, that he spent £30,000 on electioneering. That was almost certainly an over-statement, though large sums were at that time expended by candidates who, apart from experiencing a sense of triumph, placed little value on a seat in the Commons. One need only remember the gentleman-sportsman-pugilist John Mytton, who, having spent £10,000 on successfully fighting an election, went once to the House for half an hour on the day when he was sworn in, and never appeared there again.

8

After two years on half-pay as lieutenant-colonel, Lord Brudenell took a step that carried him forward in his military career and also as a public figure. He exchanged into the 15th Hussars on 16th March 1832, and three weeks later took command of the regiment which was then at Manchester.

Raised as Light Dragoons in 1759, the regiment received a new classification as the 15th (the King's) Hussars in 1807. Its uniform was the usual Hussar blue with laced jacket and a scarlet pelisse, shako and plume. The badge was the crest of England within the Garter.

Lord Brudenell took over from Lieutenant-Colonel Thackwell, a Peninsular veteran who lost an arm at Waterloo. Thackwell was a fine cavalry leader, and the regiment's reputation stood high when, under its new lieutenant-colonel, it went to join the garrison in Ireland.

There were minor outbreaks and threats of rebellion in several parts of the country, and regiments moved frequently from station to station in the course of various duties that were not always military. For apart from quelling riots and searching for arms, they were detailed to work with Excise men against smugglers. The 15th were stationed for a time at Royal Barracks, Dublin, then at Longford, Newbridge and Kilkenny. Towards the end of 1833 they arrived at Cork, where Brudenell's undisputed impact upon a regiment was fully felt for the first time.

He was a soldier by instinct, a military perfectionist who aimed at achieving a machine-like model based on uncritical obedience to orders; hard driving, both of himself and of others, and close attention to detail—the military historian Kinglake said that his love of uniformity led him to quarrel over the size of a teacup. He had the gift of concentration (which is rarer than many suppose), with the ability to hold to a main idea that he felt to be right because it served a purpose. His outlook was predominantly simple in that he was honestly surprised when others failed to share his single-minded devotion; and when he encountered opposition, he invariably put it down to more serious motives than those that inspired it.

His self-confidence was unbounded. It was based upon a stern

conscience, and the knowledge that he would never turn aside
from military duty; while his passion for detail was proper in a
commander who recognized (however ridiculous it may seem to
some) that habitual attention to pipeclay or to a button may help
to determine the holding or the breaking of a battle line.

The state of the 15th Hussars left little or nothing to be
desired. But it was known that discipline throughout the army in
general had been somewhat relaxed during the past twenty years;
and Brudenell in Ireland, with a regiment to command, was
determined to maintain it as a pattern of perfection for the
rest.

But the actual routine was not excessive. There were two or three
field days a week, when the general pace of movement was at the
regulation trot of eight miles an hour, with wheeling at a gallop.
Intermediate days were taken up with squadron and skirmishing
drill. There were foot parades or marches in the afternoon, a
watering parade on Saturday, and church service on Sunday. A
day's exercise in the field, from the time men left barracks until
they returned, lasted an average of five hours.

Procedure at the Mess table, where every officer was expected
to conduct himself as a gentleman, and in the riding school, was
strictly watched over by Brudenell. This might be Ireland, but
the horses had to be clipped and groomed as though for a review
on Woolwich Common; while being an expert horseman himself, he knew how men should sit in the saddle; firmly down, with
the body inclining, as the horse rose, from the hips, and not from
the knees, a faulty pose which meant that the man's seat would be
jerked upward. To 'show daylight' between the seat and the
saddle, in the days of cavalry, was to break an essential rule of
horsemanship.

The rule of a martinet provokes admiration, which is often
silent, together with resentment and irritation. Some officers
grumbled at rules they thought to be unnecessary; and this to
Brudenell meant insubordination, an offence against discipline.
His temper suffered; he became more independent and confident,
more over-bearing. The discontented officers retaliated with
whatever means were within their power. But the explosion, when
it came, was over a trifle.

It was greatly exaggerated at the time, and it has since been
rendered quite incomprehensible by writers who tell only part

of the story, and who use that part to emphasize Brudenell's high-handedness and lack of reason.

The colonel of a regiment was then responsible for clothing his men. He received a sum of money, called 'off-reckonings', for each man, and he and the quartermaster between them undertook the supplying of jackets, overalls and boots. One type of jacket was that worn in stables by men engaged in foraging duties, the carrying of hay and straw. These jackets were inspected at certain parades by the colonel who, again with the quartermaster, decided which jackets were in need of repair, or which could be replaced by new ones.

Each troop of cavalry kept an account book in which the cost of new clothing items were entered. This cost generally exceeded the amount of 'off-reckonings', and consequently there was a standing or surplus debt recorded in each book. The average debt was in the region of £10, and troop officers were naturally concerned to keep this moderate and so avoid complaints.

Throughout his career Brudenell aimed at making his men among the best equipped in the army; and after one of the dismounted parades, when the men offered their stable-jackets for inspection, he ordered a supply of new jackets for the troop commanded by Captain Augustus Wathen.

According to the Captain, this was done without his knowledge; and he was therefore surprised when jackets were sent in from the tailor's shop, thus increasing his troop debt to something over £28.

Brudenell complained that Wathen's bad management had caused him to exceed the regulation allowance, and reported it to General Arbuthnot, the officer commanding the district. He also called Wathen to account, and a shouting match developed between them in the regimental office.

Brudenell considered that Wathen's behaviour was disrespectful, and he instructed the Adjutant, who was present, to take down written notes of the Captain's remarks. At the same time he ordered two sergeants to write down whatever was said by the men of Wathen's troop touching the affair.

Wathen complained that some of the stable-jackets were still quite serviceable and not in need of replacement. To evidence this he held one out for Brudenell's inspection, but the Colonel snatched it from his hand and flung it across the room. The upshot was that Wathen was placed under arrest and the Colonel demanded a court martial. This was refused by the Commander-in-Chief, Lord Hill, who also ordered Wathen's release.

The dispute gathered force and assumed a more personal basis over work in the field. At one of the exercises, when the regiment trotted past in open column of troops, Wathen placed himself in front of the second file from the left. Brudenell fumed, as the official ruling in that respect had recently been changed. He told Wathen, within the men's hearing, that if he couldn't command his troop he would bring up the youngest cornet in the regiment to take over.

On another occasion, Wathen sat at ease on his horse, right hand on hip, and occasionally pointing, with the other that held his sword, to emphasize some point to the men in the ranks. Brudenell barked, "Carry your sword, sir. Can't you carry your sword properly?" Wathen 'sloped' his sword, as commanded, but he afterwards lapsed into holding it as before. In both these instances Brudenell, intent on preserving a disciplined appearance, was strictly correct. He also criticized Captain Wathen's riding and his method of holding the reins.

After an inspection of the regiment, Major-General Arbuthnot expressed, in writing, his approval of the men's smart bearing and appearance. Brudenell marked this triumph for his discipline by asking the troop commanders to assemble their men, after evening stables, and convey to them the General's appreciation. A few days later Brudenell asked whether this duty had been discharged.

Wathen replied that he had delivered the General's message to his troop, but verbally. On being told to write down what he had said Wathen refused and was promptly placed under arrest.

This time, when Brudenell asked for a court martial, it was granted. The court, under the presidency of Major-General Sir John Buchan, opened at Cork Barracks on Monday, 23rd December 1833.

Captain Wathen was a capable, steady officer. He had twenty years' service to his credit, and had seen action at Waterloo. There was nothing in this, nor in his predominantly quiet nature, which took soldiering seriously, to incite wrath. Yet "the mere presence of Captain Wathen" says C. Woodham Smith,* "was sufficient to drive the Lieutenant-Colonel into a rage". This and similar

* *The Reason Why*, Constable, 1956.

James Thomas Brudenell, seventh Earl of Cardigan, leads the Charge
of the Light Brigade

(*Above*) Deene Park,
Northamptonshire,
home of the Brudenell
family. (*Left*) Lord
Cardigan, from a
drawing by William
Simpson

remarks account for nothing, though they do serve the writer's purpose of presenting Lord Brudenell as a man of violent unreasonable temper. But the fact that he could and did lose control, often over apparent trifles, does not explain the Captain Wathen affair, which developed out of little and yet was consistently built up to its quite inexplicable climax.

In order to get to the heart of the matter we must look to the ladies of the regiment. Lady Brudenell had joined her husband in Cork, with her good looks, the stigma of adultery and divorce, and an increasingly doubtful reputation, fresh upon her; and, judging by current remarks, she was obviously making a stir among the military mashers and 'swells' of the Cork garrison.

Captain Wathen's wife was also there—a lady in her own right, with a mind that placed her infinitely and consciously above a mere butterfly like Lady Brudenell. She let it be known that she was descended from the diarist John Evelyn. She could, as will be seen, use her pen to some effect, and ladies of the blue-stocking variety have seldom been a far remove from self-righteousness. She was probably well aware, perhaps jealously so, that the frivolous Lady Brudenell far exceeded her in charm and attraction.

At any rate a journal of the day,* discussing the military entourage in Cork, baldly states that Lady Brudenell "is not exactly *comme il faut*". The ladies of the regiment, it goes on to say, did not accept the honour of her invitations, and did not invite her to their gatherings. It then continues: "Whether they were correct in sending her ladyship to Coventry, may be guessed from the fact that she was the wife of a gallant major of infantry [*sic*]—the friend of another—the attaché of a third—and, at last, the lady of the——."

It thus becomes clear that the Brudenells were made to suffer, at least socially, for their indiscretions, a state of affairs that was more than enough to make a man of the Colonel's temper see red. He was later, as a much older man, when married to his second wife, to cut himself off from friends and relations who gave her the cold shoulder. But when faced with a feminine cabal against Elizabeth, he could only retaliate against the husband of one who, if not their leader, was certainly a party to the plot. Hence his apparently blind rage towards Captain Wathen, who for his part did little to smooth things out.

* *New Weekly Dispatch.*

4

9

The trial lasted eighteen days. Enough rumours connected with it had filtered out of barracks to create a stir, and each morning, as soon as the doors opened, there was a great rush of people for places. Those officers who were off duty were among the spectators.

Lord Brudenell, in his opening statement, referred to the almost unprecedented manner in which aspects of the case had been presented, and pre-judged, by the public Press. The trifles on which the case turned, such as the issue of stable-jackets and a troop debt, were of no real matter to the public.

He claimed that Captain Wathen had stated, "in an invidious manner to Major-General Sir Thomas Arbuthnot, that an unusual number of new stable-jackets had been issued to the men of his troop, and which had been sent from the tailor's shop without his knowledge, thereby imputing improper conduct to Lieutenant-Colonel Lord Brudenell, his commanding officer, although it is the custom of the service to issue new stable-jackets to cavalry soldiers as they may require them".

He went on to say that Captain Wathen had told the General that the men were discontented at having new stable-jackets issued to them. This was "directly contrary to truth and fact". One of Captain Wathen's officers had said there was no discontent, while the quartermaster confirmed that the supply of jackets to Wathen's troop, eighty in the last two years, was in no way excessive or unusual.

Wathen's conduct as troop commander left much to be desired. His troop was the worst in the regiment. Some half-dozen horses had sore backs and broken knees; nearly half the number of sick horses in the regiment, over the past six months, were in Wathen's troop, a state of affairs that was likely to bring the 15th Hussars into contempt. These facts could be borne out by the weekly returns that were signed by commissioned officers. The men were careless in their riding and in stable duties, including such details as folding their blankets. The list of defaulters, cases of drunkenness and of being absent without leave, were heavier in Wathen's troop than in any other.

Further charges, according to Brudenell, were that Wathen had opposed, thwarted and disobeyed him. When corrected at field exercises, he had repeated the errors several times and did not fall in with or act upon corrections. His mode of addressing Lord Brudenell, as commanding officer, was disrespectful and improper, and he had intrigued with the public Press.

Some of the conversations between himself, Captain Wathen and the Adjutant, had been presented in garbled or perverted form. Brudenell had, on that account, and to guard against inaccurate memories, given instructions for remarks to be taken down. This practice had never been concealed from the officers concerned, though he (Brudenell) had come to doubt its wisdom in view of the malignant motives that had been placed upon it.

When asked if he could account for the trouble, Brudenell replied that he could "assign no other cause whatever for it but a temporary evil which had spread like a contagion in the regiment, and which required the most prompt and strong measures on my part in order to stop it".

Captain Wathen made his defence on the fourth day of the trial, a day of tempest and black clouds when lamps and candles were called for in the court room. It was common knowledge that his defence, a well-constructed and reasoned document, had been penned by his wife.

He recalled his service at Waterloo, and at the mention of that "loud Sabbath" many veterans among the spectators reached for their handkerchief to wipe the tears from dim eyes and furrowed cheeks. He referred to the time he had spent under arrest, and produced letters from responsible officers who had found him competent and of excellent character. At the end of his defence, which occupied two hours twenty-five minutes, a witness observed that the "whole powers of Wathen's mind and body appeared to be exhausted".

Brudenell's reply, on the last day of the trial, lasted some ninety minutes. Speaking very quickly and distinctly, he admitted that during some of the interviews with Wathen he had raised his voice above the ordinary tone, and went on to say, "This, I fear, has often been the case in the presence of this honourable court."

The details of the trial were submitted to the Horse Guards. Before the verdict was announced Major-General Buchan, who had presided at the court martial, inspected the 15th Hussars together with three regiments of Foot. The General paid special attention to Brudenell's regiment, and concerning them a local witness said, "There could not be a finer nor a more warlike body of men, while the horses looked in excellent condition."

On the first day of February 1834, Lord Brudenell was at Mess with his officers when a document, announcing the result of the court martial, was brought to him. He scanned it, rose, and left the table. Regimental exercises for the next day were cancelled.

The document, signed by Lieutenant-General Sir John Macdonald, Adjutant-General, was a complete exoneration of Captain Wathen. It declared he was honourably acquitted of each and all the charges preferred against him. He was given back his sword.

Lord Brudenell, who had resorted to "peculiar and extra-ordinary measures", came off badly. He was censured for having advanced various and weighty assertions without some grounds of establishing the facts, and for introducing "the system of having the conversation of officers taken down in the orderly room without their knowledge; a practice which cannot be considered otherwise than revolting to every proper and honourable feeling of a gentleman, and as being certain to create disunion and to be most injurious to His Majesty's service".

There was a partial sugaring of the pill in the admission that some of the court's findings had been slanted in a way unfavour-able to the prosecutor; but then came the really bitter part of the pronouncement: "Upon a full consideration of all the circum-stances of the case, His Majesty has been pleased to order that Lieutenant-Colonel Lord Brudenell shall be removed from the command of the 15th Hussars." These findings were ordered to be read at every regimental Mess room in the service.

Lord Brudenell, in a tearing hurry, left Cork at midnight. The weather was bad and the roads were in poor condition. But he rode hard through the darkness, travelling by way of Fermoy to Clonmel, where he picked up the Dublin coach and so left for England. Lady Brudenell also turned her back on the regimental wives who had treated her so coolly, boarding the *Victory* steamer at Cork and landing at Bristol. From now on what-ever Lord Brudenell did or said was to receive the utmost publicity; and, following the fashion set by *The Times*, it was mostly hostile. Other courts martial, of more general interest than the issue of stable-jackets or a troop debt, caused little or no stir. But the Cork affair, greatly exaggerated, became a subject for leader writers and for talk in the clubs.

Brudenell, the haughty and over-bearing, was held up to ridicule as an "unripe gallant". An officer spoke for many when he said that the only thing Brudenell could do now was to put five guineas in his pocket, then make his will and a purchase at Mantons (the gun makers). But the *United Service Gazette* took a less personal view. It regretted that courts martial, no longer what they were, could now be used to injure the character of military men; while the *Naval and Military Gazette* commented upon the "singular treatment which Lord Brudenell appears to have received during the prosecution from the President of the Court and several of its members".

10

Troops in Britain were then under the control of the Horse Guards in Whitehall, the edifice built in 1750 and so named since its original purpose was to serve as quarters for part of the Royal Horse Guards. A Peninsular veteran, Lord Hill, known as 'Daddy', or (on account of his red face and country interests) as 'Farmer' Hill, was Commander-in-Chief from 1825 to 1840, and his secretary was Lord Fitzroy Somerset, the future Lord Raglan. Apart from governing home troops the Staff at the Horse Guards dealt with requests for patronage, rewards, honours, and with complaints.

As soon as he returned to London, where he resided at 17 Carlton House Terrace in the Mall*, Lord Brudenell bombarded them with protests. He declared that he had been tried on charges upon which he had never been arraigned, and "punished by a sentence the injustice of which I have no opportunity of proving". He demanded a reconsideration of the court martial, even with himself as defendant. Lord Hill regretted that he could not recommend the King to comply with such an application—a refusal which strengthened Brudenell's conviction that he had been unjustly dealt with for political reasons. The temper of the Horse Guards was conservative, but Lord Hill found it prudent to fall

* Now the Federation of British Artists.

in with the wishes of the Whig Government under Lord Grey.

Brudenell then applied to the King, expressing his deep morti-
fication at the censure and asking that he might be allowed to
vindicate his own character; but the King took refuge in the fact
that the army authorities, whom he could not gainsay, had
sentenced Brudenell.

Nothing daunted, and sustained by the belief that members of
the Cabinet were on his side, Brudenell carried his grievances and
his demands to Lord Fitzroy Somerset. He saw Lord Melbourne,
and even his opponent over the Reform Bill, Lord John Russell,
insisting that a court of inquiry must be set up to review his
conduct.

Finally he obtained an interview with the Duke of Wellington,
who advised Brudenell to quieten down and to stop pestering the
army authorities for about a year. "I can't say I owe my success
to any favour or confidence from the Horse Guards," observed
the Duke sniffily. Brudenell, who by then must have exhausted
the patience of nearly everyone he knew, decided to follow the
Duke's advice by remaining quiet. Convinced that justice was on
his side, he was confident of being restored to the active list.
Meanwhile a new commander had been appointed to the 15th
Hussars "for the good of the regiment", and in March 1834
Brudenell was placed on half-pay.

These events had told heavily upon Brudenell's near relatives.
His father, Lord Cardigan, was naturally most affected; and almost
equally distressed was a sister, Harriet, who had married Richard
Penn Curzon, Earl Howe. The latter was appointed chamberlain
to Queen Adelaide, the wife of William IV, who was said to have
a weakness for the Earl. These combined influences led the two
women, Queen and Countess, to approach the King on
Brudenell's behalf; but although they begged, and resorted to
tears, the placid William said he was unable to interfere with Lord
Hill's righteous judgment.

They succeeded, however, in persuading the King to see Lord
Cardigan. Though obviously infirm, the head of the Brudenells
could yet comport himself with a certain magnificence: and
when he fell upon his knees, begging for the disgrace inflicted
upon his family and his son to be removed, the King yielded,
being more overcome by the aged Earl, as someone said, than by
all the petticoats put together.

Lord Hill was summoned, and he too seemed visibly affected by the distress of the Brudenell family. The King withdrew his former objection to the errant Colonel being reinstated, and the Commander-in-Chief promised to secure him a new appointment. It was hoped that Lord Brudenell had learnt a valuable lesson, and that he would henceforth cease to follow the dictates of his own temper; but his return to favour only confirmed Lord Brudenell's steadfast belief that he had been in the right from the start.

His new appointment, dated 25th March 1836, was to the command of the 11th Light Dragoons. The purchase price was rumoured to exceed £40,000. The regiment had been in India for the past seventeen years, and it was obviously hoped that by joining there Lord Brudenell would figure less prominently in the public eye, and so escape attacks from the many enemies now gathered about him.

The findings of the court martial had not meant, of course, that he was dismissed from the army. The fact of his being placed on half-pay indicated that he would ultimately be given another command. But his appointment to the 11th Light Dragoons provoked a sharp reaction in the Commons. It was led by Sir William Molesworth, M.P. for East Cornwall, a sadly embittered man whose marriage plans had twice gone awry on account of his Radical and anti-Christian opinions. He was supported by Joseph Hume, a Radical sitting for Aberdeen, and whom even *The Times* called "a clap-trap for vulgar publicity".

They wanted to know if the Secretary for War, Lord Howick, approved Lord Brudenell's appointment. Lord Howick, and after him Lord John Russell, replied that only the Commander-in-Chief had authority in such matters, which incited Mr. Hume to ask further whether the Secretary for War was merely a clerk to the Commander-in-Chief. A distinguished Peninsular soldier and a future Commander-in-Chief, Major-General Sir Henry Hardinge, who from the first had regarded the Wathen verdict as "an erroneous decision", spoke in favour of Brudenell, and welcomed his re-appointment on full pay.

Brudenell was in the House on 3rd May when Molesworth charged the Commander-in-Chief with having made an improper appointment. In reply, Brudenell said he had a delicate task to perform. On the one hand, he was bound to abstain from impugning the decision of the court martial, which was held for an officer of the regiment he had then commanded; and on the other hand, he must avoid saying anything which might appear disrespectful with reference to the exercise of the King's prerogative.

He was willing to take his share of whatever blame might be attached to the court martial. "But", he added, "it must be clearly understood that I acted under the guidance, more or less by the advice, and certainly with the full sanction, of the General Officer Commanding the District."

Letters were quoted from two general officers who commanded districts in which the 15th Hussars, under Brudenell's command, had been stationed. Major-General Sir Edward Blakeney said of Brudenell, "In field movements, and the ready application of cavalry, I considered you one of the most intelligent officers that served under my orders." Sir Henry Bouverie praised the riding, the appearance, the efficiency and precision with which the 15th moved in the field.

Lieutenant-General Sir Richard Hussey Vivian, Master-General of Ordnance, agreed that Lord Brudenell had faults, for which he had suffered severely. But he had never seen a more zealous officer than Lord Brudenell, nor a regiment in finer order than the one he had commanded. Another Peninsular veteran, Major-General Sir William Ponsonby, thought that Brudenell had been unfairly treated. Ponsonby had conversed with many officers of all classes, and scarcely anyone held a different opinion. Lieutenant-General Lord Stafford more bluntly affirmed that he was ready to defend Lord Brudenell's appointment in Parliament or in private society.

But the testimony of eminent soldiers meant nothing to the 'Destructive Party', as Radicals were called, who hated all things to do with the army, from the pipeclay on a private's belt to the feathers in a general's hat. Mr. Hume wanted to know whether Lord Hill would have dealt so favourably with Lord Brudenell had he been a poor unsupported subaltern, instead of being a nobleman's son. Molesworth brought forward a motion for an inquiry into the Commander-in-Chief's conduct in appointing Lord Brudenell to a new post. It was rejected by a large majority.

A correspondent writing to the *Alligator*, a journal mainly unfriendly to Brudenell, pointed out that it was by no means unheard of for an officer to be dismissed from command and then reinstated through the interest of the Horse Guards. He quoted the case of a general officer who, having been dismissed, was later given a new appointment. That officer had been sentenced for charges that included fraud—"and I do not recollect", said the correspondent, "such a fuss being made about it".

The 'fuss' called forth a disclaimer on the part of Wellington, who said he had never interposed his influence in favour of Lord Brudenell on any occasion whatever.

II

The 11th Light Dragoons had been formed in 1715, one of several regiments that came into being to support the House of Hanover when the Jacobite standard was raised. They saw service in the 'Forty-Five' against Prince Charlie. Their officers appear to have been outstanding, being described on two different occasions as "very genteel" and again as "most genteel young men".

During the Peninsular War their uniform was blue with buff facings. Their nickname, the 'Cherry-pickers', derived from an incident that occurred at Saint Martin de Trebego in August 1811. A patrol of the regiment, having turned aside to pick cherries in an orchard, was surprised by a force of French cavalry and had to fight a dismounted action. At Waterloo the 11th broke an infantry square, and later, towards evening, they captured the last of the French batteries to remain in action.

A few months after his appointment Lord Brudenell, accompanied by his lady, started for India. On the way through France they stopped at Compiègne, where the Duke of Orleans put on a military review for the visitors' benefit. Passing through Italy they went on to Malta, then Egypt, where, according to Brudenell, they hired a coal ship that was bound for Bombay.

The 'coal ship' was probably a steamer that stopped to take in coal, as the Brudenells were hardly likely to travel in a collier. After a passage of more than seventy days they arrived at Bombay where they stayed for several weeks as the guests of Sir John Keane, Commander-in-Chief of the Presidency. Then came a voyage by Government steamer along the coast of Bangalore, round the lower point of Ceylon and so to Madras. The steamers,

of iron construction, were uncomfortable affairs infested with
mosquitoes, cockroaches and rats, where the only furniture in a
first-class cabin, hired for 300 rupees, was a bedstead.

The Brudenells toured Madras, the 'Benighted City' overlooked by the dome of Government House that was surmounted
by Britannia with her trident, and where Fort William mounted
its massive defence of more than six hundred guns. Then came the
equally strong fortress of Seringapatam, a place to make any
soldier pause since it was here, in 1799, that the young Lieutenant
Wellesley, after the failure of a night attack, felt his nerve wear
thin for the first and perhaps only time in his life.

At Calcutta the Brudenells were received by the Governor
General, Lord Auckland. A trip by steamer took them to
Allahabad, the 'City of God', a place of Hindu pilgrimage where
the dull yellow waters of the Ganges mingle with the blue of the
Jumna. It was at Cawnpore, a large military station where the
cantonments, or military lodgings, extended for a distance of 7
miles, that Lord Brudenell saw his new regiment for the first time.
He took over from Lieutenant-Colonel Brutton, who was
retiring.

The newly arrived Colonel was not favourably impressed by
the state of the British troops in India. Discipline was relaxed.
The men were weakened by the intolerable heat, and kept in a
state of almost perpetual boredom since parade ground discipline
and military duties, under a sun that could be fatal, were not
rigidly enforced. In the hot-weather season, men were kept in
barracks from eight in the morning until five o'clock in the
evening. There was nothing to do but to sprawl on beds, tortured
by swarms of bugs and fleas; meals meant eating with one hand
and using the other to drive off pests that invaded the mouth.
Roads, when it came to marching, could be knee-deep in dust
that settled on the face and made breathing difficult. Men went
nearly mad for want of water that, when available, was often
swarming with animal life.

The canteen was their only refuge and cheap liquor their only
comfort. Heavy drinking led to quarrels and bloodshed; some of
the worst offenders struck their officers, and flogging for drunkenness became so common that the sepoys called the British 'bloody
backs', and felt a little less reverence for them.

Brudenell spent only a short time in India. But it was long

enough for his steel-like brand of discipline to make itself felt. He demanded respect for his officers, and their support for himself; and he enforced it by short-term punishments or by regular courts martial as in England. He overcame the men's boredom by increased drill and exercises, and, in spite of the climate, he would sometimes keep them, fully equipped, on their feet for an hour at a time.

His self-confidence, never in short supply, was strengthened during these months since he was now, as he wrote in his *Journal*, commanding a brigade in the field, the 11th Light Dragoons and two native regiments, and this without the slightest assistance from the Horse Guards. When he appeared at balls and dinners, given by prominent British and Indian residents, he impressed those present by his "fine military bearing".

One of the officers serving under him, who was to have some bearing on his future, was a certain Captain Harvey Garnett Phipps Tuckett. He had taken part in operations against the fortified town of Bhurtpore, when it fell to the British in 1825. Tuckett could use a pen to some effect, and he was often called on to write to the Indian papers, satirizing some peculiarity or airing a grievance on behalf of the regiment.

Meanwhile the England to which Lord Brudenell would soon return was moving into a virtually new era. Railroad tracks, by replacing the turnpike road and the stage coach, were changing the aspect of the country he had known and the spirit of his Midland heritage; Dickens, whose *Pickwick Papers* had already appeared, was giving a jolt to the public conscience by exposing social abuses and pretentious officialdom; the Oxford Movement was imparting a colourful and ritualistic impetus to the Established Church; King William IV died in 1837, and on an early June morning, when the hall of Kensington Palace was in partial darkness behind its curtains, a sleepy-eyed girl of 18, who was still in her dressing-gown and slippers, was addressed for the first time as "Your Majesty". The Brudenells, with minds not unduly troubled by events but little calculated to impose upon their ordered peace and security, continued their expedition—Delhi, on its rocky mountain range, with its picturesque ruins, mosques, palaces and cornfields, its palms and cypresses, was spread out before them. The family residence in Portman Square was very far away. But now came news of a happening there that was to affect them more closely than did any change in the character or in the monarchy of England.

The old Lord Cardigan had been taken ill at his London house. He asked the doctor if there was any hope of recovery. "You must tell me the truth."

After some hesitation, the doctor told him that he had two or three days to live.

The Earl sat up, rang a bell that stood on a table by the bedside, and ordered his carriage. The doctor protested that the sick man couldn't know what he was doing.

"If I'm going to die," the Earl said calmly, "I will die at Deene." He was carried downstairs to his carriage, travelled over poor roads the 80 miles into Northamptonshire, and died at Deene on 14th August 1837.

His son, aware of the dignity and fortune awaiting him in England, concluded his tour of India. He was entertained at the headquarters of the 16th Lancers at Meerut, where, as he wrote, he "had the amusement of tiger shooting". He went by *dak*, or relays of horses, to Calcutta, where he saw the Staff of his regiment go on board the *Repulse* and start for home. Then came further visits to Madras and Bombay, where he embarked on a private ship. The main body of the 11th Light Dragoons, a force of 340 non-commissioned officers and privates (many were left in the graveyard at Cawnpore) followed later.

They landed at Gravesend and marched to the Royal Cavalry Barracks, near Barton Mills, some half a mile to the north-east of Canterbury. The barracks, standing upon three sides of a quadrangle, had handsome apartments for officers in the centre of the building. But Lord and Lady Cardigan took a twelve months' tenancy of Hales Place, outside the city and conveniently near the barracks.

PART TWO

The Military Nuisance

I

The Cardigan estates covered 15,000 acres in Northamptonshire, Leicestershire and Yorkshire. Deene Park, surrounded by its extensive grounds, was a landmark in the county. The new earl was one of the richest peers in Britain; yet—and this says much for his character—he never once thought of falling into a life of ease. He remained a soldier. The army, as he said, was the mainspring of his existence; and together with the army he revered the sound conservative principles which buttressed the Constitution, and the Church which (again to quote) "God had given to lead them to eternal welfare".

As a nobleman he was to become a representative figure of the age that followed the death of William IV; but he was by no means typical of the time as a private character. He never courted the good opinion of others; and while standing on form, in a military and a social capacity, he discarded the props with which many men supported the respectable public image that passed for themselves.

The country was looking forward to a change in manners and morals. People had for too long been treated to the spectacle of vice and grossness in high quarters. William IV had been only a slight improvement on his riotous brother George who, according to Byron, was so blown up by feeding and disease that he weighed half a ton; and William, who had served at sea, overdid the Jolly Jack Tar pose when, between the whiles of shouting "Larboard" or "Starboard" to direct the grooms, he spat through the window of his carriage, much to the annoyance of people pressing forward for a sight of the Presence. And it was widely

known that the bluff monarch, who sometimes wandered alone
at night about the metropolis, had been pounced on and kissed by
a whore in St. James's Street.

It was hoped that "our dear little Queen", as diarist Thomas
Creevey called her, would restore the monarchy to at least an
abbreviated pedestal. She may have gobbled food, laughed with
her mouth wide open and displayed "not very pretty gums", as
Creevey went on to observe. But she was so intent on official
business that she even pored over documents when a maid was
combing her hair. It needed the superior insight of Lady Tavistock
to detect in this amiable young woman, whose reign was to strike
a tone that emphasized the discord of Lord Cardigan's life, the
makings of a "resolute little tit".

With his regiment now settled for service in home garrisons,
all Cardigan's ability and discipline were devoted to licking it into
expert shape; and that he was a master in that respect could never
be questioned. The regiment was brought up to strength and
formed into six troops. New Victoria percussion carbines were
issued, together with new sword-belts, sabretaches and pouches.
An order directed that the name 'Salamanca' should be inscribed
on regimental appointments, in honour of the Peninsular battle
when the English horse charged and broke the French cavalry
under Marmont.

There were field days on Barham Downs, parades on the
barrack field near Canterbury, reviews on Wimbledon Common.
The young Queen rode up and down the lines of the regiment.
The Duke of Wellington, and the Duke of Cambridge; Lord
Hill, the Commander-in-Chief; Major-General Sleigh, Inspector-
General of Cavalry, and Lieutenant-General Sir Hussey Vivian,
all agreed on the splendid appearance and performance of the 11th
Light Dragoons, who were brought to "a very high state of
discipline by the unremitting exertions of the Earl of Cardigan
and the officers under his command".

Those officers unanimously subscribed to and published in the
papers a declaration of esteem for Lord Cardigan's conduct as
commander; and the same standard of perfection that Cardigan
applied to the men was extended to the horses. The Government
made a payment towards every mount, and to each of these pay-
ments Cardigan added £10, from his private purse, to ensure the
worth of the breeds that arrived at the Canterbury stables.

The Cardigans entertained on a lavish scale at Hales Place, where the regimental band attended; and they in turn were fêted, especially by the people of Northamptonshire. A dinner on a "most imposing scale" was given in a tent on the premises of the White Hart Hotel, Kettering, by the political associates of the Earl, who had, of course, now left the Commons. Under a profusion of flags, banners and variegated lamps, the dinner was supervised by 164 stewards, headed by the Duke of Buccleuch.

Among the foreign royalties who inspected the regiment were Prince Ernest of Saxe-Coburg and his son, Albert. Soon after the visit a rumour, spread by the *Examiner*, announced that the Queen had "placed her affections on a most amiable Prince". But it proved to be more than a rumour since, on 7th February 1840, Prince Albert arrived in England for his marriage to the Queen.

The 11th Light Dragoons were called on to furnish escorts during the Prince's journey from Dover to London. Cardigan, mounted on a magnificent Arab charger, rode with two troops, just over one hundred men, to meet the Prince. It drizzled rain, and Albert looked pale and sickly after a rough crossing. But the cathedral bells pealed when they entered Canterbury, and at five o'clock in the evening the Prince was well enough to dine with Cardigan and two majors of the regiment at the Royal Hotel. Next morning a squadron of the 11th provided an escort along the road to Sittingbourne, and so the Prince reached London.

In recognition of this service, Cardigan received the following notification from Lieutenant-General Sir John Macdonald, the Adjutant-General: "My Lord, I have the honour to acquaint you, by the direction of the General Commanding-in-Chief, that Her Majesty has been graciously pleased to direct that the 11th regiment of Light Dragoons shall be armed, clothed and equipped as Hussars, and styled the 'Eleventh' or 'Prince Albert's Own Hussars'."

Some at once saw this as a concession to the Earl, who appeared to show some preference for the new title. In any event, it certainly gave him a chance to indulge his liking for a brilliant uniform. It was hoped that the regiment would be fitted out early in June, and fifty men, with orders to work quickly, were engaged to help the regimental tailor. Cardigan's critics said later that he defrayed the cost of the uniforms out of his own pocket, in order to impress the authorities at the Horse Guards. Others, less extreme, declared that he shared the cost with Prince Albert, who became Colonel-in-Chief of the regiment.

The change over from Dragoon scarlet to Hussar blue was made with as much magnificence as military requirements permitted. The jacket was plentifully decorated and edged with gold lace; more lace and braid glittered on the pelisse, which was trimmed with fur collar and cuffs. The distinctive crimson overalls (crimson was the colour of the Saxe-Coburg livery) had two yellow stripes. The headdress was a sealskin busby with white and crimson plume and a crimson busby bag. There was more gold lace on the sword belt. The shabrack (or saddlecloth that draped each horse) was of crimson ornamented with silver. Prince Albert's motto, *Treu und Fest* (True and Faithful) became the motto of the regiment: and his crest, a pillar charged with the arms of Saxony rising out of a ducal coronet, figured as the regimental badge.

The 11th Hussars thus presented a glorious, eye-catching spectacle; and the regiment was watched, closely. Newsmen kept their pens and imaginations ready to record the acts and utterances of its lieutenant-colonel. There were no less important sayings and doings connected with other regiments and other commanders; but readers were given the impression that the Earl of Cardigan and his splendid regiment were the sole progenitors of military scandal and publicity. There was much in the character and attitude of the Earl to justify his critics. But he was never prepared to surrender his sword, though from the start of his career he found himself in a hostile world where he encountered such storms of abuse that few would have been able to live down. Secure in the knowledge that he owed nothing, and disdaining the mask of humbug behind which many of his enemies sheltered, he adjusted his busby, set spur to his horse, and continued the regardless going forward that was his own way, and the way expected of him.

2

The nibbling process went on. When a certain Captain Smith wished to transfer into the 11th Hussars, Cardigan assented. But he later opposed the transfer. Whatever his reason was, we cannot

Adeline, second Lady Cardigan

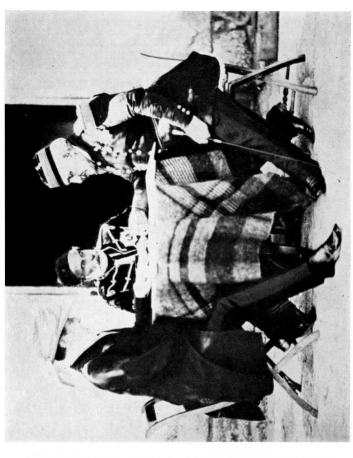

(*Left*) Lord Hill, Commander-in-Chief of the Army during the early part of Lord Cardigan's career. (*Right*) War council between the Commanders-in-Chief of the Allies in the Crimea, Britain, Turkey and France. Left to right: Lord Raglan, Omar Pasha and General Pelissier

now know it. But when it was stated that Captain Smith was about to marry, the *Observer* pounced. Cardigan, the paper said, had some objection to accepting married men in his regiment, though its records show that such a statement was arrant nonsense. "He is himself a married man," went on the *Observer*, "and what madness possesses him to oppose the introduction of an officer with an honourable and virtuous wife into his regiment? Really, the Earl of Cardigan should seek better counsel."

In the month of July 1839, while the regiment was still at Canterbury, a party of officers went out coursing. They rode across the fields towards Herne Bay, forded the Stour on their way back, then crossed a piece of high grass that had a narrow road or path running through it. There they were met by the owner of the ground, John Brent, a well-to-do miller who was also a city alderman and magistrate.

He accused the officers of trespassing; told them that he was a magistrate and a gentleman, and called them blackguards. One of the officers shook his whip at Brent and said he ought to be horse-whipped. The indignant miller then seized the curb rein of one of the riders, Cornet Brotherton. The Cornet caused his horse to rear and nearly forced the miller against a wall. The miller demanded to know the names of the officers. One of them shouted, "Mr. Snooks," and the party rode off.

The miller went to the barracks. There, however, in spite of advertising himself as a power in the district, he was refused entry. He then complained to Cardigan, saying that the field where the trespass occurred was laid in for hay, and that hedges enclosing it were broken. He intended to prosecute, and asked to know the officers' names.

Cardigan refused to give them, and offered to pay for the damage—which, according to a local paper, amounted to four-pennyworth of uncut hay. Brent replied that he wanted justice, not money, and demanded a public apology. That too Cardigan refused. Brent followed up by saying that, not knowing the names of the trespassers, he would not be able to call any of them out, and so obtain the satisfaction "that one gentleman usually requires of another". Cardigan sent a message to the effect that *he* was ready to give Mr. Brent satisfaction on behalf of the officers of the regiment. But Mr. Brent declined.

This trifle was taken up by the papers. Cardigan's attitude was

5

assailed in a number of anonymous letters, the writers of which, when challenged, chose to remain hidden. One that appeared in the *Morning Chronicle* purported to come from an officer of the 11th. But on investigation it was later admitted to be apocryphal. Cardigan, in one of his replies, said of Brent, "That he is a magistrate there can be no doubt; that he is a gentleman is quite another question."

The *Morning Chronicle* in a leader retorted that Cardigan "had an imperfect idea of what is due from one gentleman to another". This moved Cardigan to reply that the writer was fortunate in being the *anonymous* editor of a paper. The same editor then said that the country was, as yet, governed by law and not by swords; and went on to add, somewhat nervously, that if Cardigan forgot himself further he would have no hesitation in handing him over to the police.

The local papers knew Mr. Brent as a Whig and a Radical, which, they claimed, fully accounted for the opposition he had whipped up; while the *Kentish Gazette*, in a welter of impoliteness, referred to him as a "pugnacious and flour-feathered magistrate".

After some inquiries Cardigan sent the officers concerned in the affair to apologize to the miller. This was one of several petty incidents connected with Cardigan that from time to time reached the Commander-in-Chief at Whitehall. But Lord Hill, after observing that the officers' account of the trouble differed from Mr. Brent's, allowed it to lapse.

Cardigan, however, continued to be attacked in some of the local papers. After one outburst, which appeared over the name of the mayor of Canterbury, Cardigan sent a challenge to the mayor; but it then came to light that the letter had been written, and the mayor's signature forged, by a lawyer's clerk. The Earl was prepared, for the sake of his regiment's reputation, to stretch a point by confronting a miller; but he could not be expected, whatever the provocation, to exchange shots with a somewhat humbler scribe.

The final shot in the newspaper campaign was fired in a letter from a citizen of Canterbury. He wrote to say that he owed it to his own respectability, and to his business interests, to make it known that he was in no way connected with the affairs of Lord Cardigan's regiment. He was a greengrocer, trading in Cathedral Lane under his own name, which happened to be Snooks.

3

Cardigan took a personal interest in the living arrangements of his officers. He felt that his own dignity, and that of the regiment, demanded the highest standards in barrack life. The rules and regulations of the Mess were strictly observed. The menus and the style in which they were served came under his scrutiny. To dine with the officers of the 11th Hussars was a social experience and a privilege. It therefore happened that on the evening of 18th May 1840, when Major-General Sleigh, Inspector-General of Cavalry, and his Staff, were entertained at the Canterbury barracks, the Mess table of Cardigan's regiment excelled in hospitality and show.

The regimental silver and glass glittered under the chandeliers. The waiters, aware of being overlooked by the President of the Mess Committee, Captain Inigo Jones, moved with swift, silent and careful precision about their duties. Cardigan was seated by his guest at the head of the table. His eagle eye noted with satisfaction that the dinner was going well. But when champagne was being served Cardigan, glancing down the table, saw that a bottle, an ordinary bottle at that, and a black one, had been placed before one of his captains, John William Reynolds.

Could it be bottled porter? The drink was common enough in India, and Reynolds had served there. Whatever it was, it stood out like a blot on the immaculate tablecloth. And it wasn't even decanted! Cardigan inwardly fumed.

Next day he sent Captain Jones with a complaint to Reynolds. "The Colonel has desired me to tell you that you were wrong in having a black bottle placed on the table last night. The Mess should be conducted like a gentleman's table and not like a tavern dinner."

Reynolds considered he had not been in the wrong. One of General Sleigh's Staff had asked if he could have Moselle instead of champagne, and Reynolds had ordered it from a Mess waiter who placed it, in its bottle, on the table. Reynolds resented Cardigan's message, and he told Captain Jones that, as a brother officer, he would have shown better taste in declining to deliver it.

Cardigan summoned Reynolds to the orderly room, where the Adjutant and Captain Jones were present. Tempers ran high. "If you cannot behave properly, sir," said Cardigan, "why don't you leave the regiment? This is just the way with you Indian officers. You think you know everything; but I tell you, sir, you neither know your duty nor discipline." On second thoughts, Cardigan conceded that Reynolds knew his duty, but had no idea of discipline.

Captain Jones, who thought that in taking the message he was partly responsible for the difference, wanted to shake hands with Reynolds. But Reynolds refused, saying that he had no quarrel with Jones and it was therefore unnecessary to shake hands.

Cardigan broke in. "You have insulted Captain Jones."

"I have not, my lord," said Reynolds.

"I say you have." Cardigan raised his voice. "You are under arrest, and I shall report the matter to the Horse Guards."

Reynolds replied that he was sorry for it. He was placed under arrest, and summoned for further interviews with Cardigan, who confused Reynolds by sometimes addressing him in a private capacity, sometimes as his commanding officer. The interviews led nowhere, and were brought to an end when Lord Hill gave his judgment.

He advised Reynolds to admit that he had behaved improperly towards his colonel, and to resume friendship with Captain Jones. But though Reynolds fell in with the first direction, he showed a difficult side of his nature by still resenting the part that Captain Jones had played in the affair. He refused to shake hands with Jones, and remained under arrest.

On 9th June General Sleigh returned to Canterbury, and read before the officers of the 11th a condemnation of Reynolds from the Horse Guards. His behaviour had been "pernicious and vindictive", and through it Reynolds had forfeited the sympathy of every officer of rank in the service.

It was hardly possible, after that, for Reynolds to remain in the regiment. He applied to sell out, and to become a student at the Senior Department of the Royal Military College. Lord Fitzroy Somerset, as secretary at the Horse Guards, persuaded Reynolds to change his mind. He was given six months' leave of absence, with full pay as a captain in the 11th Hussars. The one condition Reynolds insisted upon was that he never again served, for even a single day, under Cardigan. He complained that the Earl's language had been habitually abusive, though Reynolds couldn't say that he actually swore at his officers.

The black bottle affair, greatly exaggerated by those who were ready to regard it as yet another instance of Cardigan's irascibility (without knowing the reasons for his objection) became a sensation. It figured as a joke, or as a means of abusing Cardigan, in many of the papers. Some who wrote letters deploring his conduct claimed to be old soldiers; if genuinely so, they were surprisingly ignorant (as will be seen) of Mess regulations pertaining to England.

Many of the letters, overlooking the fact that the case in question concerned the Canterbury Mess, pointed out that beer and porter appeared on Army tables in India. It was cheaper, and healthier in that climate, to drink porter than wine. One such letter in the *Morning Chronicle* ran: "Allow an old soldier to say a word about that feather-bed soldier, and great buzzing blue-bottle Lord Cardigan. In India bottled porter is always on the table at Mess." Another, claiming to come from an old soldier of thirty years' standing, said that "many a time and oft have I asked the fair sex, from Europe, and equally as respectable as Lady Cardigan herself, to take a glass of Hodgson's or Abbott's pale ale".

Some took the occasion to remark on the wounds they had suffered in the service, the number of children they had to support, and the paucity of their pensions. One who, judging by his statements, must have moved in high social circles, said that he had seen black bottles on the tables of noblemen equal in rank and fortune to Lord Cardigan. This writer signed himself, "Not one of the 11th, thank God!" One cannot help wondering why these gallant old soldiers, who were proud of having faced enemy fire, now shrank from signing their names.

"Cardigan may dislike the sight of black bottles," said the *Morning Chronicle*, "as some men faint at the sight of a spider." Besides filling columns, the 'Battle of Moselle', as it was called, gave rise to quarrels. A private of the 11th Hussars struck a guardsman in the street. When summoned before Cardigan, he exclaimed, "But, my lord, he called me a black bottle!" Captain Reynolds was the guest at a dinner where the host ordered his cook to prepare a dish of "the most *recherché* character". When placed in the centre of the table, and when the cover was removed, the dish was seen to consist of a large black bottle, decorated with flowers and with the word "Moselle" inscribed upon it. We are not told of its ingredients, but, says a report, "the black bottle was in great demand during the evening".

The impression was thus given that Cardigan was angered by the sight of a black bottle. This makes him appear as a man easily upset by the merest of trifles, without reason or a sense of proportion. But though he was doubtless annoyed by the appearance of a bottle on a table set out in all its brilliance, and with an important guest present, the continual mention of the object, and its colour, so engages and tickles the attention that Cardigan's critics are content to leave the matter there.

The truth is, however, that Cardigan's complaint was justified, as Captain Reynolds had committed a breach of regulations.

It was forbidden for any officer, at Mess, to order or to appropriate any particular drink. This was partly to avoid over-drinking, and also to prevent any officer from being extravagant, and making a show, by ordering a rare wine that might be beyond the means of his fellows. Such orders could only be given through the President of the Day, who passed them on to the Vice-President, who then conveyed them to a Mess waiter: and the fact of orders being hedged round by rules could make an officer think twice, and follow his taste in drink, rather than merely indulge a fancy of the moment. The order that Reynolds placed should have been given to Captain Jones, as President, which is why Cardigan sent the latter to remonstrate with Captain Reynolds.

This also explains Cardigan's reference to a gentleman's table, and his contrasting it with a tavern dinner. At a gentleman's table (and Cardigan took it for granted that the Mess of the 11th Hussars was a company of gentlemen) wine could, of course, only be ordered by the presiding host, while in free and easy taverns each man called for himself.

It was customary for those offending as Reynolds did to be admonished, by the regimental commander, before their fellow officers, for having compromised the character of the Mess.

Cardigan's reference to Indian officers was similarly strained and misrepresented in the Press. It was said, and it is still being repeated, that he could not endure officers who had served in

India; and that the phrase "Indian officers", as used by him, implied denigration or abuse.

The usual spate of protesting letters poured in to the Press. It was demanded that a meeting be convened at which Cardigan could be asked to explain and apologize for the offending words. He had "stigmatized a whole class of meritorious officers". The *Sussex Advertiser* rounded off its reproach with an attempt at humour, saying that His Lordship "would find the curries, the mulligatawny, and even the iced wines too hot for his palate at a *table d'hôte* at which Indian officers formed the principal guests".

The ridiculous idea that Cardigan was opposed to an officer merely because he had served in India has helped to confirm him as a quite incomprehensible character, with an absence of brain, and governed by unreasonable moods and tempers. But the phrase Indian officer was never considered to have had an offensive meaning. It was used by officers in the Queen's service who, having been in India, had observed the relaxed discipline that characterized the officers of the East India Company.

Those officers were often impatient of rules and authority. They professed an independent spirit that was foreign to the Queen's troops, who were, however, because of the climate, insensibly drawn into some of the prevailing East India Company ways; and Reynolds, by acting in defiance of Mess regulations, was showing the effects of the easy-going atmosphere in which he had lived for several years.

Wellington and many other distinguished soldiers served in India. Cardigan had joined his regiment there; and that Cardigan's attitude, far from being peculiar to him, was widespread at the time, is amply borne out by the words of Wellington, who said that the authorities in his day had little use for anyone who had served in India. Even a victory there, he found, was a cause of suspicion.

In the Peninsular, and at Waterloo, certain indulgences in the carrying of weapons and the wearing of equipment were allowed. They were attributed to the effects that Indian service and warfare had had upon Wellington, on which account he was sometimes referred to as 'an old Indian'. But no one regarded it as a term of reproach.

Cardigan soon accepted and remained immune to the blame or ridicule of the many-sided propaganda that was being built up against him. But some of his friends, unable to share his patrician remoteness, wrote a pamphlet vindicating his conduct and sent it to Prince Albert for his commendation. The Prince, however, was not to be drawn into anything so forthright, and he replied that he was unable to patronize any application written in defence of the one side or the other.

The eyes of half England were now turned upon Canterbury, and Canterbury watched the 11th Hussars as they exercised on Barham Downs or marched through the streets of the city. Carriages rolled up to Hales Place when the Colonel entertained. Parties of officers, and ladies in full skirts and big bonnets, walked on the lawn. Privates and their girls paraded by the river in the cool evening. The strains of the fine military band floated over the water. Recruits were never lacking, and the regiment was kept up to full strength; for Cardigan's Hussars, if only because of the stories told about them, enjoyed a popular prestige that was normally restricted to Household troops.

One of the 'recruits' who attached himself to the regiment was a black and white terrier, the property of a butcher in Northgate, named Jennings. The terrier deserted the shop, was given a home in a sentry box, turned up at every Mess, and became well versed in the complicated cavalry manœuvres. He was present at field days and reviews, wheeled and charged, without impeding the horses or causing confusion, and showed marked attention to the music of the band.

It was said that, according to the teaching of Pythagoras on the transmigration of souls, there could be no doubt but that the soul of some defunct drum-major had passed into the body of the martial dog, who because of that was called Major.

The 11th Hussars, after nearly two years in the cathedral city, were ordered to Brighton. The news was regretted. The troops had added gaiety, interest and colour to local life, and a deputation arrived at the barracks to present Cardigan with an address expressing approval of his regiment's good conduct on all occasions. It was noted that nearly as many Whigs as Conservatives joined in this tribute to the Colonel's discipline.

With the barracks in a turmoil of preparation, Major returned to the comfort of his old home. Small detachments of the regiment, the baggage wagons and their escorts, left almost daily. Each time Major went to the door and watched them pass.

Finally, the sound of drum and trumpet announced the coming of the main body; and at its head, riding before the band, was Lieutenant-Colonel the Earl of Cardigan and his lady. This time Major bounded away from those who were holding him, placed himself between the two leading horses, and trotted with the regiment at marching pace out of the city.

Brighton, with the sea and the Downs, was one of the best of the cavalry stations; and no less a critic than the political adventurer William Cobbett, some twenty years earlier, had surveyed the barracks on the Lewes Road, a mile and a half from Brighton, and thought them splendid.

4

The Cardigans took up residence at 45 Brunswick Square. It was then a part where houses were often let to army officers, furnished and for the season; and Number 45 was a typical town house with domestic offices in the basement, the hall and dining-room on the ground floor, a double drawing-room over that, and with two floors of bedrooms above. Only the inhabitants of Brunswick Square and Brunswick Place were admitted to the gardens. A rule forbade the wearing of pattens there, and no horse could be tied to the railings as it was likely to eat the shrubs in the gardens. The district had been lighted by gas since 1831.

Brighton owed its prominence as a provincial town to the patronage afforded it by the future George IV when Prince of Wales. There was a good coaching service to London, the railway was opened in 1841, and visitors flocked to join in the glory reflected by the Pavilion, where the Prince had resided for the summer and where he had indulged the caprices of a miniature but extravagant Court. It was quite "the thing", as the Countess of Granville said, to sit at a window "like citizens on a Sunday to see the folk go by". The afternoons were given over to 'carriage airings', when quality visitors and local gentry drove up and down the front. The one place for fashionable walking was on the Steine, where ladies exercised their pugs.

With the main part of the 11th Hussars at the cavalry barracks, two troops were quartered opposite the Pavilion, where they were privileged to use the royal stables. Except in the bigger manufacturing towns, a smart regiment was widely welcomed as an asset to social life; and Brighton entered fully into the round of military spectacles afforded by Cardigan's men.

There were reviews and mock battles on the Downs, and parades on Harvey's Cricket Ground, attended by crowds of local inhabitants who arrived in coaches, curricles, gigs, and even fish-carts. The regimental band played on the Steine and in Brunswick Square Gardens, "attracting thither a large concourse of fashionable company". Cardigan and his officers entertained a large party of 'elegantes' at the Swiss Gardens, New Shoreham. They travelled by train, took an early dinner, and danced quadrilles to the music of a band engaged by Cardigan.

The regiment turned out in marching order on Mondays; and on 10th September it paraded through the main streets fully equipped in its new uniform. First came the mounted band, headed by its silver kettle drums, draped, and beating out the pace as the sticks came down with alternating force; then the riders in their blue with slung jackets glittering with lace, coloured busby bags and plumes; the cherry-coloured legs of each rider, with their shining accoutrements, forked over the glistening coats of the horses; a pageant of mingled sight and sound that brought a sting of emotion to the eyes, and that summoned crowds of people to leave their doors and windows and to follow the regiment on its route. More scenes of enthusiasm occurred when the regiment, on the following Sunday, and led by Cardigan in all the richness of his uniform, attended St. Peter's Church.

The long series of troubles involving Cardigan continued, with growing force, at Brighton: and the next occasion was a private party given at his house in August. There were thirty guests. The band of the 11th played for the dancing which went on till two o'clock in the morning.

Now it needs to be understood that there were two captains, each named Reynolds, in the 11th. One was John William, of the black bottle affair; the other was Richard Anthony Reynolds, a good officer who had served for fifteen years, mostly in India; and in the course of the evening Cardigan was asked by a young lady, Mrs. Cunningham, whose husband was a lieutenant in the regiment, why neither of these captains was at the party.

Cardigan replied that they had not been invited; and on being asked, "Why not?" he continued, "Because I am not on good terms with them; and I fear if you are very anxious to see them you are not likely to see them here."

Richard Anthony Reynolds had fallen foul of Cardigan over his riding. The Captain resented this, and had since made himself so difficult that the General Commanding-in-Chief thought fit to reprove him for his improper conduct. But Reynolds, according to Cardigan, had continued to be fractious, troublesome and insubordinate.

Young Mrs. Cunningham was persistent. Perhaps she was a mischief-maker, for she pressed Cardigan to explain why he and Captain Reynolds were not on good terms. Cardigan tried to put her off by saying, "That is a very long story. I don't wish to enter into it." But those harmless remarks gathered strength. On the following morning (when the hard-worked band of the 11th was again playing, this time in Sussex Square, and to the usual gathering) another young lady retailed her version of the conversation to Lieutenant Cunningham.

The latter was a recently commissioned officer of 20. His wife seems to have been a snatcher-up of scandal; the second young lady may not have been a reliable witness; and their combined accounts of what Cardigan had said reached Captain Reynolds in slightly exaggerated form. Cardigan was quoted as saying, "As long as I live they [the two captains named Reynolds] shall never enter my house."

Captain Richard Anthony Reynolds complained of this to Cardigan in the following terms: "I cannot but consider this report highly objectionable, as it is calculated to convey an impression prejudicial to my character, and I therefore trust your Lordship will be good enough to authorize me to contradict it."

There was no written reply from Cardigan. But when next the regiment paraded on the Downs he summoned Reynolds to join himself, the Adjutant and Captain Jones. In their hearing Cardigan said that he had received a letter of an "improper nature" from Reynolds, to which he was not replying.

The matter might well have stopped there. But Reynolds carried his grievance to others who, he knew, shared his dislike of Cardigan; and he was spurred on by a concentration of resentment to pen a foolish and highly inflammatory letter.

Reynolds knew perfectly well that any officer who challenged another to a duel was liable to be cashiered; but after taunting

Cardigan with being a "professional duellist" who had challenged a miller and an attorney's clerk (the latter affair, as we have seen, was brought about by a forgery) he went on to say that such a reputation "does not admit of your privately offering insult to me, and then screening yourself under the cloak of Commanding Officer, and I must be allowed to tell your Lordship that it would far better become you to select a man whose hands are untied for the object of your Lordship's vindictive approaches, or to react as a more gallant fellow than yourself has done, and waive that rank which your wealth and Earldom alone entitle you to hold."

The letter was more than a little foolish, since, apart from placing the writer in the wrong as regards military law, it implied a sneer at Cardigan's personal courage, a quality in which, whatever his other faults, he was never found wanting: and it left Cardigan with no alternative but to report Reynolds to the Horse Guards, and to order his arrest. Reynolds was allowed two hours' exercise in the artillery barrack yard daily, but he could not leave the gates. Meanwhile the authorities at the Horse Guards, having taken stock of the case, prepared for a court martial.

5

The *Morning Chronicle* was the most disparaging and the most consistent of all the journals that opposed Lord Cardigan; and on 4th September 1840 a letter, stringent in its condemnation of his conduct, appeared in its columns.

It referred to the way in which he had "grossly and wantonly" insulted an officer at the Mess table, by telling him to hold his tongue. The insult had been repeated, but when charges were sent in against his Lordship, "superior authority" refused to hold an inquiry. Appeals were sent to Prince Albert and to Lord Melbourne, the Prime Minister, but with the same negative result.

The letter continued:

Lord Cardigan has now insulted the senior Captain of the regiment —a private insult—and when called upon for redress has again claimed his privilege as Commanding Officer and placed Captain ——under arrest for resenting such an insult. Many a gallant officer has waived the privilege which nothing but wealth and Earldom obtained for Lord Cardigan. The Army are supposed to be particularly tenacious of their honour, and to regard with repugnance any violation of it. I therefore, sincerely trust, Gentlemen, that you will aid me in calling for an inquiry, and that it may no longer be imagined that a Commanding Officer may outrage every gentlemanly feeling of others under his command with impunity.

This letter, a part of which suggests that its writer was familiar with the letter sent by Captain Reynolds to Cardigan, was signed "An Old Soldier".

Its appearance called forth a protest from the *United Service Gazette*, to which the letter was originally sent. The *Gazette* had refused to print it, saying that, "Old Soldiers do not usually offer bribes to newspapers to publish anonymous libels on their superiors." We do not know the circumstances referred to: but the *Gazette* also said that, for attacks on Lord Cardigan that appeared in the *Morning Chronicle* from time to time, "a very liberal price has been paid". This accusation was never taken up or answered by the paper.

Cardigan applied directly to the *Morning Chronicle*, demanding to know who had written the letter: and the editor, perhaps a weak man who was intimidated by the furious Colonel, broke a rule of his trade by giving the writer's name. It was Harvey Tuckett, ex-Captain of the 11th Hussars, whom Cardigan had first met in India, an amateur gentleman of the pen who, Cardigan believed, had stirred up trouble in the past by making him the subject of frothy slanders. Tuckett was now in business as an Indian and colonial agent in the City.

Cardigan sent his friend, Captain Douglas, to seek an apology. This Tuckett refused, stating that his letter was correct in every detail. The outcome was that Cardigan challenged Tuckett to a duel, which was arranged for 12th September, on Wimbledon Common.

For some years now the law had been unable to make up its mind about the old practice of duelling. Officially it was proscribed and treated as murder, to be punished by hard labour with the treadmill or by various periods of transportation. But such penalties were seldom if ever enforced, especially as there was still a keen regard for the code of honour. There were certain insults, or causes of quarrel, that a man of spirit could not be expected to overlook, even though satisfaction meant merely an exchange of shots without either party being injured; and it was generally accepted that public figures such as Wellington, Fox, Canning, Pitt, Castlereagh, and the Duke of York, all of whom figured in duels, had been justified in taking up or issuing a challenge.

But even allowing for the code of honour, the case of an army officer who challenged another was more difficult. He was committing a breach of certain articles of war, which forbade duelling; though if he swallowed an insult, or refused a challenge, he risked inviting the contempt of his fellows. The army's prohibition of duelling, however, could not be applied to the Cardigan–Tuckett controversy, as the latter had resigned his commission.

6

The afternoon of Saturday, 12th September, was clear and sunny. The air was calm, as shown by the sails of the windmill on Wimbledon Common; and on the gallery of the mill its occupier, Thomas Hunt Dann, stood airing himself and surveying the roads that crossed the Common. One led by the palings of Earl Spencer's park, and by the spot where the parishes of Wimbledon, Wandsworth and Putney meet.

Dann was suddenly aware of movement on the road, caused by two carriages and a chaise. One carriage halted by the park, the other drew up on the north side of the Common. A party of men alighted from the vehicles, and appeared to be marking the ground. Thomas Dann, who was a constable as well as a miller, and who had seen such happenings before, noted the time. It was five o'clock. He then called his wife, Sarah, and his son, Sebastian Byron Dann, descended from the gallery and hurried across the couple of hundred yards to where two of the men, after standing back to back, walked twelve measured paces from each other.

Shots were fired as Dann hurried towards them, but neither of the principals appeared to be hurt. He noticed that the taller of the two, who was Cardigan, made an impatient gesture, and signed for his second to give him another pistol. There was a further exchange of shots when Dann was about 15 yards distant from the group, and following this the taller man's opponent (Tuckett) was seen to be wounded.

He was bleeding copiously when Dann came hurrying up, and

Cardigan, still holding his pistol and in what the miller thought was a lordly voice, demanded to know why Dann was interfering.

"You have been committing a breach of the peace," said Dann, "and I now take you into custody in the name of Her Majesty." The party consisting of Captain Douglas, Captain Wainwright of the 47th Infantry, who was Tuckett's second, and Sir James Anderson, who was present as a surgeon, then repaired to the mill where Mrs. Dann provided a basin of water and a towel.

Tuckett's wound was by no means serious. The bullet had entered the upper part of the hip bone, and then come out near the spine. His second gave the constable a card, bearing Tuckett's address, and the surgeon then arranged to take the wounded man to his London house for treatment.

Dann asked the others to accompany him to the police station, which was nearby. But in all these proceedings it was not the constable, but Cardigan, who took control. He was first out of the carriage. He knocked on the station door, and Inspector John Busain, of the Metropolitan Police, was sufficiently impressed by his bearing as to bow when asking their business.

"I have been fighting a duel," Cardigan told him, "and I have wounded my man. Not seriously, I believe; slightly, a mere graze across the back."

Cardigan then produced a number of cards, letting some fall at the inspector's feet as he did so. The inspector read on the one that was given him, "The Earl of Cardigan, 11th Light Dragoons."

The inspector, of course, read the papers. He understood now why the sight of the visitor had impressed him. But he could not forbear saying that he hoped the duel had not been with Captain Reynolds.

Cardigan was scornful. "Dear me, no!" (What could this dolt of a policeman know of military decorum?) "Do you think I would condescend to fight with one of my own officers?"

He was then required to enter a recognizance to appear, when summoned, before a bench of magistrates at Wandsworth; and late that evening he returned with Lady Cardigan to Brighton. On the journey his mind went over the events of the day, and he reached the barracks, where he was not expected, in a bad temper.

As he passed through the gate he noticed that the sentry was not at his post. It was a cold night, and the sentry explained, when summoned, that he left his post in order to put more coals on the guard-room fire. Cardigan had the man arrested and sentenced him to be drilled, for a month, in the vicinity of the gate he had deserted, in order to make him fully aware of a sentry's duty.

A few days later a trifling regimental occurrence, that might have been quietly handled, brought forth another of the ever-ready complaints with which Cardigan, when the devil of irritability moved him, pestered the Horse Guards.

A subaltern was sent each week from the barracks to the Pavilion stables on special guard, and on 17th September this duty devolved upon Lieutenant William Forrest. Before leaving barracks he locked his room, which held his belongings, and pocketed the key. Meanwhile Cardigan had told another young officer, Lieutenant Jenkinson, that he could make temporary use of the room that Forrest had vacated; but when he attempted to do so Jenkinson could not, of course, get in.

Cardigan fumed, and shortly afterwards, when driving his phaeton along the Steine, he caught sight of Forrest who was coming from the Pavilion. It was late afternoon and the place was busy; but Cardigan stopped, jumped out, called Forrest across the street, and demanded to know, in a loud voice, why he was still retaining the key of his room. "Do you suppose, sir, you can hold two rooms? I have sent an order for the key to be given up, and given up it shall be."

Forrest replied that his possessions were still in the room at the barracks. There was nowhere else to keep them, and no place to dress at the Pavilion. He was not breaking any regulation by holding the key, and since it was only for a week it was unreasonable to require him to give it up.

To Cardigan the rules of the army were sacred. He broke none himself; he enforced their observance by others; and now to hear a junior officer, to justify his own temerity, refer to those rules, drove Cardigan into a fury.

"So you mean to come the letter of the law over me, sir, do you? I must tell you that military lawyers do not get on in the service. I could understand your feeling inconvenience if you had been accustomed to two or three suites of apartments at St. James's, but really—for you . . . !" Cardigan, now bent on pinpointing faults, suddenly switched his attack. "And what were you doing in the Mess room this morning after the stable trumpet had sounded?"

Since he had neither stabling nor a servant at the Pavilion, Forrest replied, he was compelled to take his horse back to barracks himself, and he had then gone into the Mess room for breakfast.

"Do you suppose, sir," Cardigan inquired, at his most intolerant, "that it is necessary for an officer to eat after field exercises?" To that there could be no adequate reply, and Cardigan went on, "I am the Commanding Officer of this regiment, and I order you to give up the key of your room, and that instantly, to Lieutenant Jenkinson."

But by the end of the day the key had not been handed over, and Cardigan reported the matter to Lord Hill. When asked for an explanation, Forrest admitted he had been at fault, but said it was due to the Lieutenant-Colonel's "offensive and irritating manner and language. . . . Had I received the slightest courtesy I should not now find myself in the painful position of being reported to the General Commanding-in-Chief."

Lord Hill requested Cardigan, more than once, to give a fuller version of the story; but Cardigan, as he sometimes did when he felt that his never-great stock of patience had been exhausted, failed to reply. The matter came to an end when Forrest received a mild reprimand from 'Daddy' Hill.

This was the period when opposition to Cardigan's command became most marked. He was advised by the *United Service Gazette*, a mainly friendly publication, to abrogate a little of his aristocratic *hauteur*, and to "cease to trample on the feelings of his subordinates". Some officers applied to sell out or to be exchanged, though in fairness it needs to be stated that Cardigan had been held responsible for officers who petitioned to leave the 11th before he took command. At least one who did so, Major Morse Cooper, wished to return to the regiment under Cardigan, though he afterwards joined the ranks of the Earl's critics.

7

Cardigan and his second, Captain Douglas, appeared before the Wandsworth magistrates on 28th September. The courtroom was

6

crowded, and people gathered outside for a glimpse of the privileged being who was also cutting a figure in the popular Press.

The main part of the hearing turned on a statement read by the police inspector, Busain, to the effect that Cardigan's duelling pistols had rifled barrels and hair triggers. Rifled barrels have spiral grooves that produce a rotatory motion in whatever is fired, thus adding precision to a steady aim; a hair or detented trigger releases the main one by only a slight touch. The pistols had been examined on behalf of the police by a gunsmith named Field.

It was part of a second's duty to examine the pistols before a duel, and Captain Douglas declared, "I looked at the barrels to ascertain whether they were rifled, and satisfied my mind they were not." This was later supported by Tuckett, who exonerated his opponent from any blame in the matter of weapons. Inspector Busain, having read Field's statement, afterwards agreed that the barrels of Cardigan's pistols were not rifled.

The pistols were taken from their case, which bore the Cardigan crest, and passed to the members of the bench. "No one would think of fighting a duel with hair triggers," Cardigan told them. It was easy enough to discover that the triggers were perfectly normal, and one of the magistrates, Captain Page, put his finger in the barrel to feel for grooves.

"You see, they are not rifled," Cardigan said.

"Yes," answered Page, "I perceive they are not."

Later he contradicted himself, expressed concern as to the length of the pistols—had one been longer than the other?—and finally left the court.

A statement was obtained from the Dover Street firm of Manton and Hudson, who had made and supplied the pistols to Cardigan shortly before he left for India. This certified that the pistols were, in every respect, similar to the ordinary duelling kind that they had manufactured for the past fifty years.

Another statement, that might have been read at the hearing, occurred in the columns of *John Bull*. This spoke of Field, the gunsmith applied to by the police, as a one-time comic actor who had played at Covent Garden Theatre.

The case was referred to the Central Criminal Court at the Old Bailey where, some weeks later, a grand jury found true bills, for feloniously shooting, against Cardigan and Captain Douglas. His rank precluded Cardigan from being tried in an ordinary criminal court, and it was arranged that he be tried, by his peers assembled in full Parliament, on 16th February 1841. He was admitted to bail, on his own recognizance and with two other sureties, for £20,000.

Although accepted by many as a remote possibility, Cardigan was liable, if convicted as a felon, to suffer the forfeiture of his possessions to the Crown. With this in mind he executed a deed of gift, making his estates over to Viscount Curzon, the eldest son of his sister Harriet, who had married Earl Howe. The cost of duty on this transaction was £10,000.

The news of the coming trial was a signal for Cardigan's enemies again to line up against him. *The Times* anticipated his being sentenced by demanding that his head be cropped, that he be put on a felon's diet and sent to the treadmill. But there was no outcry against the equally guilty Tuckett. The surgeon reported that he was "pretty well", and walking about the drawing-room of his house. But he was not called before the magistrates. No Bill was passed against him, and it was never suggested that the prosecution, intent on pressing the case against the unpopular Cardigan, should demand the appearance of Tuckett at the Bar.

8

At this period Cardigan might well be likened to an actor who becomes conspicuous, in a succession of different roles, on as many different stages. For while affairs such as the black bottle were fresh in the public mind, and while his trial at the House of Lords was pending, preparations were under way for the court martial of Captain Reynolds at Brighton.

It began on 24th September, and early in the morning a large crowd, mostly of ladies, gathered outside the Gloucester Hotel to see Captain Reynolds, a fine figure with jet black hair and moustachios, and dark flashing eyes, make his way to the court, which met in a ward of the hospital at Preston Barracks.

When the doors opened, people who had waited for hours surged forward, breaking the glazed panels and finally wrenching the doors off their hinges. The room was so hot that the windows

were flung open, whereupon more people climbed in, or stood
outside on any kind of stand so that the apertures were filled with
their craning heads and faces. Orderlies were kept busy restraining
excited movements and exclamations when the members of the
court came in, officers in the full dress of various regiments,
including Guardsmen, with Major Pipon as Judge Advocate, and
Lieutenant-General the Hon. Sir Hercules Pakenham in the
President's chair.

Lord Cardigan spoke first. "On his appearance," said a
reporter, "it is not necessary to make any remark, as he is
generally known." Cardigan referred to the "torrent of misre-
presentation and obloquy" which had been poured upon him by
a section of the Press, and to the "ungracious and derogatory
words" put into his mouth, and which he solemnly declared had
never issued from it. The words he denied saying were, "As long
as I live, they [the two captains named Reynolds] shall never enter
my house."

He then read the letter which formed the basis of the charge
against Reynolds, "a most disrespectful, insubordinate, offensive
and insulting letter". Cardigan was almost overwhelmed with
emotion during the reading, and had to wipe his eyes several
times.

On succeeding days, barriers were erected to keep back the
people when the court opened. As part of his defence, Reynolds
declared that Cardigan's conduct as commanding officer was
irritating and insulting in the extreme. He was unable to call the
young lady to whom Cardigan had spoken on the evening of the
party, as a witness, since she had left for Paris. He agreed that Lord
Cardigan had a perfect right to choose his guests. He had visited
Cardigan's house at Deene, and they had been on good terms
when the regiment was in India. But the offensive remark made
by Lord Cardigan, and which had called forth his letter, was calculated to rob him of his good name and to injure his status in
society. As he sat down, Reynolds was applauded by some of the
officers present.

When next he spoke, Cardigan answered the charge that he
could not endure Indian officers. When Captain Reynolds
returned from India, Cardigan, in the face of opposition from
certain disgruntled officers, had seen to it that Reynolds remained
with the regiment. "Does this", Cardigan asked the court, "look

like undervaluing Indian services? Is it the conduct of one who is held up falsely to the public as speaking contemptuously of Indian officers? This is only one instance out of many of the exertions I have used in support of Indian officers whom I am charged with affronting."

Before the hearing ended, and on one of the days when the court was not in session, Cardigan led his regiment to exercise on the Downs. Half Brighton, including many 'fashionables', and officers from the court still in full dress, gathered to witness this demonstration of discipline and efficiency by the commander who was engaging the attention of the public. Military judges and civilian enthusiasts alike were considerably impressed by the regiment's bearing. "Lord Cardigan", said a journalist on the spot, "must feel justly proud of being placed at the head of so truly soldier-like a corps."

The offence committed by Reynolds, in seeking to promote a duel with his commanding officer, admitted of only one verdict, which the court delivered on 19th October. He was found guilty and sentenced to be cashiered. But at the same time Cardigan received some advice from the Commander-in-Chief.

Lord Hill reminded him that the officers of the 11th had recently returned from a tropical climate, "in which the habits and the customs of the service must differ from those in European service. It was hoped that in future Lord Cardigan would exercise moderation and forbearance." Lord Hill considered that the numerous complaints which had been made to him as commander-in-chief would never have occurred "if the Lieutenant-Colonel of the 11th Hussars had evinced the proper degree of temper and discretion in the exercise of his command".

A reporter on the scene said that Cardigan was obviously delighted by the court's verdict; but when the admonition from Lord Hill was read "his countenance changed, and the agony on his face was perceptible to all". However, whatever abashment Cardigan felt was short lived; for a few days later he was heard to say that Lord Hill, who had landed interests, was more fitted to fatten bullocks on his pet farm than to have command of the army.

The Duke of Wellington agreed that Reynolds, by intending provocation to his commanding officer, had committed a serious breach of discipline. But a section of the public, and most of the

Press, knew better. The result of the trial was greeted as yet another proof of Cardigan's tyranny and harshness. Letters attacking him, and demanding some recompense for Reynolds, filled columns of the *Morning Chronicle*, the *Globe*, and the *Sun*, some couched in over-enthusiastic language on behalf of Reynolds, some sadly lacking in humour.

It was stated that the result of the court martial, another addition to the "dark catalogue of events in Lord Cardigan's military command", was enough to make the country rise; that Cardigan "had snatched from the brow of a gallant young officer the blood-stained helmet he had worn in distant climes". The women of England were called on to present Reynolds with a memorial of their regard for his high character and spirited conduct. One oddly constructed letter said that the verdict now made it possible for a commanding officer to spit in the face of an inferior, or to be found in a delicate situation with an inferior's wife, and then to launch a complaint about it. Favourites with the Horse Guards (the letter continued) like the Earl of Cardigan, could now whisper away the character and reputation of deserving men, a back-biting and abominable practice which had driven many an officer from the service he was calculated to honour.

Committees were formed on behalf of Reynolds, and penny subscriptions were started in several towns. His sympathizers were not always wise in their selection of meeting places. One such place was the 'Portland Arms', a Marylebone public house; another was a low tavern, the 'Lord Nelson', in Southwark.

"The Lord Nelson Southwark!" commented the *Brighton Gazette*, a paper which had been favourably impressed by the conduct of Cardigan's regiment in the town. "A fine place, truly, to originate a national fund!"

Reynolds had private means, and he was not so badly hit by the loss of his commission as some of his sympathizers liked to imagine; and he realized that some of the methods they employed to recompense him, and to collect money for a possible appeal to the Queen, were not reacting to his credit. So he published a disclaimer, to the effect that his loss, though a bitter one, "was not of a nature to be alleviated by pecuniary compensation; and that he was even more anxious that no attempt should be made to influence the Crown on his behalf".

But the anti-Cardigan agitation continued, spreading to all

circles and to many different occasions. Boys at school took sides for or against him. Edmund Yates, a son of the actor-manager Frederick Henry Yates, was then at a preparatory school at Highgate. One of his uncles, Colonel Brunton, had brought Cardigan to the house of the Yates family in the Strand, and young Edmund formed an admiring impression of Cardigan's character and personality. His defence of Cardigan made him unpopular at school.

Stories were manufactured or worked up for the benefit of the papers. Lord Hill, at a dinner party, was seated next to a lady who took and cracked a walnut. She remarked that its variegated skin reminded her of the uniform of the 11th Hussars (to which, of course, it bore not the slightest resemblance). But a wit who was present provided a finishing touch by saying that walnuts, like the officers of the 11th, were broken for the sake of their *kernel*; and thus embroidered the incident found its way to the columns of a paper, the *Alligator*.

An effigy of Lord Cardigan, grotesquely attired as a Hussar complete with whiskers, cigar, a black bottle, and perched on a donkey, was paraded, before being burnt, through the streets of Brighton on Guy Fawkes day. A paper remarked that the people had exchanged the satisfaction of burning the Pope for the pleasure of roasting an earl.

There were certain incidents connected with Cardigan about this time that had no grounding in fact, and were plainly meant to disparage him; others were at least contradictory. The *Morning Chronicle* reported his attendance at the Brighton Theatre Royal, where the celebrated Mr. Betty was appearing in *Hamlet*. Cardigan was recognized when he took his seat in a box, and was immediately assailed by a storm of hisses. This continued, without the curtain being raised, for half an hour, after which Cardigan rose and left the theatre. Three loud groans from the audience followed him out, then three cheers were given for Captain Reynolds.

According to a local paper, however, the disturbance that night at the theatre was directed towards a stranger, who stood at the side of the stage accompanied by "a lady of a certain description". Lord Cardigan was in London on the night in question, and had not been to the theatre during the whole of the week.

The announcement of a special performance at the theatre,

under the patronage of Lord Cardigan and the officers of the 11th Hussars, at which the regimental band would play several overtures, caused much resentment and speculation. It was said that Cardigan would obviously buy up all the tickets and fill the house with his hirelings, and the performance was denounced in advance as a revelation of his callous disregard for public opinion.

But a few days before it was billed to take place notice was given of its cancellation. "The public is most respectfully informed that, in consequence of the very dangerous illness of Major Jenkins, Lieutenant-Colonel the Earl of Cardigan and the officers of the 11th Hussars have been under the necessity of postponing their patronage of the theatre to some future day."

But the performance never took place. Major Jenkins died, and Cardigan spent nearly the whole of the two nights before his death sitting at his bedside. "Yet this is the man", one of the few pro-Cardigan papers pointed out, "who was painted as regardless of his officers' comfort and welfare!" Cardigan walked in the imposing funeral procession to St. Peter's Church, and defrayed all the funeral expenses. But even this happening was taken up and distorted to swell the agitation against him.

An anonymous letter declared that the Major's death had been caused by anxiety over Reynolds. In the very moment before he died he was heard to whisper, "Poor Reynolds!" But this attempt to heap more discredit upon Cardigan by wringing the heart called forth a denial from the dead man's son, of Balliol College, who said that after his first seizure his father was attacked by delirium. He then became totally insensible until he expired, and those who waited beside him for some lucid interval never heard him utter a single word.

But still the papers gave Cardigan no rest. When it was known that he had invited his officers to Deene Park, the *Morning Chronicle* asked, "Who will be mean enough to go?" It then provided the answer, "Only Cardigan's toadies!" But prolonged and concentrated propaganda attacks cannot fail to have some effect, and those directed against Cardigan culminated in a scene at Drury Lane Theatre on the day before Christmas Eve 1840.

It was at a promenade concert conducted by Monsieur Jullien, an eccentric or a charlatan, if not both, who performed by waving his arms with electric vigour, now whirling, now soothing, and then giving way to a frenzy of gesticulation and finally sinking, gasping and exhausted, and with his huge white waistcoat heaving, into a gilded chair that was placed by the rostrum to cushion his collapse.

His musical machine, for such it was, consisted of ninety instrumentalists and a chorus of eighty. On the night in question the programme included the overture to *Fidelio*, the overture to *Robert le Diable* and to Auber's *Bronze Horse*; a madrigal "Down in a Flowery Vale", and a flute fantasia on Weber's air "The Hermit Song".

Some of the items had been performed when a group of people, gathered near a corner of the stage, commenced pointing at a box where Cardigan was seated with one or two friends and some ladies. People in other parts of the house turned and craned their necks till even Monsieur Jullien's antics were forgotten. There were cries of "Shame! Black bottle! Turn him out!" Cardigan sat unmoved.

Even Byron had stayed away from the theatre for fear of being assailed by the self-righteous, in whom the sight of prey arouses a veritable frenzy. But Cardigan's attitude agreed with that of Wellington, who, during one of his unpopular spells, said that he wouldn't allow the mob of London to deprive him of his temper or his spirits. For two hours, from nine until eleven o'clock, the noise continued. Not a note of music was heard, though Monsieur Jullien bounced up and down, as explosive as ever, and some of the demonstrators cooled off. But Cardigan sat on for as long as he wished.

He finally advanced to the front of the box, donned his cloak with great coolness, bowed to those who continued the uproar, and retired.

The endemic effect of the opposition to Cardigan may be judged by the fact that the scene was welcomed by the *Spectator*, as showing "a healthy state of public sentiment". But a letter in *The Times* on 29th January, from one who was at Drury Lane, stated that "Lord Cardigan's demeanour throughout was perfectly correct and dignified, respectful towards the audience, but firm and determined not to be bullied from a place where he had as good a right to be as all those clamourers". The same writer also observed that the trouble had been started "by two or three members of the Hebrew community".

Cardigan's inborn self-confidence never diminished. But his

assurance also derived from the fact that he was answerable only to the military authorities appointed by the Queen. He was therefore not over concerned when the Press used its influence against him; and a letter explaining his silence was sent by his solicitors to *The Times*. It referred to the numerous and unsparing attacks being made upon him, and observed that "His Lordship's forbearance to reply to them through the same channels has been construed into a tacit admission of the truth of the allegations." But so far from admitting that, "his silence is entirely owing to the orders of the Army forbidding any communications between officers on full pay and the public Press on military matters".

The plain-spoken *John Bull* printed an article on Cardigan's behalf that went directly to the heart of the matter. "Lord Cardigan is an Earl—that is one horrid fault. He is, we believe, a conservative Earl—that is another horrid fault. He is an active, able, and vigilant officer, devoted to his profession, and anxious to keep his regiment in a state or order and discipline. All these circumstances in the outset are confessedly very much against Lord Cardigan."

Touching the effects of that discipline, and the harshness with which he was said to rule his regiment, the punishment return showed that, at the time of the Brighton court martial, there were only four men of the 11th Hussars on punishment drill. This meant parading up and down for a given time in heavy marching order. "Perhaps a similar return cannot be made from any other regiment in Her Majesty's service," concluded *John Bull*; for this was a time when punishments were frequent and often severe.

The *Brighton Gazette*, after observing the behaviour of the regiment and its commander at close quarters, had this to say: "Of Lord Cardigan we know, personally, nothing; but no unpopularity should deter us from stating that under his command the 11th Hussars have attained a superiority of discipline and order which, any of our readers may see with their own eyes, is superseded by no regiment in the service. We also know that His Lordship is popular with the men, as indeed good officers always are, strict as may be the discipline to which they are subjected."

Cardigan's most consistent champion among the London papers was the *Morning Post*, which confessed itself unable to discover "the motive of this virulent enmity to the noble lord". The opinion of Lord John Russell was that because of Lord

Cardigan's rank, a great deal more was made of the Brighton court martial than there would have been in any ordinary case; and Sir Robert Peel echoed this when he spoke of Cardigan's unjust treatment by the greater portion of the Press, "from which a man of inferior rank would have been exempt".

But apart from these considerations, and the extent to which political and social bias counted at the time, it was generally recognized that in every regiment, and especially in what are called crack regiments, there were certain young men of fashion who resented being called to parade at six o'clock in the morning, and being kept closely to duty. It was probably their organized resentment which caused Sir Henry Hardinge to state in the Commons: "That there existed, in Cardigan's regiment, something in the nature of a cabal": and the term 'cabal' occurred in a document, drawn up for the information of the Prime Minister, and kept at the Horse Guards, which spoke of differences that rose between Lord Cardigan and his subordinates. There were, it went on to say, "four or five officers in the regiment who were resolved to contest, and if possible to control, the authority of their Commanding Officer".

One of the officers who stood apart from any such design expressed the opinion that, if war came, they might "look in vain for a commanding officer more thoroughly initiated in all military operations, more inured to fatigue, more deeply interested in the success of his regiment, than the Earl of Cardigan".

Finally, even the far from friendly *Times* was compelled to admit that few persons, exposed to the same pressure, would have refrained as he (Cardigan) had from taking the slightest notice of attacks.

The Victorian love of skits, parodies and trifling rhymes gave rise to what was called "The English Battle Song", which appeared in the *Morning Post*. It emphasized Cardigan's right to choose his own guests when giving a party, and ridiculed the offence, the subsequent court martial and widespread agitation that followed from a perfectly harmless remark.

Lord Cardigan's given a party at Brighton,
And Reynolds has not been invited at all!

There, there, there is an insult
This British nation will never withstand;

So up with your monkeys, and out with your weapons,
And show them the pride of a passionate land!

Hear, hear, hear the dread story
Let your proud heart by its terrors be rent;
There was a young lady, a Whig or a Tory,
Who made a sensation wherever she went.

She, she with Lord Cardigan walking,
All in the party room, and arm in arm,
Asked, in the slightest of amiable talking,
For Captain Reynolds, and where was the harm?
But then His Lordship, though good were his manners,
(He did not familiarly utter "my dear")
Insulted the whole of the nation's bright banners
By saying, "I'm sure that you'll not find him here."
"Why, why, why?" asked the lady.
"Because," said His Lordship, "we're not on good terms."
(We think there's a case of revolt here already,
At least, we are sure we discover the germs.)
"But, but, but—" then the lady
Added significant, pleasing and well,
"Why not on terms?" and his Lordship, quite steady,
Responded, "The story is too long to tell."

There, there, there is an insult
This British nation will never withstand;
So up with your monkeys, and out with your weapons,
And show them the pride of a passionate land!

9

One of the most unreasonable sides of Cardigan's nature was
shown by his persistent disregard of warnings. The authorities at
the Horse Guards were tired of his series of complaints; yet he
continued to make them, on the slightest excuse, and to order the
arrest of anyone who appeared to act in defiance of his orders.
His lack of wisdom in this, and his imperious manner, provided
more ammunition for his opponents.

The next to incur his wrath was Doctor Backshall Sandham,
the junior surgeon of the regiment, who had served with the army
for more than thirty years.

Cardigan was as meticulous in the ordering of church parades as he was over the most active exercise; and on 8th December he instructed Doctor Sandham to go with the troops who were attending St. Peter's Church, and afterwards to return with them to barracks. There were two gates leading to the church, and the troops would naturally enter and leave by the main one.

At the conclusion of the service Sandham had some difficulty in adjusting the fastening of his cap. By the time he was ready the troops were on their way back, and Sandham managed to catch up with them by using the smaller of the two gates leading from the churchyard.

The Adjutant was waiting for him when he reached barracks. "It is his Lordship's order", he was told, "that you fall in with the troops." The surgeon, sensing that he had offended, but not understanding how, later told Cardigan that he thought his orders had been to fall in with the troops.

"Those are my orders, sir," said Cardigan, who then asked, "Did you not come out at the small gate?"

Sandham agreed that he had. "Then I order you in future, sir, to come out of the main gate," rapped Cardigan.

The indignant doctor repeated this conversation to others in the regiment; and when Cardigan heard of it he summoned Sandham, who, after telling Cardigan that he was unjust, was placed under arrest.

The doctor and Cardigan both sent written complaints to Lord Hill, and Cardigan hastened to the Horse Guards to make his explanation. But Lord Hill's reply was unexpectedly severe. Mr. Sandham, it said, was unaware of his fault, which was of an unimportant character. Lord Hill hoped that his valuable time would not again be taken up by regimental controversies, and he ended by telling Cardigan that he would "best consult his own integrity, comply with the wishes of the Army in general, and more particularly of his own regiment, and would conciliate the feelings of the British public towards himself, were he at once, by retiring from the Army, to restore that harmony and good fellowship again to the 11th Hussars which, until His Lordship joined the regiment, previously existed". The Commander-in-Chief directed that this letter be placed in Mr. Sandham's hands.

But Cardigan had no intention of leaving the army, nor of showing the letter to Mr. Sandham. He likewise refused to answer Lord Hill when the latter wrote, more than once, asking if his direction had been followed. Cardigan blissfully ignored whatever opposition or difficulty stood in his way; the proof of the rightness of his conduct was in the perfect appearance and performance of the regiment he had virtually created.

But here again it needs to be pointed out that the affair of Doctor Sandham and the two gates was, as in the case of the black bottle, not quite so ridiculous as some modern writers on the subject make it appear. The question was not whether Sandham emerged by the large or small gate, as is thoughtlessly suggested; it was rather that Sandham, by letting the troops pass through the larger exit without him, and then having to catch them up by using another way, had failed to obey Cardigan's order to fall in with and keep with the men. It was an instance, as appears so often in the Cardigan story, of a martinet's rigid insistence upon the letter of the law.

The next phase of that story, eagerly awaited by the public and the Press, was the trial in the House of Lords.

The Houses of Parliament had been burnt down in 1834, and the peers were now meeting in the Painted Chamber, a part of the building which escaped the fire. An army of carpenters, labourers, upholsterers and seamstresses was employed in the fitting of extra seats and galleries. New crimson carpets and cushions were provided. The cost of the preparation, including fees for counsel, for officers of the House, for witnesses, and the hire of a shorthand writer, was £1,290 12s. 6d.

The office of the Lord High Steward, or Judge, was filled by the Lord Chief Justice, Lord Denman, in place of the Lord Chancellor, who was indisposed. Counsel for the Crown were Sir John Campbell (the Attorney-General) and Mr. Waddington. Lord Cardigan retained Sir William Follett, Mr. Serjeant Wrangham, and Mr. Adolphus to conduct his defence.

10

Extra police were on duty at the approaches to the House on the morning of the trial, 16th February 1841. Soon after nine o'clock a number of carriages, occupied mostly by ladies, formed a line leading to the principal door. Peeresses were conducted to the

Strangers' Gallery. Others, with the sons and the friends of peers, filled the Great Gallery. Members of the Diplomatic Corps were present. Judges in their robes sat in front of the woolsack.

The House stood when Lord Denman entered, preceded by the Sergeant with the Mace, Black Rod bearing the Lord High Steward's staff, and Garter holding his sceptre. After prayers, read by the Bishop of Chichester, the roll of Lords was called. Then the Sergeant-at-Arms summoned the Yeoman Usher to bring James Thomas, Earl of Cardigan, to the bar.

Cardigan entered, tall and dignified. He bowed three times, and when he was seated the Lord High Steward preferred the charge—"Of shooting at Harvey Garnett Phipps Tuckett with intent to murder, or to maim and disable him." Cardigan pleaded not guilty, in a firm voice. "How will your Lordship be tried?" asked the Deputy Clerk of the Crown.

"By my peers," answered Cardigan. "God send your Lordship a good deliverance," responded the Clerk.

The trial was a farce that might have come direct from the pages of Dickens. The first quibble turned on the card that Tuckett had given, after the duel, when asked his name.

Sir William Follett declared that the card was not admissible in evidence. Unless the card was given with the full knowledge of the prisoner at the bar, he protested, it could not be used as evidence against him. The prisoner was no party to the giving of the card; he never saw it, and so was not aware of its contents.

"Therefore I take the liberty", said Follett, "of submitting to your lordships that the card cannot be read in evidence against the noble earl at this time."

The cross-examination of the miller's wife and son was typical of the many-sided and repeated questions by which the law seeks to perplex witnesses who are likely to be awed by their surroundings. What was the position of the post-chaises Mrs. Dann had seen on the Common? How far were they apart—how far were the parties from each other, and from the post-chaises?

It was stated, Follett said, that the distance from the mill to where the parties had taken their stand was about 220 yards. Could Mrs. Dann distinguish the features of the parties at that distance?

Mrs. Dann replied (unwisely for her) that she could see if their faces were red or pale.

Follett repeated his question. Could she distinguish the faces of gentlemen some 220 yards off, and whether they were red or pale?

Mrs. Dann replied that they appeared to have red faces "in the sun".

"All the gentlemen had red faces, had they?" queried Follett.

"No, I do not know if all of them had."

But Follett persisted. "Had they all red faces?"

The miller's wife again said, "No." Her cross-questioning ended with Follett again asking, as a refinement to diminish the worth of her evidence, "How many had red faces?"

Sir James Anderson, the doctor who attended Tuckett, was called next. But he brought the case no further, for he refused to answer any of the questions put to him, and in so decided a fashion that the people in the galleries were reduced to laughter.

The prosecution then called Mr. Walthew, a chemist who lived in the Poultry.

Tuckett rented rooms in his house and used them as offices, and Mr. Walthew was asked what were the Christian names of that Tuckett. But Mr. Follett again objected, on the grounds that the question could only be relevant if the person whose Christian names were being inquired into was connected in some way with the transaction.

Next to be summoned was an army agent named Codd, who was responsible for making over to Captain Tuckett his half-pay. Codd knew his client's full name to be Harvey Garnett Phipps Tuckett. But Tuckett called at Codd's office to collect his pay, and the agent had never seen Tuckett at his own house. So it was ruled that there was no link between the half-pay Tuckett and the captain of that name who had been on Wimbledon Common.

The disputed card now appeared in the evidence. It bore the name and address of Captain Harvey Tuckett, 13 Hamilton Place, New Road (in the parish of St. Pancras).

Sir William Follett, in Cardigan's defence, said that the only point established was that "a person of the name of Codd" received and made over the half-pay of someone named Harvey Garnett Phipps Tuckett. There was nothing to identify that person with the party whom the noble Earl was charged with having shot. The prosecution must prove the Christian names and surname of the person against whom the offence is alleged to have been committed. There was no such positive evidence, nothing to prove that the Tuckett mentioned by Codd was the Captain Tuckett referred to by other witnesses.

The Attorney-General replied by saying that the gentleman who was wounded by Lord Cardigan on 12th September was a Captain Harvey Tuckett. The same Captain Tuckett lived in Hamilton Place, New Road, and he rented premises in the Poultry. Sufficient evidence had been given to show that the aforesaid Captain Tuckett had been Lord Cardigan's opponent on the Common.

The Attorney-General went on, "Am I obliged to call the clerk of the parish where he (Captain Harvey Tuckett) was baptized, in order to prove his baptismal register? Am I obliged to call his father or his mother, or his godfathers or godmothers, to prove the name that was given to him at the baptismal font?"

Sir William Follett reiterated his point—that there was nothing to connect a Captain Tuckett, who bore certain Christian names, with the Captain Tuckett who was at Wimbledon Common on the day in question.

This principle of strict proof was best debated behind closed doors, and strangers were asked to withdraw. In their absence, the Lord High Steward reviewed the main point of Follett's defence. The link of identity had not been established between the half-pay officer known to Mr. Codd, and the person who had been wounded on 12th September. To name that person as Captain Tuckett, or as Captain Harvey Tuckett, was not sufficient. It was for the Crown to prove that the accused had fired at Captain Harvey Garnett Phipps Tuckett; and since that had not been done, the Earl of Cardigan could be declared 'not guilty'.

Judgment was given by each of the peers placing his hand upon his heart and announcing, in set terms, that the Earl was "not guilty, upon my honour". The Duke of Cleveland varied the formula slightly by declaring, "Not guilty *legally*, upon my honour", with marked stress upon the adverb. The white staff of the Lord High Steward was then broken in two; and another manifestation of legal hair-splitting, or a superb example of trickery, or an exploitation of absurdly over-stressed 'nice points', passed into the history of law.

Such, at least, may be the views of the ordinary man. But it needs to be emphasized that strict proof of the injured party's

7

name, according to his description in the indictment, is a principle of evidence; for without the safeguard of such strict proof, it might be possible for a man to be prosecuted for offending against a person whom he never saw.

The Crown, however, had not conducted the charge in a convincing manner. For the failure in proof of nomenclature would have been overcome by the appearance of Captain Tuckett at the bar, and his identification by those who witnessed the duel, and by the army agent who had business with him from time to time. But so obvious a method of proof was never insisted upon by the prosecution.

The result of the trial was greeted with more shrill expressions of disapproval. Several papers, mostly Radical, again opened their columns to the Earl's personal and political opponents, until even *The Times*, after deprecating his acquittal on an "absurd technical deficiency of proof", deplored the personal malevolence now heaped upon Cardigan as "a pitiful manifestation of popular rancour". A similar note was struck by the Attorney-General who said, in his summary of the trial, that there was "no propriety in trying to load the accused with unjust obloquy".

The greatest loss occasioned to Cardigan by the trial was a financial one. We have seen how, to guard against the remote possibility of his being convicted, he had already paid £10,000 for his property to be made over to his nephew; and the cost of duty on now having his property re-transferred was another £10,000.

The case was yet another cardinal instance of the inveterate one-sidedness displayed by Cardigan's critics. They were justified in condemning the conduct of the trial which turned on an over-refined point (or so it appeared to the man in the street) such as failure of proof. But the law against duelling declared that if any person shot, drew a trigger, or discharged any kind of loaded arms at another, he was guilty of felony.

Yet there was no demand for Captain Tuckett to go on trial. He had aimed twice at Cardigan, but Press and public stayed silent over his offence. At the same time the Earl of Mountcashel pointed out that while Lord Cardigan's trial was under way, another duel had been fought. One of the parties had been wounded. But not a single protest was raised by those who, professing a hatred of duels on social or humanitarian grounds, demanded the condemnation of Cardigan.

II

The question of corporal punishment in the army had for some years (roughly, it may be said, since Waterloo) been debated by prominent soldiers, reformers, and by those who consistently and for any reason opposed the military system. The word 'flogging' has come to acquire a most sinister meaning, beyond what it originally had, as time goes on. It was for long regarded, by those best qualified to know such as the Duke of Wellington, as the one punishment which made any impression on hardened offenders. The effect of solitary confinement was generally admitted to be nil. One of the most humane men of the period—the Hon. Henry Clifford, a future V.C. and major-general—declared that, "You must not look upon the soldier as a responsible agent. . . . Give him one farthing more than he really wants, and he gives way to his brutal propensities and immediately gets drunk. . . . He is only kept in order by strict discipline. . . . Soldiers are all very well when ruled by soldiers' laws. . . . Fine soldiers are so in comparison with the amount of discipline used over them."

Wellington, who was more proud of his 'scum' and 'rabble' than he cared to admit, regarded the wish to alter army discipline as one of the morbid symptoms of the age. "It is like the notion that thieves ought not to be punished"; and he knew by experience that the army thought less of the punishment than did most of the ardent civilian reformers. One need only consider the nickname 'Shellbacks' given to the old 48th Foot (Northamptonshire), because its ranks accepted being flogged as part of their calling.

The fact that men were sometimes flogged for an apparently minor misdemeanour, such as getting drunk, inspired the criticism of those who failed to realize that most serious crimes in the army were caused by drink.

A vote for the abolition or retention of flogging had been taken in 1836. Cardigan was one of the large majority who favoured its retention. But it remained the wish of most commanding officers to restrict corporal punishment, and to lessen the number of lashes inflicted, as much as possible; and in course of time most victims of flogging were generally looked upon as confirmed bad characters in uniform.

The mental picture called up by mention of a flogging seems almost equal to the shocked impression produced in those who witnessed the punishment—the victim stripped, except for trousers or overalls, and boots; strapped to a wooden frame, or triangle, by the wrists and ankles; a couple of farriers taking it in turn to administer the lashes, and the victim's back, at first numb or frozen, changing colour until the blood flowed to hide it; with the doctor standing by to call a halt if he thought the man was unable to bear more; and finally a cloak being flung over the victim who was then led away for hospital treatment.

In the spring of 1841 the 11th Hussars left Brighton for barracks at Hounslow; and there shortly after the regiment had settled in, Lord Cardigan became the centre of another storm.

The commonly accepted reason for it is that he had a man flogged, just after a church service, on Easter Sunday. But this story, like most of those connected with Cardigan, calls for some clarification.

In the first place, the sentence of flogging had nothing whatever to do with him. The offender was Private William Rogers, one of the Queen's hard bargains who was left under arrest at Brighton, for having been drunk, when the regiment marched out. There he remained for eleven days, and after being sentenced by a district court martial to one hundred lashes, he was taken as a prisoner to Hounslow.

Cardigan received the order, to see that the sentence was carried out, from the General Commanding-in-Chief at the Horse Guards, by the first post on the morning of 11th April. It was Easter Sunday, and the regiment, with a detachment of the 14th Foot, was about to parade for church service in the riding school.

Cardigan considered he was bound to execute the order as quickly as possible, but only after a proper interval between the service and the flogging had been established. So at first the infantry, and then his own regiment, marched away from the scene of the service. Soon afterwards the Hussars re-assembled. They were inspected for half an hour, and then marched back to the riding school. There the trumpet-major was making things ready; the prisoner was escorted in, and the sentence was put into effect.

Directly the news reached the public a cry went up that Lord

Cardigan, by sanctioning the enactment of a barbarous, a savage, a disgusting spectacle on such a day, had outraged the country's religious feelings. How strong those feelings were in a country whose mainly materialistic outlook was opposed to belief in the supreme miracle of Easter, is open to question. But the sentiments expressed so vigorously showed whole-hearted respect for "the great event which the Church" (to quote *The Times*) "commemorates at Easter". The same paper went on to ask what should be done with "this inveterate offender, this plague-spot of the British Army, who seems to exist for the single purpose of setting public opinion at defiance?"

The *Globe* followed much the same lines by asking, "What shall be done with Lord Cardigan? There is generally something new and unprecedented in each successive escapade. . . . He commits a thousand indecencies, each more shattering than the last one."

It was elsewhere stated that the flogging had taken place on the very spot where the chaplain had read the service *a few minutes earlier*, and that the soldiers were kept in place, in the riding school, and the punishment inflicted, "as if it were a continuance of divine service".

On 20th April Joseph Hume, Cardigan's old Radical opponent, rose in the House to ask whether the happenings at Hounslow, as reported in the Press, were true, and whether regulations permitted the carrying out of military punishment on a Sunday.

He was answered by Mr. Thomas Babington Macaulay, then Secretary-at-War, the devout Whig historian, who now, by virtue of the office he held, did not feel that his principles were compromised by having to make out a case for a high Tory like Cardigan.

Mr. Macaulay denied some of the falsehoods that were spread by the Press. The troops had not been detained, after the service, for the purpose of witnessing the flogging. It had not been inflicted as though it were a continuance of that service. "But", he went on, "the immediate infliction of punishment on a Sunday after divine service was clearly contrary to the religious feelings and habits of the people of this country, and could not be reconciled with either good sense or good feeling."

A gentleman of doubtful origin, Mr. Muntz, who was a member for Birmingham, said that if floggings on Sunday were to be permitted they would soon have hangings on Sundays. He then proceeded to read out a list of punishments relating, over the past two years, to the 11th Hussars, which were calculated to illustrate their colonel's harshness. During that time, according to Mr. Muntz, 105 courts martial had been held, and upwards of seven hundred men had been named as defaulters.

Apart from the fact that the total strength of the regiment averaged some 350 men, no flogging had taken place in the 11th Hussars since 1839, and that was at a time when Cardigan was absent from the regiment. It was likewise true that during the recent march from Brighton a man had been tried, for drunkenness, by regimental court martial, and sentenced to one hundred lashes. But in view of the man's previous good behaviour, Cardigan had remitted the whole of the sentence.

The member for Birmingham was answered by Lord George Lennox, who said he did not know the list of punishments to which Mr. Muntz was referring. "But he did know that when regiments returned to the United Kingdom, after an absence of twenty years in India, soldiers were in the habit of squandering their money, and that the discipline of regiments, returning from foreign stations, was, generally speaking, more lax than that of regiments which had passed the same period at home."

Following a censure from Lord Hill, Cardigan was requested to report on the flogging, "which could only be justified by necessity, or by a case of the most urgent emergency", to the Horse Guards; and for some days Wellington (to quote his own words) "was up to the ears as usual in Lord Cardigan's last indiscretion".

The Prime Minister, Lord Melbourne, expressed his concern to the Queen lest the affair should provide an excuse for the House of Commons to interfere with the discipline and control of the army. There was a move in that direction when a motion was made for removing Cardigan from his command; and it again fell to Mr. Macaulay to defend the military system, and to state, of the Sunday flogging, that the case was not peculiar, "as similar instances had occurred in the army, as well as in other branches of the service".

He was supported in that by the *Naval and Military Gazette*, which said that there were many precedents, both in the army and the navy, of corporal punishment being inflicted on Sundays. This called forth a spate of denials in the Press, which were countered by a letter from an ex-member of the 14th Light Dragoons. He recalled that when the regiment was quartered at Canterbury, under Colonel Egerton, he had witnessed a Sunday flogging.

Cardigan remained, as ever, impervious to hostile clamour. Secure in the knowledge of his own deserts, he kept the command of his regiment. Between periods of duty he hunted and rode, excessively; he entertained at Deene Park, at his residence in Portman Square, and aboard his yacht at Cowes. He was proof against scandal. He had been hissed at the theatre and when entering a train; he had lately been compelled to travel in his carriage with drawn blinds. But his frank estimate of his self-inspired stature remained unimpaired; and when he came to look round, he considered that he was entitled to more recognition from his country, and from his own county in particular, than he had so far received.

12

The recognition Cardigan had in mind was to be appointed Lord Lieutenant of Northamptonshire. He based his claim upon being a Brudenell, with no mean stake in the land, and a consistent Tory. The post fell vacant in December 1841, when the holder, Lord Westmorland, died. Cardigan had already put forward his claim in a letter to Peel, who was then Prime Minister, and to the Duke of Wellington. But both disappointed him. Lord Exeter succeeded to the post, and Cardigan lost no time in carrying his grievance to Sir James Graham, Secretary of State.

His hurt feelings gave way to resentment when he was told that his military record precluded such an appointment. There were more letters to Peel and to Wellington, insisting upon his right to the Lord Lieutenancy. He expressed surprise that he was being made to pay because of an outcry in the Press, and because he had committed "a single act of indiscretion"—one wonders which 'single act' was in Cardigan's mind?

Nothing daunted, however, his aspiration soared some degrees higher when, in March 1842, a vacancy occurred in the Order of the Garter. It was most unusual for a candidate to solicit for the highest honour within the gift of the British Crown; but

Cardigan again applied to Peel for the necessary recommendation, only to encounter another rebuff from the Prime Minister.

Two more vacancies occurred in the order within the next sixteen months, and each time Cardigan, with amazing pertinacity, advanced his claim. But Peel was still adamant, though the Queen had expressed her readiness to grant some show of favour to the importunate Earl. Some time later, in 1844, Cardigan wrote to Wellington with the object of being appointed an aide-de-camp to the Queen; but Wellington, as before, remained politely immovable.

Cardigan's domestic life had long since proved as unsatisfactory as were his several attempts to overcome the disapproving front shown by official circles. He and his wife were badly matched; both pursued a casual and promiscuous way; they might still appear together, but neither complained if the other stepped aside to welcome some passing adventure. The close of the London season found them at Cowes, where the yachting world gathered to affect appreciation of simple pleasure offered by a quiet little town and the sea.

The day's programme began with a morning spent on board the various craft that put out from the Cowes Roads. Then came a gathering at the King's House, a former residence of George III, or in the Royal Yacht Club gardens. Ladies appeared on the Parade in dresses of blue serge and neat hats that reflected the current vogue of simplicity. Parties assembled in the gardens, under the coloured glow of Chinese lanterns, for dinner, while out at sea the lights of anchored yachts twinkled under the moon.

The Cardigans occupied a villa, Rose Cottage, when not on board either of the yachts, *Dryad* and *Seahorse*, that carried the Earl's pennon. The commodore of the Royal Yacht Club was Lord Wilton, whom gossip Creevey described as "a sulky, selfish chap", with the worst countenance he ever saw. Lady Ailesbury, who was there with her husband, was having an affair with Wilton; but that did not prevent her spending a night with Cardigan when his yacht was lying off Calshot. It led to quite a scene between Wilton and Cardigan. The lady, though attractive to men, was thin to the point of being scraggy; which caused a looker-on to liken the angry lords to dogs fighting over a bone.

Cardigan's striking appearance, his handsome figure and colourful reputation, enabled him to take full advantage of the mutual freedom that he and his wife allowed each other. Lady Cardigan was fully prepared to derive what entertainment she could from awareness of her husband's amorous associations, and about this time she stage-managed a little scene that recalls a situation in *Measure for Measure*.

A certain Mrs. Browne, described as a woman "well known in society", who visited Deene Park, developed a passion for the Earl. She sent him letters imploring a meeting, and one of these letters found its way to Lady Cardigan. The agent employed by Cardigan at the time, Mr. Baldwin, was somewhat like Cardigan in build, and he was persuaded to arrange and keep a meeting with the lovesick Mrs. Browne. A condition made by the bogus Cardigan, in his letter, was that the meeting must be secret, to avoid any servant knowing, and carried out in complete darkness.

Had Mrs. Browne paused to reflect, it might have occurred to her that Cardigan was not the sort of man to seek any cover. Some of his deeds, according to moralists, might be dark; but he himself was never averse to standing in daylight. But no suspicion crossed the mind of the infatuated Mrs. Browne. The meeting took place; Mr. Baldwin left the lady in the still total blackness of a wintry morning; and one need not be too much of a cynic to imagine the pleasure Lady Cardigan took in acquainting her friend with the facts, and thus depriving her of a deep, though vicarious, sense of well-satisfied passion.

Those were the great days of hospitality. The stately houses, the spacious rooms, and the broad acres seemed to demand that a host should spread himself, generously and magnanimously, to please his guests; and Cardigan fulfilled those duties on a lavish scale. His hunting, shooting and house parties were in keeping with their expensive Midland setting. He was then no longer a martinet, and was a soldier only in orderliness and precision, when he entertained; and at one of the parties given at Deene, in the winter of 1842, he noticed the arrival of a young girl who had just been presented at Court.

She was Adeline, the daughter of Mr. Spencer Horsey de Horsey, M.P., and Lady Lavinia Maria Judith, youngest daughter of the Earl of Stradbroke. Adeline, then 17, had been accustomed to holding her own in the world of Vanity Fair from her early days. As a child, she had acted in miniature plays before private audiences that included Wellington, and she may have been one of those screaming children who crawled on all-fours with the Duke and who pelted him with pillows. She had been greeted, with all the grace that belonged to the salons of the *ancien régime*, by the French ambassador, Prince de Talleyrand, the ex-priest who hobbled his way from the Republic, via the Directory, to St. James's. She had met Lord Hertford, who figured as Thackeray's Marquess of Steyne, bald, buck-toothed, with underhung jaw and bow legs. She had heard the light Irish voice of Thomas Moore touch the heartstrings with nostalgia in the Tavistocks' drawing-room; and she had watched Queen Victoria being attired for a State ball at Buckingham Palace.

At 16 Adeline had lost her mother, and since then she had played the part of a fully accomplished hostess at Number 8 Upper Grosvenor Street, where she lived with her father. She was good at languages and at music; she sang well. Her figure was slight, but rounded. She was proud of her small hands and feet, and of what she herself referred to, with delightful freshness, as her "beautiful legs". She described her hair, perhaps with a little pardonable exaggeration, as falling below her knees. At the time of her visit to Deene, her face was alive with the promise of coming beauty.

Her mental and social development, without the supervision of a careful Victorian mother, was therefore something exceptional for that period. She was free, high spirited, and ready for adventure—the more so after a visit she made, wearing a borrowed cloak and bonnet and a thick veil, to a fortune-teller in Bridge Street, Westminster. There a pack of greasy cards, as interpreted by the seer, revealed that she would one day marry a widower who occupied an exalted position. The prediction, prominent in her mind from the time it was uttered, stayed with her all her life.

She recalled it when entering a room, when meeting strangers; and it was uppermost when she walked, for the first time, into the hall at Deene. The dim light of a late January afternoon was casting shadows over the walls and ceiling. The staircase ascended into obscurity; the recesses were dark. But there were figures in the hall, distinct, definite; figures of women clustered about a solitary man.

The *Court Journal* spoke of Deene as a social centre "where England's reputation for female beauty was well sustained". The Earl saw to that; and on this particular afternoon the beauties included the Duchess of Montrose, Lady Clementina Villiers, and Mrs. Dudley Ward; a bevy of early Victorian womanhood whose dresses in stripes, plaids, or plain satin reflected every shade of red, blue, green or yellow. Their skirts, long and full, flowed down from tiny waists; their hair was worn in ringlets or drawn smoothly back from a middle parting. They regarded the girl with none too friendly eyes. She possessed uninvaded beauty, outward youth and inward maturity—a dangerous combination.

The air of frigidity was broken by Cardigan who advanced from the circle of women to welcome Adeline. It is easy to picture his tall lithe figure, tightly buttoned in a frock coat, with flowered waistcoat and a large bow tie; his high bridged nose and pronounced cheekbones; the ingrained sense of being in command that stamped him with rarity of breeding.

He flashed the challenge that he habitually directed at women into the sparkling brown eyes of the 17-year-old girl; and the impulsive, chivalrous rake was at once swept off his feet by her demure response. Adeline, for her part, had seen enough of the world to recognize his type. She was also thinking. The Earl was not actually a widower . . . not yet. . . . But everyone knew that his marriage was a failure. The Countess of Cardigan was on the brink of another affair, this time with Lord Colville. . . . The fortune-teller had said. . . .

Lady Cardigan felt none of the concern that was shared by Lady Clementina and the rest over the new arrival. She showed marked attention to Adeline, and they became, on the surface, temporary friends. She gave the girl some samples of Northamptonshire lace.

The Earl, with Adeline's help, soon persuaded himself that he was Mr. Horsey's 'particular friend'; and when the couple returned to London he followed them. He became a frequent visitor to the house in Upper Grosvenor Street, and Adeline's presence cast a welcome glow of youthful charm over Cardigan's parties. She readily responded to his gallant treatment of her as a *jeune fille*; and Mr. de Horsey, although himself a man about town, was late in realizing the effect that a man of Cardigan's maturity and character was exerting upon his (apparently) inexperienced daughter. He was also soon made aware of the current gossip. Tongues were let loose in the drawing-rooms of Mayfair and Portman Square, where circles of interested ladies discussed the notorious Cardigan's latest involvement. The crux of the scandal was his obvious affair with a young girl whilst his wife was still alive; the fact that Lady Cardigan's reputation was certainly no better than her husband's seemed less offensive to the guardians of outward social convention.

When in London, Cardigan rode daily in the park. On his way he passed the de Horsey residence. Adeline would watch for him at a window, and when he appeared she went out upon the balcony. From there she lowered a length of string, to which was attached a piece of coal to secure its passage down. Cardigan stopped, took a letter from his pocket and tied it to the string, which Adeline quickly hauled up.

This little manœuvre was watched by children from their nursery window in a nearby house. The children were so intrigued that they arranged, with the help of a coachman and his wife who lived in the basement below, to let down their own piece of string. To this the coachman's obliging wife fastened a little basket holding cakes and tarts, which the children pulled up to their balcony. These two sets of stratagems did not pass unnoticed in the neighbourhood. They were awaited and watched for, by as many of the household staffs and residents whose windows admitted a view. Mr. de Horsey advised, then ordered, his daughter to break with Cardigan; but Adeline, who resembled the Earl in several ways, shared his spirit of independence. Both were disdainful of opinion, and she was ready to leave home if her father made life unpleasant.

One morning Cardigan received a note from Adeline. A new play was being performed at the Princess's Theatre, and Adeline had heard that it was very bold and daring. Would Cardigan accompany her there? She had broached the subject to her father, but he had read her a lecture on morals. The play was degrading, and it was the duty of every self-respecting person to keep away. But in any case her father could not take her, as he was dining that evening with General Cavendish, at his club.

When the coast was clear, Adeline and her maid went to the box she had reserved at the theatre. The overture had commenced when Cardigan, obviously agitated, joined them. He told Adeline that she must leave the theatre at once, and when pressed for an explanation he said that her father and General Cavendish were in the opposite box. Not only that, but (and the amoral

Cardigan showed some embarrassment) they were with their mistresses.

Adeline was highly amused, and barely suppressing her desire to laugh she peeped through the curtains of the box. There, sure enough, were the upright Mr. de Horsey, the General and two pretty women who were strangers to Adeline. She insisted on seeing the play, though dividing her attention between what passed on the stage and the quartet opposite; but she agreed to leave before the end and so reach home before her father. Cardigan summoned a hackney carriage and they set off.

It seemed a long drive to Upper Grosvenor Street, but the night was foggy, and no one was very disturbed until Cardigan, stopping the carriage to inquire as to their progress, discovered that the driver, who was drunk, had brought them to Islington. When Adeline reached home it was past midnight. Her angry father met her in the hall and demanded to know where she had been. To the theatre, she told him, "where I saw you with General Cavendish and . . .".

"Go to bed at once," ordered her father. "We'll talk about your behaviour in the morning." But during the hours of darkness the subject must have passed from his mind, for it never recurred.

Relations between father and daughter, however, became so strained that Adeline left home. She had her own income, and attended by her father's valet, Matthews, she lived for a time at a hotel in Hyde Park Square. Before long Cardigan joined her at a furnished house in Norfolk Street, Park Lane. They kept three servants, apart from Matthews, who became the Earl's valet and stayed with him all his life. They were 'cut' by many of their kind and, except for a few close friends, lived very much in a world of their own where riding, in Rotten Row or Kensington Gardens, was a paramount recreation.

The fashionable time for appearing in the park, either on horseback or passing up and down in a carriage, was between eleven and one p.m. Cardigan in dark frock coat, tight trousers, and silk top hat, was always stiff in the saddle. Adeline, wearing one of her *outré* riding-habits, of green cloth or black or purple velvet, and a saucily perched hat with nodding plume, rode her favourite 'Don Juan'. Facial make-up was then the mark of a latent or a practising whore, and Adeline, at the most polite, was judged to be "a very painted lady".

They joined the procession of riders, some of whom could be recognized by the lookers-on pressed against the railings—Lord Palmerston; Lord Lucan, always serious and unbending; the Duke, who kept his fore-finger almost permanently raised to his fore-head acknowledging salutes; ladies such as the Duchess of Sutherland, Lady Dufferin and Lady Duff Gordon, elegant yet sedate in their bodices trimmed with white collar and cuffs, and buttoned to the neck; some of them looking the other way when Cardigan and Adeline, easily the handsomest couple there, inclined towards them.

About this time the Countess of Cardigan and Lord Colville entered upon a more or less permanent liaison. Everyone knew how threadbare the Cardigans' relationship had become, but good breeding demanded that Colville should confront the forsaken husband if only to tender an apology; while a duel was by no means out of the question. But Cardigan was at his most affable, and more than met the diffident Colville half-way. "My dear sir," he told him, "you have done the greatest service that one man can render to another."

So Elizabeth passed out of Cardigan's life. He retained a link with the Tollemache family, however, through one of his very few intimate male friends. He was Hubert de Burgh, whose country house was at West Drayton, Middlesex. His wife was Elizabeth's sister, Marianne. De Burgh was a curious, flabby character who served as a foil to the razor-like edge presented by Cardigan. He was known as 'the Squire'; he always wore country clothes, even at the height of the season in London, and his person and general appearance once caused him to be described as an "unlovely gent".

13

A cavalry regiment quartered in or near the metropolis undertook a number of duties connected with the Queen or with foreign royalties who visited England; and while Cardigan was at Hounslow Barracks he was called upon to furnish escorts for the King of Prussia, who made two visits about this time—first to attend the christening of the young Prince of Wales (the future Edward VII) at Windsor, and later a military review at

Woolwich. The 11th Hussars escorted the Queen to Woolwich when the warship *Trafalgar* was launched; and they guarded or patrolled the way from Buckingham Palace to Nuneham, near Oxford, when the Queen visited Edward Harcourt Vernon, Archbishop of York.

A detachment of Cardigan's regiment was stationed at Little Barracks, which then stood near the top of Queen's Gate at the entrance to Hyde Park, to carry out what was known as 'Queen's duty'. This meant the escorting of her carriage whenever she went on short journeys. Three privates formed on either side of the carriage, which was drawn up at the palace gates, facing inwards. An officer rode on one side of the Queen, and a sergeant on the other, when she reviewed the escort before entering the carriage; and each man knew that he was being 'looked over' in earnest, from the tip of his plume to the soles of his Wellington boots. From the time the carriage left the palace the two leading men rode some 100 yards ahead, with the remaining four following close behind.

It was not easy to catch a glimpse of Cardigan out of uniform or the strictly formal dress of the period; but an incident when he was 'off guard' for a moment occurred at Hounslow. The 13th Light Dragoons were also in barracks there, and one night the officers of the two regiments met for dinner. A few hours later the older men retired. There was a watering parade early next morning, so the juniors, some sitting about on the floor, and all talking in loud after-dinner tones, decided to see the rest of the night out.

It had been sharp and frosty, but at three o'clock in the morning rain started to fall. Some suggested a hunt as a fitting way to end the celebration. Lord Cardigan's room was near at hand, and they went along to ask his permission. They found the Colonel with a severe cold, still sitting on his bed, for the noise had kept him awake, wearing a dressing-gown and with his head muffled in a shawl. He gave permission at once, doubtless glad to get rid of them; and some time later he put his head cautiously round the door and asked in a hoarse voice, "Have all those damned fellows gone?"

The latter half of the year 1842 found Cardigan and his regiment quartered at various towns in the North and the Midlands. Riots were still frequent in manufacturing centres, and extra force, apart from that available to civil powers, was needed to clear the streets.

The perfectly disciplined Hussars were expert at this, and at marching prisoners off to gaol, without a single one of the 'bludgeon men', or their dupes, being seriously injured.

In the spring of 1843 the 11th Hussars were at Royal Barracks, Dublin. There were more troubles in Ireland, after the passing of an Act that deprived large numbers of the peasantry of political rights; but the regiment and its colonel were soon involved in their own problems of authority, as well as the usual journalistic campaign that was still waged about Cardigan.

The slightest detail connected with him provided fuel for unfavourable comment. Two of his hunters were killed in different accidents. *The Times* decided that they were two of Cardigan's favourite possessions and "highly prized" by him. "But," said the newsman, "His Lordship heard of these losses with his usual equanimity and indifference, speaking of them as ordinary casualties."

The senior Lieutenant withdrew one of the horses, judged to be unsuitable because it was "a confirmed roarer", from the riding school. Cardigan ordered the horse to be taken back, and in doing this the Lieutenant was late at morning stables. He was arrested. Other officers complained of the language used by Cardigan when addressing them in field-drill. But when these matters were probed, letters from the General commanding the district, approving Cardigan's conduct and reprimanding the officers concerned, were read aloud in the Mess room.

Following a field day in Phoenix Park, a report was published illustrating the highly unreasonable conduct and demands attributed to Cardigan. It was said that the regiment, having carried out a four-hour exercise, returned to barracks. There the men dismounted, and were in the act of filing off to the stables when Cardigan suddenly ordered them back into the saddle. Those officers whose horses had been taken away by their grooms, could not obey. "Where is your horse?" Cardigan demanded of one, and when told what had happened, he ordered the officer to go for the horse himself. The officer declined, and Cardigan placed him under arrest.

So much for the story that was circulated. But the truth was very different. During the exercise, Cardigan had ordered a subaltern to leave the ranks and receive instructions. Instead of spurring forward at a gallop, the subaltern, described as young

(*Right*) Captain Louis Nolan. (*Below left*) Mrs Fanny Duberly. (*Below right*) Major-General Lord George Paget

The Allied encampment at Balaclava photographed in 1855 by Roger Fenton

A lithograph of the Charge of the Light Brigade on 25th October 1854

and dandified, lounged towards the front at a slow and listless pace. Cardigan told him to go back and to repeat the move in a more soldier-like fashion. "But," says the corrected version of the report, "either from a willingness to try Cardigan's temper, or from a desire to incommode himself as little as possible," the lounge to the front was repeated.

Cardigan administered a well-deserved rebuke, which was repeated by General Blakeney, commanding the cavalry in the garrison, who rode down on witnessing the scene.

Even *The Times* was driven to contradict its first and false account of the incident; while the *Satirist* commented, "This comes of employing reporters who, for half a crown or a glass of gin and water, will pervert the truth and belie themselves. . . . We begin to think that Lord Cardigan is more sinned against than sinning."

Another affair that was greatly magnified occurred when William Forrest, now a captain in the 11th (he had already crossed swords with Cardigan over the trifle of the key) obtained leave to visit his wife, who was expecting a baby, in England. Her illness, it was said, took a serious turn, and Forrest applied for an extension. Cardigan, for some reason that was never made clear, refused, and Forrest overstayed his time of leave.

The papers relating to this affair were sent to the Horse Guards, where Wellington had replaced Lord Hill, who died in 1842, as Commander-in-Chief for life. The Duke, aged 83, was not over disposed to give his time to regimental matters, especially when Cardigan, with his passion for detail, added complaints about the resignation of his adjutant, and even about a drunken batman.

The Duke supported Forrest's application for extra leave, and told Cardigan that

nothing could be more fair and proper than that Captain Forrest should apply for leave to escort his wife to her friends under circumstances of her approaching confinement. . . . It became necessary for Captain Forrest to apply for an extension, and the Duke considers that Captain Forrest had a perfect right to do so until after such time as her medical advisers and her friends should cease to wish for his presence. . . .

The Duke must observe that in the whole of his experience he has never known the time of the Staff of the Army to be taken up

8

in so useless a manner as in the present instance, that if any other regiment in Her Majesty's service gave such trouble and could not be commanded without such voluminous correspondence, and such futile details, an additional Staff would be necessary for conducting the affairs of that regiment.

If the foolish quarrels of the officers of the 11th among themselves continued, the Duke might think it necessary to submit to Her Majesty some plan to relieve the Department from an intolerable nuisance.

It may be that so stern a rebuke, coming from such a quarter, was well deserved. But in view of certain facts that are less commonly reported than is Cardigan's lack of reason, it may be that his attitude was influenced by what he already knew of the characters of Captain and Annie Forrest. They were certainly a very odd couple.

It is true that Forrest, who transferred from the 11th Hussars to the 4th Dragoon Guards, reached the rank of lieutenant-general in 1877. But according to the evidence of his colonel, Edward Cooper Hodge, Forrest was "a vulgar selfish man" and a bad regimental officer who neglected his duties.

When the 4th Dragoon Guards were in Glasgow, in makeshift quarters, Forrest brought his kept woman to reside in the passage that he shared with another officer: while later on, in the Crimea, the two Forrests occupied one-half of a hut, the other part of which was tenanted by Colonel Hodge.

The latter's life was made miserable by "horrid Mrs. Forrest's infernal cackle, like that of an idiot". All their conversation, and their movements, were perfectly audible to the Colonel, who thought the arrangement disgusting. They had no female servant, but only a Dragoon orderly who was employed to do everything —literally *everything*—from emptying the leather bucket that held their slops to picking fleas out of Mrs. Forrest's drawers.

The Forrest controversy was soon turned to account by those who were ever ready to pounce on Cardigan. According to the *Court Journal*, the wife of the officer was actually dying when he applied for further leave. Because this was not granted he returned to duty, and the eyes of his dead wife "were closed by the hand of strangers".

Cardigan, aware that the lady in question was very much alive, wrote to *The Times* and said he was taking legal proceedings against those who manufactured such falsehoods; and in view of Cardigan's readiness to follow up threats, there must have been some private apology, for the affair fizzled out.

From time to time letters defending Cardigan appeared in the Press, but these, of course, did not receive the publicity that followed attacks upon him. A letter signed "A soldier of the 11th Hussars", which appeared in *The Times* in October 1843, complained that the paper's Irish correspondent "had been made the victim of some of the many misrepresentations afloat against the Earl of Cardigan. It is not for me" (the writer went on) "to enter into a defence which his Lordship deems unnecessary, but I think it is only due to the Army in general, and the regiment in particular which he commands, to state that there is no truth in the reports which represent him to have treated his officers with harshness or incivility. I believe him incapable of either. It is possible that he may have had occasion to exert his authority in order to maintain due discipline among his officers; but I am convinced that any investigation into the circumstances would amply justify His Lordship in anything he has done."

Another letter which also appeared about that time stated: "It does appear somewhat strange that, in spite of all the vagaries, real or imaginary, laid to the charge of the noble Earl, he should have contrived to win, since his arrival in Dublin, golden opinions from all classes as well as by his noble demeanour as by the exercise of princely though unostentatious benevolences."

A ranker of superior standing, named Pennington, overstayed his leave by several hours. When he reached the barrack gate he was arrested by the sergeant of the guard, and next day he was marched to the orderly room where Cardigan was sitting in judgment upon offenders.

"What have you to say?" growled Cardigan.

Pennington looked his commanding officer squarely in the face. It was borne in upon him that here was a man who would appreciate frankness as much as he despised excuse.

"Nothing, my lord," Pennington replied. "But it shall not occur again."

Pennington had not misjudged. He saw Cardigan's stern look relax and give way to a gratified expression. Cardigan then turned to the sergeant of the guard. "What sort of character?" he asked.

"Very good, my lord," said the sergeant.

Cardigan stared at Pennington, fixedly; and another realization came to the offender—not to shrink from scrutiny. Then Cardigan dismissed him with the words, "Fall away. Make yourself scarce." Pennington wrote later that Cardigan impressed him strongly during that interview.

The 11th went to Newbridge for summer training. There was a period of service at Dundalk and another at Belfast, followed by a return to Dublin, where the regiment proceeded to add a military aspect to the city's social and artistic traditions. Albani, Mario and Grisi were singing there in opera: Charles Kean, Toole and Robson were appearing at the Queen's and the Theatre Royal: and the 11th Hussars staged colourful reviews and miracles of precision in Phoenix Park, some attended by Prince Albert, but all carried out under the vigilant supervision of Jim the Bear, as Cardigan was nicknamed.

Whilst in Dublin, Cardigan came under the spell of a young married woman, one of the acknowledged beauties in a society where, at that time, feminine charm and graces were by no means rare. She left her husband and went to live with Cardigan on his yacht, where, not long afterwards, she died; but no great scandal resulted.

14

For some time past the public had been titillated by rumours of a pending law-suit. It promised to be no ordinary action, since it was being brought by Lord William Paget, second son of the Marquess of Anglesey, against Lord Cardigan. Paget's wife was Frances, daughter of Lieutenant-General Sir Francis Rottenberg. She had married Paget (who was in the navy) at the age of 18, in 1827, and they had two sons. Cardigan had for long been a friend of the family.

The rumours found expression in an anonymous letter, which Lord William said he had received, confirming his previously held suspicion that an "improper intimacy" existed between his wife and Cardigan. A statement regarding this appeared in the *Satirist* on 3rd September 1843: "The reports which have been current in the circles of *ton* during the past fortnight, inculpating the matrimonial fidelity of Lady William Paget, and implicating in the dishonour of her husband the Earl of Cardigan, unfortunately turn out to be too true."

Things were carried a step further when Paget challenged Cardigan to a duel. Cardigan declined, saying that he would never again fight a duel in England. Lord William then aired the matter in a letter he sent to a number of papers. He was, apparently, chiefly concerned to satisfy himself that his wife was virtuous. In his reply, Cardigan declared that the statements in the letter were false, and that he would give them the most "unqualified contradiction".

The action brought by Lord William was listed to be heard at the Guildhall, London, just before Christmas 1843. Cardigan was accused of "criminal conversation" (a polite term for adultery) with Lady Frances. But on the morning of the trial Paget stated that his principal witness, a man named Winter, could not be found. The clerk therefore announced that the case had been withdrawn; the scandal-loving public who had packed the court from the time it opened, at nine o'clock, pulled disappointed faces; the special jurors pocketed their guinea.

Paget, still bent on making his grievance public, again wrote to the Press. This time he accused Cardigan of having bribed his witness, Winter, to keep out of the way. Cardigan replied that he had never had, authorized or sanctioned any communication with any witness. At the same time Paget applied to the Duke, asking for his case to be made the subject of a full military inquiry. But Wellington, who was heartily sick of the endless differences in which Cardigan was involved, said that he could not interfere in social matters.

The case was eventually heard at the Guildhall, before Lord Chief Justice Tindal, on 27th February 1844. Public excitement was intense, with the crowd that packed the court overflowing into the passages where people craned necks and stood on tip-toe, signalizing their concurrence, by nods and murmurs, when Mr. Wordsworth, who appeared for the plaintiff, opened the proceedings by declaring that the defendant, Lord Cardigan, could not be unknown to them.

The story that emerged as the hearing proceeded began with Paget's decision, when his suspicions had been aroused, to have the couple watched. In this he was aided by his valet, John Thomas, and by a certain Frederick Winter, who was specially engaged for the purpose.

Preparations were made for a Saturday in August, when Cardigan had arranged to call at the house then occupied by the Pagets in Queen Street, Mayfair. There were two drawing-rooms, connected by folding doors, with a sofa in each room. Winter managed to squeeze himself under the sofa in the back room, and Thomas made sure that the valance hid him from view. After Cardigan's double knock was heard Winter, who was twisting his head and squinting sideways with one eye, narrowly escaped having his face scratched by Cardigan's spurs. The couple exchanged kisses; Winter described their conversation as having been of a "familiar nature"; but nothing more intimate occurred.

The visit was repeated next day. Winter was not in position when Cardigan was admitted. He attempted to dive under the front sofa, but hearing footsteps approach he had to retreat down-stairs. When the couple were seated in the front, Winter was able to hide himself again beneath the other sofa. The windows were closed and the blinds were drawn, but the connecting doors were left open.

Winter heard Lady Frances say that her husband had gone to Woolwich, where their 15-year-old son was a cadet at the Royal Military Academy. They discussed the previous night's opera, which Cardigan said he would have enjoyed more had he been able to have "a little closer conversation with Lady William". This was followed by whispers and a distinct sound of kissing. Winter heard nothing for a while. Then he heard the creak of the sofa, a cracking of boots, and hard breathing "like that of persons distressed for breath after running".

Winter resolved to see what was happening. He worked his way from under the sofa, moved worm-like over the carpet that rubbed his face, and peeped round a corner of the door. A "distinct criminal conversation" was taking place between the couple, but the papers reporting this could not enlarge upon it as some of the things the witness saw and heard were "unfit for publication".

Back in his hiding-place, Winter heard Cardigan get up and walk about the room adjusting his dress. Lady Frances pulled up the blinds. In the course of more conversation, she said that she was

dining at the Duchess of Richmond's house. Cardigan asked
whether she could plead a headache and meet him.

"Don't you know Lord William better than that?" she
answered. "If he should call and not find me there, he'd go stark
staring mad and go to all the policemen in town."

Cardigan questioned her as to Lord William's behaviour. "He
is very unkind," she told him. "He calls me all the damned
bitches he can think of."

"That is very unkind of him," said the protective Cardigan,
who then (still according to Winter) attempted to make up for her
infelicitous married state by leading her to repeat with him, after
more toying and kissing, the "distinct criminal conversation".
This visit of Cardigan's lasted for about two hours.

Winter crawled out from under the sofa. He was heated and
perspiring freely, a condition doubtless brought on by the
cramped position he had occupied as well as by what he claimed
to have witnessed. When he reported to Lord William the latter
became quite violent, and the valet noticed that Lady Frances
appeared with a black eye.

The Solicitor-General's speech, influenced by a number of
salient facts which invalidated the accusations, ensured a verdict
for the defendant.

Lord William was the black sheep of the Anglesey family,
always short of money and heavily in debt. The man Winter was
typical of the company he kept. Formerly an attorney's clerk,
Winter had been dismissed for embezzlement. He then became a
valet, and afterwards a 'hand' in a soda-water factory. Paget had
been putting up at the 'White Bear', Piccadilly, a disreputable
place to which he had taken a woman from the streets. His valet
had let her out early in the morning.

The house in Mayfair had been taken for a very short period and
obviously for a set purpose. Lord William had arranged for
Cardigan to call there on the days when Lady Frances was alone,
and during their meetings he had waited below in a cab, where
Winter had joined him to report. Winter explained that he had
not appeared when the case first came up because Lord William
had failed to pay the money he was promised. Later, Winter was
heard to say that when it was over he would be better off and
hoped to take a public house.

Lord William had openly discussed the affair with his valet

Thomas. It was Thomas who suggested where Lord William should sleep, whether with his wife or in the dressing-room, on the night following the encounters on which the accusations were based. Thomas advised Lord William to sleep with his wife in order to prevent her suspecting that her name was to be coupled with that of Cardigan.

In concluding the trial, the Solicitor-General described it as "an atrocious attempt to extort money from a wealthy nobleman who was unpopular with the public, at the sacrifice of the honour and reputation of an amiable lady". These observations left Cardigan in the unusual position (for him) of hearing a judgment, given in his favour, greeted by popular applause; though the people's approval probably derived as much from the entertaining evidence they had heard as from their agreement with the result.

But even allowing for the rightness of the verdict in so far as the happenings reported by Winter are concerned, one may still wonder whether Cardigan's relations with Lady Frances had always been completely innocent; or whether they had at some time given rise to Lord William's suspicions, and so to his plan for brightening his financial horizon.

15

For the next few years Cardigan and his regiment carried out duties, mostly in support of civil authorities, in several of the larger towns where riots were prevalent. There was Chartist agitation in Manchester; there were disturbances in Norwich, and Yarmouth was taken over for a time by riotous seamen; labouring mobs, worked up by Radical orators, interfered with a new rail-way cutting that was being completed at Grantham. In all these operations Cardigan, who was now a full colonel, controlled his regiment so that it moved with absolute firmness and efficiency yet without causing the bloodshed that served as fuel for further trouble.

There were the customary reviews on Wimbledon Common, and parades at Woolwich in honour of the Queen's birthday. In May 1850 Wellington rode along the ranks of the 11th for the last time; for on 14th September 1852, when the regiment was again in Dublin, the Duke was found dead in his high-backed chair at

Walmer Castle. A captain, a subaltern, and six privates were sent to represent the 11th Hussars in the long military procession that escorted the ponderous funeral car through the rain-soaked streets of London to St. Paul's.

The Irish elections were a constant source of trouble, and voters had to be protected on their way to and from the polls. This highly disagreeable task led to an outbreak of violence at Six-Mile Bridge, County Clare, during elections in the following February, when men of the 31st Regiment were escorting a body of Protestant voters. They were attacked by a Catholic mob, urged on by priests; but when the troops stepped in Protestant and Catholic joined forces against the redcoats.

Several of the troops were felled by stones; a corporal trying to save a comrade who was on the ground was struck and wounded eleven times; another received injuries that disabled him for life. The mob only dispersed when the troops opened fire, killing seven of their attackers; and when it was announced that several of the soldiers, after twice appearing on trial, were to be prosecuted by Crown lawyers, Cardigan, who was ever watchful for the reputation of troops even though they were not of his regiment, raised a motion on their behalf.

He doubted the wisdom of calling on the military to protect voters. At the same time, he admitted, that owing to the conditions of the sister kingdom, "it would be difficult to know how a general election could be got through without disturbance and the military being called in". But if the soldiers were to be prosecuted for defending their own lives, who would defend the soldiers? There was not the slightest doubt that the trouble had been started by priests. Were they not to be tried?

The Prime Minister, Lord Aberdeen, said it would not be expedient to institute any proceedings against priests. Such a step would be improper, unwise; and Cardigan withdrew his motion reluctantly.

A few days later his voice was heard again, when he spoke in favour of abolishing the office of Lord Lieutenant of Ireland. His reasons for doing this were mainly economic; but he put them forward in a way so light and humorous that a reading of his speech should dispose of the notion, so glibly advanced by modern writers, that Cardigan was brainless and without ideas.

He invited the lords to see a picture of one of their kind, of unblemished and highly respectable nature, though perhaps not of transcendent ability, young in years, who was selected to pass over to the other side of the water to fill the office of Viceroy in that part of Her Majesty's dominions.

He arrived in the country in the midst of a great parade of troops; he then proceeded to take the oaths, and immediately afterwards held a number of levees and drawing-rooms, at which he had to undergo the task of saluting three hundred or four hundred ladies; an amusement very innocent in itself, but it appeared to him (Cardigan) very extraordinary that any of their lordships should be placed in a position where he had to undergo such a ceremony as a point of duty.

This was followed up by several great fêtes and dinners at the castle, which were, no doubt, very agreeable both as acts of hospitality and as an encouragement of trade. But it ought to be recollected that it was not necessary that anyone should assume royal habits in order to entertain.

At these fêtes and dinners there appeared a numerous and splendid staff, and various high officers of the household, such as a chamberlain, a controller, treasurer, and a Master of Horse. He believed that one of the principal duties of the Staff officers on such occasions was to carve the massive joints on the viceregal table. The Master of the Horse had a high salary for superintending an establishment of some eight or ten horses; and he probably knew as little about the selection of horses as did the Masters of the Horse in other countries.

Cardigan then went on to say that the Viceroy had to appear at the theatre, where, if the well-known farce of *King Charming* was being presented, "the Viceroy might see a not very unfaithful representation of his own very equivocal and somewhat ludicrous position". But like his motion on behalf of the prosecuted soldiers, Cardigan's suggestion that the Lord Lieutenancy was "exceedingly inconvenient", and should be abolished, was rejected by Prime Minister Aberdeen. It was contrary to the will of Her Majesty's government; and the office remained in existence for the best part of another century.

Meanwhile talk of a growing Russian menace was filling the air. The shadow of the Czar had for some time been looming over Europe by way of the tottering Turkish Empire, and in the sum-

mer of 1853 England thought it advisable to look at her meagre
and pitifully neglected military strength.

A 'camp of instruction' was organized at Chobham Common,
near Windsor, at which regiments of the home garrisons, under
Lieutenant-General Lord Seaton, were to carry out manœuvres.
Big crowds, in holiday mood, created an atmosphere that was
likened to a combination of Greenwich Fair and Derby Day. The
Queen, riding a black charger and attended by Prince Albert, the
King of Hanover, and Prince Lucien Bonaparte, appeared in a
blue riding habit that was adorned, in military style, with brass
buttons. There is no actual record of the 11th Hussars forming
part of the cavalry contingent; but a critical and observant young
lady, Miss Bessie Carew, who witnessed the exercises and
parades, referred in her diary to the magnificent appearance of
Cardigan at the head of his splendid regiment.

The high spirits of the troops, and their colourful uniforms,
were declared to be excellent. The Life Guards brandished swords
and made a dashing charge over the Common; the infantry
deployed, retired, and then swept forward over the heathland and
the hills. When it was over the favoured guests sat down to a six-
course luncheon, with champagne and sherry. Finally a storm
broke that threatened to wash away the tents; the more fortunate
of the female visitors, gathering up their skirts, were glad to shelter in the cavalry stables; but it was generally hoped that the
Czar, at the head of his unnumbered legions, would be sufficiently warned by this demonstration of 10,000 horse, foot and
gunners, to call a halt to any intended aggression.

Cardigan responded to the turn of events, and the sudden
revival of England's military spirit, by continuing to keep his regiment at the highest possible pitch. Officers and men were
stretched to the limit in a system of training that never spared himself. But there were high days when it was commonly agreed that
he was not too oppressive (though he had made them sweat);
when the outside world was largely forgotten, and only a breath
of chill wind, blowing from the Russian steppes, crept into the
drawing-rooms of Merrion Square, partially dimming the light of
chandeliers and muting the violins. Czar Nicholas extended his
hand still nearer towards Turkey, whose independence meant
nothing to Britain or France. But the growth of Russian power in
central Europe had to be resisted. English commerce in the

Mediterranean could be threatened by a Russian fleet based on the Bosphorus; while Napoleon III wished for a war, waged on the side of Britain, as a means of strengthening his new imperial power, and giving it an air of military prowess and traditional respectability.

The excuse came when a quarrel developed, in the Holy Land, between the Greek Orthodox and the Latin Churches. The Orthodox monks, who claimed Russian protection, and the Latins, who were supported by Napoleon, came to blows; after that it was comparatively easy for propaganda, and differing appeals to supernatural power, to do the rest.

The Czar had three successive visions of St. Nicholas, patron of Russia, who after some hesitation declared that the Orthodox Faith would triumph. In furtherance of that promise two Russian army corps marched into the Balkans, that were then Turkish provinces, and laid siege to Silistria, an important town on the Danube, from which a road struck due south to Constantinople. A combined fleet of British and French warships entered the Dardanelles. Soon afterwards British troops sailed for Malta, within striking distance of the Balkans that promised to become the seat of war.

Britain called on Russia to evacuate the Turkish provinces; and Czar Nicholas, surrendering to the mystic fervour that so readily gripped his subjects, raised his eyes and a quivering hand to heaven and pronounced, "War, war, war, to the enemies of Russia!" Britain and France responded by declaring war at the end of March ... and in the Dublin drawing-rooms military notes replaced the music of quadrille, polka and gavotte. Swords were sent to the grindstone. The number of uniforms gradually lessened as spurs clicked and men bowed low over the hands of girls in sprigged muslin and sashes. A late spring mist lighter than the cloud that was soon to gather over Russian waters, swept in from the Dublin mountains. . . .

16

An order warning him to prepare his regiment for active service reached Lord Cardigan on 11th March; and not only the Royal Barracks, but the city of Dublin was in a flurry of preparation. At the first hint of war, nationalist pride and political grievances were forgotten. Men flocked to the recruiting depots. "Musha, sir, d'ye think we'll ever get a prod at the Emperor of Roosha?" was a typical question put to one of the sergeants. The questioner was gravely assured that he would certainly come face to face with the barbarian Nicholas. Archbishop Cullen told his congregation that the war was more than likely to end well, since the French fleet had been placed under the protection of the Blessed Virgin Mary. Only a few isolated voices were heard calling upon all right-minded Irishmen not to accept the Saxon shilling.

As part of their preparations, the 11th Hussars sent their swords for sharpening to a cutler named Lamprey, in Westmorland Street. It was made known that officers were having patches of black leather sewn to the seats of their cherry-coloured overalls, an event that was celebrated by some verses that appeared in *Punch*:

> Oh, pantaloons of cherry!
> Oh, redder than raspberry!
> For men to fight in things so tight
> It must be trying—very.
>
> 'Gainst wear, though fine the weather,
> They would not hold together.
> On saddle-back they'd fly and crack,
> Though seated with black leather.
>
> In overalls more spacious
> If crimson, still rapacious,
> The bold Hussar will rush to war,
> Lord Cardigan is gracious!

But apart from such good-humoured raillery, Cardigan's opponents were still on the watch for any announcement connected with him or his regiment. Another anonymous letter appeared in *The Times*, criticizing the brevity of the jackets worn by the 11th, their headgear, and the tightness of their cherry-coloured pants. Their general appearance was likened to a corps of female Hussars then appearing in ballet. The fact that Cardigan had not yet departed for the seat of war also came in for comment, as also did the mention that the regiment's swords had been sharpened.

Cardigan's reply treated each point raised by the letter (which was signed "Common-sense") in a very temperate and informed style. "The sharpening of swords," he said, "when a cavalry regiment is ordered on foreign service, is not only the invariable rule of the service, but is usually on each occasion of the sort expressly ordered by the military authorities." As for their uniforms the jackets worn by the 11th Hussars were longer, and their overalls looser, than in almost any other cavalry regiment. The colour of their overalls was not unlike that of the 'Garance' overalls worn by the French, and similar to those worn by several Hungarian and Austrian regiments. Their headgear was the precise pattern of the fur cap worn by every hussar. Cardigan might have reminded the anonymous letter-writer that the commanding officer of a regiment has no power over its uniform; also that mention had been made in the papers of the Inniskilling Dragoons, and the 4th Dragoon Guards, having had their swords sharpened—but this most ordinary fact had not been picked on for attempted ridicule.

Any soldier, subject to orders, might well have resented the reference to his not yet having left for the war zone. But here again Cardigan's reply was surprisingly moderate. "It is no part of my duty to proceed to the seat of war until I receive orders from superior military authority to do so." He then pointed out that the commanding officer of every cavalry regiment listed for service was still in Britain.

The Times, belatedly realizing that it had been foolish to publish such a letter, tried to save face by advising Lord Cardigan not to be hysterical. The continued attacks upon him occasioned an article in the *Naval and Military Gazette*, which said in his defence, "We may appeal to Lord Cardigan's own regiment against the vile slanders of those who know him not. The 11th Hussars would to a man follow Lord Cardigan to victory or death."

The first troop of the 11th Hussars to leave for the Balkans sailed from Kingstown in the troopship *Glendalough*. Many Irishmen had joined the regiment during its stay in Dublin, and crowds lined the quays, waving caps, flourishing shillelaghs, and singing "A good time coming" to the music of three bands, as the vessel was towed out of harbour. There were shouted exhortations for the departing troops to "bring back the big bear in a cage". Even in better informed circles the belief was current that the Russians would be "crumpled up like a Hyde Park mob". Their military system was said to be a corrupt and cruel criminal despotism, in which "The commander-in-chief robs the generals, and the generals after their degree rob the colonels, and the colonels rob the majors, and the majors rob the captains, and the captains rob the lieutenants, but all rob the soldiers together."

Cardigan was to say of this period, "I did not lose any time in applying for a command in the cavalry, conceiving that I might have a fair claim to employment on active service." He was not likely to pause and reflect, as some privates did, that their cause was "a rotten one". Anticipating a prolonged absence, he reduced his establishments at Deene Park and in Portman Square. His stud of valuable hunters was brought to the hammer at Tattersall's.

Cardigan was then 55. His health was far from good. He suffered from a bladder complaint, and was subject to chronic bronchitis. But no feeling save one of acute satisfaction weighed with him when, on 1st April, he was gazetted Brigadier-General and given command of the Light Cavalry Brigade, consisting of his own 11th Hussars, the 8th Hussars, the 4th and 13th Light Dragoons, and the 17th Lancers. This, with the Heavy Brigade, formed the Cavalry Division. The Heavies were commanded by Brigadier-General the Hon. James Scarlett, a sensible and popular leader with a perpetually rubicund face that (like his name) was out of keeping with his sober nature.

Lieutenant-Colonel Hodge, commanding the 4th Dragoon Guards of the Heavy Brigade, called on Cardigan about this time "to find out all I could". After saying that Cardigan was "very civil", the Colonel goes on, "I learnt much that was worth knowing."

Cardigan's enthusiasm was somewhat tempered when he found that the Cavalry Division was to be led by the Earl of Lucan. The two men were brothers-in-law, and they hated each other like poison.

George Charles, Lord Bingham, who succeeded as the third Earl of Lucan in 1839, was three years younger than Cardigan. Of Elizabethan settler stock, and therefore of a race and a religion that made him a 'foreigner' in Ireland, he had inherited large but unprofitable estates in County Mayo. He entered the army when he was 16, and ten years later, having risen, like Cardigan, by purchase, he attained command of the 17th Lancers. Also like Cardigan, he poured what money he could into equipping and mounting this regiment, which was known, on account of its splendid appearance, as 'Bingham's Dandies'; and still again like Cardigan, he was proud, highly courageous, and dedicated to his calling. A friend said that he thought of his cavalry by day, and dreamt of them by night. Possessed of dark and somewhat Byronic good looks, he gave way to bouts of temper during which his teeth would be clenched and a wild gleam flashed from his eyes.

He married Lady Anne, the youngest of the Brudenell sisters, a tall, worldly-minded beauty who never lost her zest for admiration. After a time she complained to her brother that she was ill treated, and (since Lucan was not over-wealthy) denied many of the luxuries to which she had been accustomed. Cardigan was ever jealous of his family honour and condition; the fiery Lucan resented his interference; and their mutual hatred became a common scandal, a subject for gossip wherever people, especially men, met together.

It reached such a pitch that Wellington was asked to step in between the two earls and make peace. The Duke tried, but soon gave it up, declaring that he would find it more of an ordeal than the winning of Waterloo. In the year when war broke out, the Lucans parted. This worsened, as far as it was possible, the chronic relations between the brothers-in-law; and when Lord Hardinge, who succeeded Wellington as Commander-in-Chief, appointed Lucan to command the Cavalry Division, with Cardigan serving under him as a brigade commander, speculation and gossip flared anew. Such a move could lead to unpleasant, if not hazardous, consequences; and it was reckoned that Lord Lucan's hardest task would not be the leading of ten cavalry regiments, but how to control Lord Cardigan.

The Commander-in-Chief of the army destined for the East was unlikely to fare any better than Wellington in handling the two quarrelsome earls. He was Lord Fitzroy Somerset, the youngest son of the Duke of Beaufort. Somerset, who was created Lord Raglan in 1852, was fully versed in the administrative side of the army. He had been Wellington's military secretary at Waterloo, and had since carried an empty sleeve as a trophy of the battle. He possessed the high courage that often goes with a gentle nature; he would rather give way than ask a favour or beg co-operation; whatever the strain, he exhibited the patrician calm that made him seem aloof from ordinary men; but he had never

"Balaclava", Lady Elizabeth Butler's painting of the aftermath of the Charge of the Light Brigade

"The valley of Death" in which the Charge of the
Light Brigade took place

Ronald, Lord Cardigan's famous charger

actually commanded troops in the field. At the time of his supreme appointment he was 65; in his plain blue frock coat a perfect English gentleman, whom Wellington described as the sort of man who would not tell a lie to save his life. He was an old friend of the Cardigan family.

Apart from the cavalry, the expeditionary force was made up of five infantry divisions, each division consisting of two brigades, and each brigade of three regiments. The divisional commanders were Lieutenant-General Sir George Brown, a martinet of 66 who acted as though his prime duty was to conserve army regulations; his nickname, coined of that mixture of abuse and admiration so freely indulged by the old-time soldier, was 'the old wretch'; Major-General Sir George de Lacy Evans, a year older than Brown, whom he equalled in personal valour; General the Hon. Sir George Cathcart, who could be dangerously stubborn if not given the notice he thought he deserved; and Lieutenant-General the Duke of Cambridge, an easy-going yet painstaking soldier whose promotion had come as a matter of course since he was a cousin of the Queen. Subordinate to these, but superior to them in military experience, was Brigadier-General Sir Colin Campbell, who commanded the Highland Brigade that was part of the 1st Division under the Duke of Cambridge. The Quarter-Master General was General Richard Airey, who was possessed of a superabundant energy that could make him rash and impatient of detail.

Marshal St. Arnaud, Commander-in-Chief of the French, was the exact opposite to Raglan in every respect apart from personal bravery. He was theatrical, able to voice (like most French generals) fine ringing phrases, and without a scruple in the world. At the time of his leaving France he was already in the grip of an illness that was soon to kill him.

It had been suggested that Lucan, Cardigan and Scarlett, with their cavalry, should march through France to Marseilles and there embark. The march, so far as Paris was concerned, would be a positive triumph. But the effect that the sight of English uniforms might have upon parts of the south, where Waterloo was still a painful memory, was highly doubtful; and the regiments sailed by way of Gibraltar.

Cardigan made a hurried visit to Portsmouth to overlook his personal arrangements. He himself left Liverpool, in April,

9

accompanied by his Staff, servants and five horses, and provided with a small tent, some 6 feet square, and a spring sofa bed. One of his horses, a chestnut named Ronald, was destined for fame. Among his servants was a favourite orderly, Sergeant Richard Brown, who had served for twenty-one years and who had never been listed with defaulters. He was later to become one of the survivors of Balaclava who died in a workhouse.

But though his cavalry was not to pass through France, Cardigan decided to break the journey by a brief stay in Paris. He would after that fall in with the convoys when they entered the Dardanelles, bound for the sort of venture he had in mind when he first put on uniform and rode at the head of his Yeomanry at Deene Park. He was heading for glory, part of an army whose courage and spirit of endurance, in ranker and officer alike, has never been surpassed; an army superbly drilled and splendidly dressed in scarlet, green or blue; an army that had little or nothing in the way of land transport or in medical supplies, and with not the skeleton of a reserve behind it.

PART THREE

To the Crimea

I

Paris applauded Cardigan. His tall youthful figure, his keen blue eye and trimmed auburn whiskers, the uniform that set off his long horseman's legs and fashioned waist, made him the perfect hussar for a people whose normal headiness was increased by the knowledge that they were at war.

It had been the hottest Good Friday for years and the nights were soft and warm. The cafés where people sat over drinks and ices blazed with lights; and Cardigan, who always made a brave show, threaded his way amongst them and responded to the plaudits like a seasoned actor. He dined at the Café de Paris. He attended a reception at the Tuileries, where Napoleon III led him forward to kiss the tapering finger-tips (and Cardigan was a model of grace when greeting women) of the Empress Eugénie.

From Paris he went to Marseilles, where he took ship for Athens. The Greece of King Otho and Queen Amelia was said to be "more Russian than the Czar". But French troops moved into the country at about the time of Cardigan's visit; and he was able to view the monuments of a past culture in a comparatively friendly atmosphere. The newly built royal palace was thought by many to be the ugliest thing in the world; but this visual drawback was compensated for by the good looks of the Greek women, though critical foreign visitors (and Cardigan was one) wished they would curb the spread of their over-ample bosoms by wearing stays.

He embarked for the final stage of his journey with detachments of the 30th and the 55th Foot. They entered the Dardanelles, passing through shipping where French and British colours mingled with the crimson flag of Turkey, and sailed through a region of purple hills and tall dark woods bordered by chalet-like houses. They anchored off Scutari, a fair-sized village opposite Constantinople on the Asian side of the Bosphorus, dominated by the large and contaminated barracks that were soon to be associated with pestilence and death in every form, and with the name of Florence Nightingale.

Cardigan landed and went ashore on foot. He had been ill on the voyage and suddenly looked older but even so he was still a 'great swaggerer' whose presence could not be overlooked. William Howard Russell, *The Times* correspondent, wrote, "Lord Cardigan made his appearance yesterday"; while Captain George Higginson, of the Grenadiers, was a trifle more cynical: "Lord Cardigan has appeared looking as usual highly important; whether his Hussar Brigade is to distinguish itself remains to be seen."

Cardigan called on Raglan at army headquarters, a wooden building set on a filthy beach and surrounded by sludge and animal remains washed in by the sea. He sat down to dine with Lucan, and both men, temporarily good-humoured by the prospect of glory ahead of them, managed to suppress their true feelings. They figured at the review of British troops that celebrated the Queen's birthday on 24th May. The long lines of red and blue, "regulated as though by plummet", marched past in slow or quick time, their bayonets moving like a forest of light as they flashed above their shakos in the sun, while the guns of the fleet thundered a royal salute.

A few mornings after the review Cardigan staged a little pageant for himself. Donning his full-dress uniform, he hired a pony and rode through the rough and evil-smelling streets of Constantinople, through the streaming sewage and over the carcasses of dogs and rats; past the coffee houses and cafés and small boys who stood in the way shouting offers, "Show you bazaar, sir? See St. Sophia, captain?" Money-changers stopped arguing and smokers drew thoughtfully on their pipes to stare at the brilliant figure, with plume bobbing up and down as the pony struggled over the rough stones, "like a cricket ball on a ploughed field", as one rider put it; a figure that, apart from entertaining the Turks, might also have reminded them that their world was rocking.

The Turkish pashas received Cardigan and other high ranking English officers with every mark of distinction. But their principal concern did not appear to be the Russian menace, but the threatened corruption of their faith and customs by the introduction of Western manners; while the Sultan, Abdul-Mejid I, showed more interest in a new palace that he was building than in the fate of his empire. Cardigan shared the impatience of English officers who declared, "We are ready, as we stand, to go on to St. Petersburg this instant." But the Turkish commander, Omar Pasha, had plans of his own which he laid before Raglan and St. Arnaud.

Still thinking of the Balkans as the scene of future operations, it was decided that the Allied point of concentration should be at Varna,* on the Bulgarian coast, some 180 miles across the Black Sea. Cardigan's Light Brigade was ordered to make the move at the end of May. On the 29th they struck tents, and the transports, some steam, some sailing vessels, with a flotilla of launches, cutters and paddle-box boats, put to sea. None welcomed the move more than Cardigan, who saw it as a chance to assert the independence of his command by breaking away from Lucan, who was still at Scutari.

Cardigan applied direct to Raglan for permission to travel with his brigade; and having obtained it, he and his Staff proceeded to Varna. In this both Raglan and Cardigan were wrong, as Lucan, who commanded the two cavalry brigades, was Cardigan's immediate superior.

In spite of his natural temper, however, Lucan restrained himself when he heard how his authority had been overlooked. He sent a mild reminder to Cardigan of his fault in going direct to the Commander-in-Chief. But by then the offender was with his five regiments in their camp on a sandy stretch opposite the new base, and Lucan's letter was put aside.

When approached from the sea, and at first glance, Varna appeared to be a pleasant collection of wooden houses, with a few minarets, enclosed by thickets and gently sloping hills. But beyond their outward disguise of paint and whitewash the buildings were squalid and verminous; the ways between them were deep in slush and haunted by the usual assembly of rats and mangy curs.

* Re-named Stalin from 1950 until 1958, when it was again called Varna.

Cardigan's tent was erected on one of the hills, an operation that was watched, as his arrival had been, by one of the ladies who followed the army throughout the war. She was Fanny, the wife of Captain and Paymaster Henry Duberly, of the 8th Hussars. A most dutiful wife, and a lover of horses, she was opposed to Cardigan from the start. His morals were bad; his hard riding was notorious. Hence she made only a brief reference to him in the *Journal* she kept—one of the most graphic and readable of its kind: "Lord Cardigan and Staff rode into our lines."

2

The days were intensely hot. There were sudden and frequent storms. On some nights a great red moon, such as Cardigan had seen flooding his Midland meadows, rose over the sea; but on others a damp mist filled the hollows between the hills, bringing a vaguely ominous sense to those whose business it was, with the few resources at hand, to study the welfare of the army.

There were other disturbing signs. Cavalry commanders noted the poor quality of forage provided for the horses. Many of the bales of hay were filled with dust, shavings and straw; one bale contained the body of a cat, another a half-decayed lamb. But so far the Light Brigade (the Heavies were still at Scutari) excited the admiration of all who saw it. Cardigan allowed it to parade for the express benefit of Omar Pasha, who finally insisted on leading it in a spirited charge. Watched by Cardigan, he started off, mounted on a small Turkish horse, in front of the brigade. But after a few paces, with the big British chargers gaining upon him, he only escaped being run down by plying his spurs like a madman.

While riding alone one day, in the vicinity of Varna, Cardigan became the guest of the most unusual company he was ever to encounter. They were a band of Bashi-Bazouks, mounted Turkish ruffians who preyed on their own people. We can almost see the curl of Cardigan's lip as he watched them approach, dressed in filthy finery that was heavily embroidered and covered with gold tinsel, and armed to the teeth. Their leader was a woman. She may have been the mysterious Fatima Hanoum, the so-called Black Virgin or queen, who was greatly feared for her habit of quartering her followers upon towns and villages, and then demanding 'cup and stirrup' money for their keep.

None the less, Cardigan could not avoid being courteous to all women (though it would have taken a medical examination to prove the sex of the chieftainess, who was lean and scraggy with a hooked nose, and who smoked a pipe); and when she invited Cardigan to take coffee, he accepted, while the brigands standing round stared enviously at the details of his uniform.

In mid-July cholera broke out among the French. A few days later British soldiers were reporting sick, and before the end of the month Cardigan's cavalry brigade was infected.

Years later, when there had been great improvements in medicine, and when it was known that the disease was water-borne, Rudyard Kipling was to say that cholera in camp was worse than forty fights: and the ravages it inflicted upon the Allies, before a shot had been fired or a single enemy sighted, were more disastrous than the losses to be inflicted by Russian arms throughout the campaign.

Within a few weeks the British numbered only some 27,000 effectives; the sick in makeshift hospital tents, where the only beds were often of cut grass, presented (as a medical officer said) "a ghastly spectacle of suffering beyond all human aid". Dead bodies, in process of being devoured by rats and insects, lay reeking and unburied under a torrid sun. The proudest regiments were reduced to a demoralized collection of skeletons. Tall Guardsmen drooped under the packs they were unable to carry.

But while, as it was noticed at the time, the strongest men were the first to be overcome by the several forms of sickness—and fever and dysentery were also rife—those like Cardigan, who suffered from recurring minor troubles, were practically immune to the more deadly complaints. He had now been promoted to major-general, and in keeping with the custom of splitting up camps when disease struck them, he was ordered to move his Light Brigade to the village of Devna.

It was a poor place of mud and stone huts, set in a lonely stretch of country that was subject to extremes of weather. Men sweltered in the flimsy tents by day and shivered in them when bitter night winds swept down from the hills. But Cardigan's discipline was never relaxed. He knew the danger of leaving men without tasks or supervision even in a place like Devna. Travelling merchants who followed the army had set up booths, shops and cafés; drink was cheap, and drunkenness led to pilfering and trouble with the villagers. The conduct of officers in Constantinople, who peered closely at the veiled women in the streets, as though trying to see through the yashmaks that covered their faces, greatly angered the pashas. One had, in fact, died of shock when he heard of such depredations. But over-mellow privates at Devna were not above adding profanity to insult by pulling a veil aside with their infidel fingers. Cardigan came down heavily on all offenders, and early morning floggings, with the brigade drawn up in a hollow square to witness them, became quite frequent. Russell of *The Times*, who was then in Devna, gave his opinion of flogging as being the only cure, "and even that is not a good or certain one".

The travelling merchants or canteenmen, who were one and all known as 'Johnny Turk', caused quite as much trouble as the hardest cases among the soldiers. One villainous looking seller of poisonous liquor was ordered out of the district by Cardigan. But he returned, driving his cart that was again loaded with barrels. The angry troops he had previously swindled overturned his vehicle. He snatched up a sword, and flung it with such force at his attackers that it stuck fast in a door-post. At the height of the uproar Cardigan galloped up, and on being apprised of the reason he told the troops to give the fellow a good thrashing. But when they ceased standing at attention, and came to look round, the wily Turk had disappeared.

There was another shindy when some hussars, waiting to be served in a coffee shop, found there were not enough drinking vessels to go round. One of them went to a rival establishment to borrow what was needed. The keeper of this shop was a huge negro who refused to lend anything; whereupon the hussar proceeded to help himself. The negro snatched up a large iron pestle, that was used for grinding coffee, and swung it at the hussar. The blow missed him and smashed a table, and before the negro could recover his balance another hussar struck him on the head with a heavy jug. The negro dropped like a log. His friends complained to Cardigan, who ordered inquiries throughout his brigade in order to find the culprits. But none could be recognized and every man held his tongue.

A similar silence prevailed after a large turkey, that was meant for Cardigan's table, disappeared from the tent peg to which it had been tied, leaving only the string. Several hussars had passed that way when going to fetch water. Cardigan was infuriated by the loss. His rage was such that an officer mentioned it in one of his letters. He had the camp turned upside down, without success. But when things were calmer, the turkey was produced from underground and a secret feast took place in one of the tents.

3

By this time Cardigan had finally convinced himself that his was a separate command. He had several times applied direct to the Commander-in-Chief, over Lucan's head, and he interpreted Raglan's replies as a tacit admission that the Light Brigade, although officially part of the Cavalry Division, could act independently.

This being so, he ordered a series of field exercises without regard to the climate. There was early morning drill, skirmishing drill, charging by line and in squadrons, and outpost drill. One of his movements was to advance a squadron to the front, signal it to disperse, then to have the "Rally" sounded, which brought each man quickly back to his original place. Some Turkish cavalry had been detached to serve with the brigade. Cardigan despised these and refused to give them orders. But he cursed them roundly when, completely at a loss, they fell out of formation.

It was not for a general officer to inspect the stables. But Cardigan went the rounds, and insisted that every officer of the brigade was present at morning stables, and that an officer from each of the troops attended evening stables. A patrol was ordered out for three days and nights. They were on the point of starting when Cardigan noticed that cloaks were strapped to their saddles. Declaring them to be "effeminate" he told them to leave the cloaks behind, though the night wind, in spite of it being summer, could be bitter and the dews fell like rain. Between the days of oppressive heat, and the dangerously cold nights, men fainted at the frequent 'turn-outs', and some feared that Cardigan would weaken the men, and break up the horses, at this early and bloodless stage of the campaign.

Meanwhile Lucan, who had been fretting at Scutari, crossed the Black Sea with part of the Heavy Brigade and arrived at Varna. He had several scores to settle with Cardigan, who had acted on his own. But Cardigan, he was now disappointed to find, had moved on to Devna, from where he was still in touch with the Commander-in-Chief, and with the Quarter-Master General, just as though Lucan was non-existent. Lucan was not slow in complaining, but Cardigan continued to go over his head. What also galled Lucan was that Raglan, far from reprimanding Cardigan, appeared to be acquiescing in his calm assumption of separate authority.

Since Lucan could not, while Cardigan was at Devna, actually pin him down, he tried to assert himself by making pernickety demands that were likely to try his subordinate's patience. He asked for reports of the most detailed kind on a series of unimportant military items. Cardigan retaliated by sending back the merest outlines. Lucan demanded explanations, which Cardigan either continued to parry or completely ignored. He was still, however, in close touch with headquarters, and Lucan repeated his demand that all communications and reports should be sent to him as Divisional General. Cardigan replied that he was not bound to anyone except the commander of the forces in which his brigade was serving.

The dispute was carried on by the two earls at every level that allowed for opposition. Lucan found fault with the general appearance of the cavalry, and issued an order of the day directing a more rigorous application of pipeclay and ochre to belts, leathers and facings. The fact that none of those cleaning materials were available did not affect the validity of the order, which Cardigan, as much a stickler for smartness and discipline as Lucan, at once set out to contravene.

He authorized the wearing of garments that were not strictly uniform, and requested Raglan to allow all ranks to grow beards. The using of bad razors, on sunburnt skins, was producing veritable wounds; and although Raglan disliked the wearing of whiskers and moustachios, an order from the Horse Guards compelled him to agree, with Cardigan, that hair on the face could be permitted.

In June, while Cardigan was still at Devna, he was given his first important and independent command. The Russians had withdrawn from Silistria, but Raglan, with unknown country ahead of him, had no idea as to their next probable move. They might be planning an attack on Varna, or a further withdrawal. Were they following a route that would take them to the right bank of the Danube and into the district known as the Dobrudscha? Cardigan was ordered to take a patrol and to ascertain their whereabouts.

The patrol, consisting of one squadron each of the 8th Hussars and the 13th Light Dragoons, with some Turkish cavalry, set off on 25th June. It might have been known, from the start, that whatever information was gained would be dearly purchased, since they took no more than could be carried on the horses, which were pitifully overburdened for travel through marshy and sandy country, which made heavy going, and tortured by a blinding sun that dazed and blinded the eyes.

Each horse carried its rider in average full marching order, weighing some 20 stone; extra ammunition; two blankets, 36 pounds of barley, two hay nets filled with hay, 3 pounds of meat, as many pounds of biscuit, and a keg holding 3 pints of water.

They were on the move from sunrise to sunset, riding through a country entirely treeless and without roads. They bivouacked in the open, for the few villages they passed had been ruined and plundered by the Bashi-Bazouks. The first halt was at Bazargik, where they encountered a handful of inhabitants, one of whom was called the mayor, and where dogs and cats attacked them so fiercely, and in such numbers, that they had to be repelled with swords. Then came Karasi, and a march along the banks of the Danube that brought them to Rassova. There were more ruins, and more half-wild stray animals, including pigs, nosing and rooting among them. Shots were heard; Cardigan went to investigate, and he came upon a scene that caused him to explode with fury. "Cavalry officers shooting pigs with pistols? Disgraceful!" That night, however, he sat down to a supper of pork without inquiring as to its origin.

They turned westward to Silistria, riding through a thunderstorm that covered the earth with a pall of darkness. Horses stumbled, several fell, and the men rode at funeral pace glimpsing no more than the yard or so of earth that each step covered. What was left of the town, which marked the limit of the Russian advance, bore signs of the recent siege, and as Cardigan's patrol

again followed the line of the Danube they came within a mile
or so of a large Russian force encamped on the opposite side. The
hussars and dragoons were well within range of the enemy guns;
but when a Turkish officer, bearing a flag of truce, was sent forward by Cardigan, the Russian general was content to take long
looks at the cavalry through his telescope, and inquire if they were
French or English.

Having completed his mission by locating the whereabouts of
the nearest Russian force, Cardigan started back by way of
Shumla, a hill village overlooking the Bulgarian plain, and Yeni-
Bazaar (New Market). The patrol reached Devna at three o'clock
on the morning of 11th July, after being absent sixteen days and
having covered some 330 miles. One who watched the stragglers
come in was Mrs. Fanny Duberly, and she thought it a sorry
sight, with exhausted men on foot driving and goading the
wretched horses, some of which could hardly stir.

The strain imposed upon the men, and more especially the state
of the horses, gave rise to much superficial disparagement of this
'Sore-back Reconnaissance', as Cardigan's critics still call it. But
the move into difficult and unknown country, to probe for an
enemy whose numbers and position were unknown, was one of
the many hazards of war that, although strictly necessary, yield
little in the way of practical accomplishment. It was still believed
that the coming campaign would be in that part of the Balkans;
and only the most hare-brained commander could anticipate
going forward without having reconnoitred the terrain.

Cardigan thanked all ranks of his patrol for the zeal and activity
they had shown throughout. They had borne themselves well—
except for "a few irregularities at Shumla", of which, he said, he
would take no further notice; while Raglan was "very much
obliged" to Cardigan for the pains he had taken to ascertain the
direction of the Russian withdrawal, and also that the countryside
was deserted. "These are very important facts which it is very
desirable I should be made acquainted with, and I hope that the
fatigue that you and the squadrons have undergone in obtaining
the information will not prove injurious to your health, and that
of the officers and men under your orders."

Senior officers have always come in for a great deal of criticism
from their juniors, and Cardigan, having figured so much in the
public eye, was especially open to hostile or derogatory remarks

from those he commanded. One spoke of Cardigan as "a dangerous ass". The unsavoury case brought by Lord William Paget against Cardigan had naturally caused bad feeling between the Earl and Lord George Paget, William's brother and second in command of the Light Brigade; and this in turn was reflected by an officer of the 4th Light Dragoons, Captain Robert Portal, who was Lord George's aide-de-camp and friend. In one of his letters, Portal referred to Cardigan being equalled only by Lucan in want of intellect. Cardigan, Portal went on, had no more brains than his boot, and two such fools as the brothers-in-law could hardly be found in the British Army.

There were, of course, contrary opinions of Cardigan that are seldom, if ever, repeated by those who endorse the popular case against him. A serious judge of men and events, such as Captain the Hon. Henry Clifford, V.C., was to tell his relatives in a letter that everyone who met Cardigan had the highest opinion of him as a soldier and a very brave man. Captain George Higginson, who was temperamentally opposed to Cardigan, wrote of him, at the time of the 'Sore-back Reconnaissance', "they say he is very quiet and attentive, and that he explains his orders most clearly". Later on he spoke of Cardigan as "a chivalrous cavalry leader"; while Captain Jenyns of the 13th Light Dragoons, who had taken part in the patrol, told a friend, "We got tremendous praise from Lord Cardigan, who is a capital fellow to be under at this work."

4

The Light Cavalry again broke camp and moved on to Isyteppe, another miserable village 12 miles from Devna. The march was made in sweltering weather; Mrs. Duberly rode in the van of her husband's regiment, which halted for the night at Yeni-Bazaar. A young battle-hungry officer of the 11th Hussars, surveying the ground, thought it would be "a stunner for a mill"; but Cardigan was more concerned with personal comfort, and chose the one cool place, under a tree that overlooked a stream, as the site for his tent.

But the Duberly tent was erected there first, and Cardigan, not wishing to disappoint a lady in person, sent a message to her pay-master husband and told him to settle elsewhere. Fanny was soon surrounded by a crowd of indignant sympathizers, who called down all manner of discomforts upon the Major-General's head; and Fanny next day recorded in her diary that during the night the stream overflowed and flooded into Cardigan's tent.

But apart from this little demonstration of self-interest, one of the several incidents that Cardigan's detractors slant against him occurred during this stay at Yeni-Bazaar. The stream could have supplied enough water for the camp, but since it flowed at the bottom of a hill Cardigan had reason to fear that it might be infected. A sentry was posted to prevent the troops drinking the water; and since the only other supply was a good mile distant, this vigilance on Cardigan's part is usually interpreted, by those who overlook the reason, as an act of petty tyranny.

The column reached Isyteppe in a state of general exhaustion. Fanny was hardly able to stand, while the men, without regard for the rule of regimental seniority that Cardigan insisted upon, pitched the tents. But rest was still denied them. Cardigan was never too tired to make an inspection, and he was shocked to find that the place on the right of the line, which properly belonged to the 8th Hussars as senior regiment present, had been given to the 13th Light Dragoons.

The tents had to come down again for rearrangement. But still the Major-General was not satisfied. His eagle eye detected that the canvas lines were irregular, and the weary men were called on to make another adjustment before they slept.

Mrs. Duberly decided that she frankly detested the officious Cardigan, especially when, in defiance of the boiling climate, field days were ordered twice a week. Between these spells of duty he was a frequent caller at the 'bower', that the Irishmen in her husband's corps had constructed, of branches and foliage, for Fanny. He became expansive, talking to her of military matters beyond the regimental level to which she was accustomed; and she was flattered by his attention.

She could hardly avoid comparing his gallant figure with the stolid, uncavalier-like appearance of Paymaster Henry; while Cardigan's shocking reputation, which he carried as carelessly as he did his slung-jacket, added a touch of salt to her growing appreciation of his presence.

He was standing, one evening, at the entrance to her bower. The many indiscriminate sounds of the camp had died away into a silence that was only broken, at intervals, by the chafing of horses in their lines where some were being groomed. All eyes turned as a Staff officer galloped over the flats from the direction of Varna. Fanny heard Cardigan say, "Hallo! A cocked hat, by Jove!" The rider dismounted and gave Cardigan a message. It came, as the white plumes of the messenger indicated, from general headquarters. As Cardigan read his eyes lighted up and his face flushed with pleasure. "Hurrah!" he exclaimed, like a boy, "we're for the Crimea!"

He had lived for such a moment. His brigade, in anticipation of it, had been brought to a peak of efficiency; and now it swung into a disciplined bustle. Trumpets sounded "Orders!" Sergeants moved quickly about, with book and pencil, noting down and marking off instructions. Supplies and equipment were prepared for the march back to port. Even the horses sensed the thrill of preparation. Cardigan looked beyond Fanny and saw the first hazy gleam of a Russian coastline.

5

The original object of Britain and France in declaring war— which was to safeguard Turkish independence—had now been achieved. The Russians had withdrawn from the Balkans. But the Allied governments were unwilling to relinquish their fear of Russia and to let their expeditions end in stalemate. Voices were raised in Britain and France demanding some spectacular success, which could best be achieved by invading Russia. The only point open to invasion was the Crimea, the southernmost part of the country which protruded, almost island-like, into the Black Sea. It contained the great fortress of Sebastopol; but beyond that—and estimates of Russian military strength in the peninsula that varied from forty-five thousand to one hundred and forty thousand men—very little was known of the Crimea outside Russia. Some vaguely remembered, from their schooldays, that Homer may have mentioned it. The Czar thought it a likely location for the Garden of Eden. But the reputation of Sebastopol was such that its capture would be a stab at the very heart of Russia, and a victory that the Allies could regard as the basis of an honourable peace.

Cardigan shed his years, and his physical complaints, while the expedition prepared at Varna to cross the Black Sea. He was now convinced that the Light Brigade was his own separate command; and when part of the Heavy Brigade was attached to it for a time he assumed the greater part of Lucan's authority. The latter complained to Raglan, who at last made Cardigan understand that he was subordinate to Lucan; and the better to enforce Lucan's position as commander of the Cavalry Division he was promoted to lieutenant-general.

Cardigan did not easily surrender the idea of his independence. There were several interviews between him and Raglan; and the Commander-in-Chief had to be unusually firm in stressing Lucan's superior military status. From that time, Cardigan wrote, his position in the cavalry was greatly changed. "All pleasure ceased in the command which remained to me, and I had nothing to guide me but a sense of duty to the service."

But he continued to oppose Lucan by every means in his power. The two earls carried on their warfare by exchanging angry letters, of which the main theme was Cardigan's request to know whether or not he commanded the Light Brigade. Lucan's most telling shot was a reminder to Cardigan that though his rank was that of major-general, his position as commander of the Light Brigade was essentially that of a brigadier—"and that there were many brigadiers in the six divisions of the Army".

Cardigan struck back by defying an order that Lucan determined to enforce throughout the two cavalry brigades. The order stated that officers' wives could not travel in transports to the Crimea, but only those regimental wives who were officially 'on the strength'. Cardigan's friend, Fanny Duberly (whose original dislike of the Earl had been somewhat tempered by his flattering attention) was reduced to tears. She had come so far, and had so set her heart on continuing with the army, that the disappointment threatened to make her ill; and Cardigan, overcome by the sight of a woman in distress, at once saw Raglan and asked him to make an exception on her behalf.

But Raglan stood firm; Lucan reinforced the ban where cavalry wives were concerned; and Fanny's tear-stained face was almost a reproach to Cardigan when he returned to her bower with the refusal. He had always invested orders and regulations with a sort of near-sanctity. But Fanny's broken voice, and sad tear-washed look, were more than enough to overcome the resistance of any chivalrous hussar.

Cardigan posed, stuck out his chest; his long legs in cherry-coloured overalls might have been those of a military Colossus bestriding the camp. "But, should you think proper to disregard the prohibition," he told Fanny, "I will not offer any opposition to your doing so." She looked up, through her strands of fallen hair and her tears. The martinet expression had gone from his keen blue eyes, which were kind and sympathetic. Fanny recovered, almost at once, and before long was joining in a plot to overcome the ban imposed by Raglan and Lucan.

The steamers and sailing ships that were to make the 300-mile crossing assembled off Varna. When joined by the French, the great armada would be protected by the guns of the fleet under Vice-Admiral Dundas. Cardigan was detailed to sail, with 700 men and 390 horses, on the *Himalaya*, that was generally admitted to be a 'stupendous' four-masted steamer that could rush through the waters like a dolphin. Cardigan went aboard on Friday, 6th September, and at nightfall the wives of the privates and non-commissioned officers followed. Lucan, who was sailing on the *Simla*, kept watch by the quay in search of any officer's wife who attempted to follow; but he never spied Fanny, who, wearing an old hat and shawl, went with the tattered procession up the gangway and straightway took refuge in a cabin.

Early on the 7th, as the horizon mist was giving way to a coloured dawn, the firing of three guns heralded a signal that fluttered from the mizzen mast of the flagship *Britannia*, "Prepare to weigh anchor." Bands played, and flags appeared throughout the six lines of vessels, each line carrying a division of troops, that put to sea under a warm breeze blowing from the land.

Fanny could now leave her cabin, and Cardigan at once sought her company. She still disliked him, of course; but she was none the less flattered to be seen with him, walking the deck, passing up and down between the lines of horses and judging their qualities. She knew they were being watched, and almost certainly providing food for gossip. The situation, she confessed in a letter to her sister, was intolerable. "How scandalous people are!"

But during that crossing of the Black Sea her opinion of Cardigan underwent a further change. She was amused by the boyish excitement he showed at the prospect of 'going to war'.

10

When a head-wind delayed their progress he fumed with impatience. At other times he pranced up and down (as she said) "like a soldier in a country theatre".

There were days and nights of such sheer beauty that even the most guarded emotions could be stirred. Sails fluttered in a warm wind over the calm water. On clear evenings the vessels seemed heading straight for the September sun as it sank in the west. Then the masthead lights, glimmering portholes and the blaze of lanterns, turned the great armament into a pageant of moving colour that shone till sunrise. It needed only music to add a touch of grace to the scene, and the *Himalaya* boasted a piano.

Fanny, like most of her kind, was a trained singer and a polished performer on the piano; but when Cardigan, who had a genuine love of music, asked her to play, she looked at her hands, browned by the strong Bulgarian sun and roughened by the exigencies of camp life. They were far less becoming than the hands over which Cardigan had lingered at Deene Park, and Fanny declined.

So far as they could, Cardigan on the *Himalaya*, and Lucan on the *Simla*, annoyed each other by the messages they exchanged. Lucan was further infuriated by the several attempts, made by the *Himalaya*, to forge ahead and appear to be leading the fleet. One of his Staff wrote, "We conclude Cardigan is at the bottom of this, it looks like a piece of his silly vanity."

Land was sighted on 12th September, and the vessels anchored off the spit of sand from which rose the white houses, overlooked by the usual minaret, of Eupatoria. Through his glasses Cardigan viewed the farms, the cultivated land and stubble running down to the sea, the windmills on the plateau that stretched away inland. A few Cossacks, mounted on shaggy nags that would never have been admitted to English stables, invited his scorn.

The horses of the Light Brigade were lowered by slings into paddle-box boats, or on to rafts, and towed ashore by launches and cutters. The brigade then moved some two miles in front of the main British position, and threw out detachments in skirmishing order. The horses of each troop were picketed in column of lines, with their heads facing inwards, and the gear was deposited in the spaces between each line. The horses were blanketed; the men, wrapped in their cloaks, used the saddles as pillows. The bivouac closed down with traces of sunset still in the west, but presently the sky turned leaden. A sharp wind sent heavy seas roaring into the bay, and rain lashed down, falling in floods, upon an army that had no shelter or cover, and that spent the night crowded together in little groups, or huddled in pools. General and drummer-boy were soaked to the skin. Uniforms, some of them full dress, that had to last the length of the campaign, were reduced to sodden rags.

Suddenly shots were heard from the direction of the Light Brigade lines.

6

The cry of "Cossacks!" went up. Vedettes came galloping back to the main body. Sentries in the horse-lines fired towards the undulating ground that offered cover for any attack. Horses were saddled and girthed up, and the men mounted. More shots were fired as Cardigan arrived, icy calm as he called on the lines to steady themselves and to rally, furious when the officer in charge of the vedette came in with a garbled report as to what had caused the alarm. It might have been Cossacks, or a newly landed British regiment that had stumbled on the Light Brigade in the darkness. . . . One who was there said, "The *sang-froid* of Lord Cardigan was equal to the occasion—unquestionable and remarkable."

This affair was followed by a meeting between a small advance party of the Light Brigade and a body of Cossacks. It occurred on rising ground, and the British, going forward from knoll to knoll, were suddenly confronted by a strong Russian force which had been hidden. The British retired at walking pace, and just outside the camp they encountered Cardigan.

Why were they falling back? he demanded. He rebuked the officer in charge, and said that he wished *he* had been on the spot when the Russians were sighted. One of the party, who had witnessed the Russian strength, remarked (out of hearing) that it was just as well Cardigan had not been present. The latter, when he had cooled down, while still insisting that the withdrawal had been disgraceful, apologized for some of the "nasty expressions" he had used.

Cardigan was ordered, with the 13th Light Dragoons, to make

the first reconnaissance into enemy country, and to bring back everything they found, in the way of carts and animals, that would serve to carry baggage. Before starting he formed the men in a hollow square, and keyed them up in readiness for action by a little speech that revealed his keenness as a cavalry leader:

I have received orders to proceed a few miles inland, as it is expected a couple of regiments of Russian dragoons will be marching in this direction. I am determined to cut them off if possible. I have every reason to believe—in fact I am certain—that whatever service you are ordered on, you will do with credit and honour to your name as British Dragoons. I wish to give you some little advice and caution.

In case we fall in with them, and charge them, ride close, and let the centre be a little in advance of the flanks. When you get within a hundred yards of them ride with the utmost impetuosity. But mind, whatever you do when you have passed through the ranks, don't go too far, but turn about as quick as possible, and rally together and charge back again, that is if they have not bolted by that time. That is all I have to say, except that we shall be accompanied by a couple of guns of the Horse Artillery and some of the Rifle Brigade.

Before starting the dragoons were given permission to cut off their brass epaulettes, which made it impossible for fully dressed men to sleep, in the open, on their sides. On Cardigan giving the order, "Advance guard from the left," a file of men rode forward with carbines at the ready. Thirty yards in the rear of these came a non-commissioned officer, and 60 yards in the rear of him rode a party of four. Another non-commissioned officer followed at the same distance, and then came the main body. The rearguard followed the same formation as those leading the advance.

After proceeding for 3 miles, and crossing a large salt lake, they entered the village of Sak. The inhabitants lined the road, each kneeling and making the sign of the Cross to show that they too were Christians, and offering black bread and water melons. They came to rising ground; vedettes were pushed forward, and officers peered long and anxiously through their glasses. But there was no sign of the enemy or of warlike preparations.

Cardigan turned back, with a string of carts for transport, and a mixed collection of animals to draw them, keeping his dragoons at a good sharp pace in apparent forgetfulness of the Rifles in the rear, who, even by increasing their traditional quickstep to the utmost, could not keep up with the horse.

They reached camp at two o'clock in the morning, having ascertained that the Russians must be preparing to make their first stand some miles off, in the direction of Sebastopol—though Cardigan's habitual detractors, as though expecting a mere reconnaissance to yield some truly impressive result, describe the patrol as yet another badly executed and profitless move on his part.

He and Lucan were still at loggerheads, Lucan complaining that Cardigan flouted his authority, and Cardigan accusing the other of needless interference with the Light Brigade over sundry details, even to the pitching of tents. Their attempts to hamper each other were watched with no little amusement by Lord George Paget, who noted that from the moment of landing the brothers-in-law had been "like a pair of scissors who go snip and snip and snip without doing each other any harm, but God help the poor devil who gets between them".

PART FOUR

Twenty Minutes of Glory

I

Lord Cardigan was in pride of place, leading the army that began its march inland on the morning of 19th September. He rode with the 11th Hussars and the 13th Light Dragoons. Then came the infantry divisions, some twenty-six thousand men, with the three remaining regiments of the Light Brigade covering the rear and the left flank. The French were on the right, nearest the sea. It was a fine cloudless day; the sun promised heat; larks soared overhead; bands played, Colours floated in the breeze; bayonets and lances glittered, and the guns rattled and jingled over the springy turf. Sebastopol, the goal of the expedition, was but 25 miles distant; but as noon developed a change came over the order and the spirit of the march.

With the sun at its fiercest, and the breeze gone, men who had been worn down by disease in the Balkans began to drop. The agony of thirst was upon them. Some were delirious, kneeling and begging for drink, no longer able to carry their equipment. Shakos and even rifles were thrown aside. Cardigan's men, the 'swells', 'fancy fellows', and 'silly peacock cavalry', were not so painfully afflicted. They led the way over undulating ground, and about two o'clock Cardigan drew rein on the crest of a ridge.

A valley stretched before him, rising in tiers on the other side; and in the hollow a sparkling stream of water, the Bulganak River, ran out to sea. The columns lost the last semblance of order as men rushed down into the valley to slake their thirst; and before resuming the march Cardigan, with four squadrons, went forward to reconnoitre the slopes beyond the southern bank.

He advanced for 2 miles towards a range of hills, following a dip that led downward then brought him out, on the other side, in full view of mounted men whom he knew, if only by the long 15-foot lances they carried, to be Cossacks. They were dressed in blue trousers, tightly buttoned blue coats and conical-shaped caps. Cardigan's squadrons were greatly outnumbered, but it was for moments like this that he had lived. He threw out half the right troop of dragoons in skirmishing order, so that they crossed the front at intervals of some dozen yards from each other. The Cossacks followed suit and opened fire at long range, which the British returned. But Cardigan was not prepared to leave it to the carbines of the cavalry.

He determined to charge, and was forming the dragoons in readiness when Lucan arrived. The situation offered a chance for Lucan to assert his authority, and he at once ordered changes in the disposition of the squadrons. Cardigan took no heed; an argument developed, the two leaders turning in their saddles to exchange abuse while the Cossacks and the dragoons remained facing each other.

Meanwhile Raglan, following with the main body and coming out upon a spur of hill that admitted a view beyond the some-what limited perspective that was open to Cardigan, saw a large Russian force drawn up in the rear of the Cossacks. By then twilight was settling over the hills. A general engagement was out of the question. But the advanced British cavalry was in dire peril, and Raglan despatched General Airey with an order for Cardigan's squadrons to be withdrawn.

But when Airey arrived on the scene the two earls were still wrangling. They did not calm down at the sight of the Quarter-master General, nor when he repeated the order; and Airey was finally forced to command them in Raglan's name, to fall back.

Meanwhile the Russians had pushed some artillery forward, and round shot came pitching over, harmlessly at first, in the ranks of Cardigan's dragoons. They stood their ground with admirable firmness, a tribute to the iron discipline that had forged them; and they withdrew, slowly, when Cardigan reluctantly ordered them to do so, in the same spirit. A trumpet sounded "Rally to the left", and the skirmishers trotted back, strapping their carbines and drawing swords as though preparing for action. Then came the order, "Threes right, leading threes right wheel," which brought them into line with the advanced squadrons.

They exhibited the same faultless discipline when dropping back upon the main body. The Russian cavalry made a show of following them up, but Cardigan's men turned and faced about, every 50 yards, in readiness to repel any attack. In this operation, as the Russian fire continued, the 11th Hussars had their first casualty of the war. Private Williamson suddenly moved out of line and rode up to one of the cornets. "I am hit," he announced. "May I fall out?" Glancing at him, the cornet saw that one of his feet had been carried away, with the stirrup iron, just above the ankle, and that the leg was only held in place by a mess of shattered bone and shredded overall. With such a wound the private might have ridden straight to the doctor in the rear; but the training of the Light Brigade, as though in readiness for their supreme test, had exceeded any regulation model. A second casualty, with a leg that was broken into splinters, refused to make use of a stretcher.

Cardigan was furious at having been held back when about to charge. "I don't know why it is," he complained bitterly, "but whatever I propose is always frustrated." He worked his temper off on his brigade, and when he encountered some hussar officers who, owing to the heat, had exchanged their busbies for forage caps, he rated them severely. Their lieutenant-colonel attempted to speak on their behalf, and high words followed. Some of the troops, anticipating close action that afternoon, had thrown off the forage nets that the horses normally carried, and Cardigan laid the blame on their commander. "Now mind, Colonel, I shall expect a letter from you tonight giving me full particulars as to why your regiment is without forage."

He was only partially consoled for his disappointment by Raglan's account of the operation, which said that "Major-General the Earl of Cardigan exhibited the utmost spirit and coolness, and kept his Brigade under perfect command." The part Lucan had played in interfering to stop the charge was hotly resented; and one of the officers suggested that he might fitly be called 'Lord Look-on', a nickname that followed the cavalry leader throughout the war, and after.

The two armies confronted each other some 7 miles beyond the Bulganak, where the Russians, under Prince Menshikoff, held strong positions on the heights rising above the River Alma. Batteries of guns were massed about their central strong point, called the Great Redoubt on the Kourgane Hill, which dominated the river crossings. The soft green country reminded many of those on the English side of their native Downs; a breeze blew in from the sea; and the sun, rising on the morning of Tuesday, 20th September, promised heat. The crossing of the river, and the attack on the Russian strong point, made the battle an infantry affair.

Cardigan and his cavalry were on the extreme left of the line. Their numbers were insufficient to attempt a turning of the left flank—any single regiment of Russian horse was stronger than a British cavalry brigade—and Cardigan had to rest content with the knowledge that his presence covered the left and rear of the British line. Those of his troops who drew their swords that day only used them to pick up water melons that grew in the field where they waited in reserve.

Lord George Paget who, as second in command of the Light Brigade, was positioned close to Cardigan, said that they were able to view the battle "as if we had taken an opera box". They heard the "Advance" sounded, soon after noon, when the lines of redcoats began their steady march down to the river; they saw those lines drop to the ground, without protection on the bare turf, when the Russian artillery opened fire; they then saw one of Raglan's Staff, Captain Nolan, deliver an order for a general move forward.

The redcoats rose to their feet and continued their advance, splashing into and crossing the river with rifles and ammunition held above their heads, moving up hill in the face of a veritable storm of grape, round shot, canister, and musket balls, with Colours showing through the smoke and the figures of field officers still miraculously erect on their horses.

A Colour was carried over the parapet of the Great Redoubt, then, as the Russians rallied, the decimated British infantry fell back in places, till the Guards and Colin Campbell's Highlanders, keeping impeccable formation, poured heavy and destructive fire into the densely packed Russian masses that appeared, to Cardigan's view, like dark patches of wood on the hillsides and ridges. The sun was going down, and as daylight faded the masses broke and streamed away while the victorious British infantry appeared in silhouette on top of the ridges, their bearskins and bonnets raised on bayonet points, and their cheers sounding over

the river to where Cardigan had sat in the saddle all day hoping
for a chance that never came. His only intimation of danger was
when a chance Russian round shot passed over the crupper of his
horse. Those near its rider noticed that he never moved a muscle.

Raglan's orders had been explicit. His policy was to keep his
small cavalry force "in a band-box", and not to expose it to any
risk. The most they were permitted, at the Battle of the Alma, was
to act as escort to the Horse Artillery as it moved to a forward
position; but when the Russians broke, Lucan and Cardigan could
stand it no longer.

They divided forces, with Lucan on the left and Cardigan on
the right, and crossed the river. Ascending the slopes at a gallop,
they joined the cheering infantry on the crest; the guns they had
escorted opened up on the retreating Russians, and Lucan, who
had led with the 17th Lancers, swept in a few prisoners at the
eastern end of the front. He was immediately recalled, though it
was clear to all that the cavalry, given a free hand, could have
turned Menshikoff's retreat into a rout. Lucan swallowed his rage
and let the prisoners go; Cardigan sulkily withdrew down the
slope.

On the way he met the Assistant-Commissary General,
Crookshanks, with a bullock cart, bringing rations for the troops.
"That's right," said Cardigan, stopping to survey the load, "what
have you got with you?" Crookshanks explained that he had
"plenty of everything"—meat, biscuit, coffee, sugar and rum.
"Well, I hope you will let my men have some as soon as possible,"
said Cardigan, "for they have had nothing today." He moved on
to his tent and stood at the entrance, watching the mist creep up
from the river and envelop the hillsides. The sound of martial
music and bugles echoed from the camp of the French, who had
held a limited front during the advance and had not been heavily
engaged.

Cardigan was joined by Captain Higginson of the Grenadiers,
and they discussed the part the Guards had played in the river
crossing and the final move. The moon was high over the valley
when Cardigan retired to his tent, but not to sleep. For in spite of
the prevailing after-battle tension, Cardigan penned a long letter
to Raglan, complaining of Lucan's continued interference with
the Light Brigade. Would Lord Raglan make it clear that he
(Cardigan) was its sole and independent commander? But Raglan

was now fully concerned with the serious side of war, and did not reply.

The army resumed its march towards Sebastopol before daybreak on 23rd September. Part of the way led through the valley of the Katcha, a place rich in cultivated farmland and orchards. But as the road entered the hills they encountered narrow passes, and one night the vanguard, still led by Cardigan, was held up at a dangerous point where a single battalion of riflemen could have inflicted heavy losses. When someone remarked on this to Cardigan, his only comment was that Lord Lucan commanded the cavalry.

The old rivalry continued without a break, Lucan riding with the Light Brigade as often as possible, and trying to make Cardigan feel that he was some sort of junior officer; Cardigan smarting at Raglan's reluctance to confirm his independent leadership of the brigade; both being blamed unjustly, by firebrands like Captain Nolan, for the cavalry's failure to turn the Russian retreat from the Alma into a rout. "It's too disgraceful, too infamous!" stormed Nolan. "It's enough to drive me mad. They ought to be damned!"

After crossing the Balbec River, the British gained their first sight of Sebastopol. It was on a clear sunny morning. The streets appeared to be blocks of dazzling white, with here and there a green copper dome rising above them. The Russian fleet was at anchor. Powerful forts and massed guns covered the town's approaches and the harbour.

Cardigan again went ahead, and reported that an area of marshland was immediately in front of the British. A move to the left, which would bring them to a site overlooking the Sebastopol roadstead, was therefore decided upon; and a rendezvous was arranged between Lucan and the cavalry, and Raglan and his Staff, at a spot that went by the unusual name, for those parts, of Mackenzie's Farm. It was called after a Scottish admiral who had supervised the Sebastopol defences and then settled in the Crimea at the end of the previous century. A road that connected with the highway to Sebastopol ran past the farm. Cardigan with the rest of the cavalry was to follow Lucan.

The way ahead was largely a tangle of brushwood, broken by a byroad that became a mere track forking to the left and to the right. Here Lucan, coming to a stop, took the wrong direction, and when Raglan arrived the cavalry were nowhere to be seen. The spell of indecision that followed led to a most remarkable episode, with General Airey emerging cautiously from the wood and finding the road filled by a Russian wagon train and its escort. The men were resting, but the sound of hoofs made them start up and stare as the British Commander-in-Chief, who had followed Airey, came out into the open.

The Russians could have seized Raglan, but the sight of his frock coat (he was seldom in uniform) added to their surprise and made them uncertain. Then came the unmistakable noise of artillery crashing through the wood in the wake of the Staff, and the Russians hurriedly made off.

The artillery unlimbered, wheeled out into the road, and fired some shots. Lucan, still deep in the woodland, took his bearing from the sound and came charging up. He was fuming, breathless and embarrassed, too much the military fanatic to bear his errors lightly, especially when Raglan at his coldest called out, "Lord Lucan, you're late!" Then Cardigan arrived with part of his brigade, and the normally placid Raglan turned on him. "The cavalry were not in their proper place."

Cardigan acknowledged the rebuke with a half smile that, while implying a sense of injury, was also a reproachful reminder. "I am, my Lord, no longer in command of the cavalry." Never for a moment did he moderate his wish to be independent of Lucan.

The army moved on, with the two cavalry commanders either quarrelling or maintaining a stony silence. They descended into the valley of the Tchernaya River, then gained the high ground in the region of Balaclava, a little port that remained the army's base for the rest of the war. The fleet had followed round the coastline, and the main operation now was to besiege and capture Sebastopol. In spite of its great strength, it was confidently hoped that the fortress would fall within a matter of days.

2

Cardigan wrote in his journal on 26th September, "Encamped close to Balaclava"; and on the 27th he added, "Changed our camp to opposite village of Kadikoi." The village consisted of a few stone houses and a church, while the camp was on a plateau that promised little in the way of forage for the cavalry horses. Thistles alternated with coarse grass, and the hay ration for each mount was soon restricted to 6 pounds daily.

Balaclava, a fishing village 7 miles from Sebastopol, with a narrow harbour enclosed by cliffs of red stone, and hardly more than a street of green-tiled houses, was entered without a shot being fired by the British. It was garrisoned by only a handful of militiamen who fired a single mortar, and then hung out a cambric handkerchief, followed by one of the governor's best linen shirts, in token of surrender. The infantry encamped on the plateau that thrust out spurs and ridges overlooking Sebastopol, and prepared for the siege. Although expected to be of short duration, the siege would engage the bulk of the British forces, which meant that the defence of Balaclava, on the possession of which the existence of the army depended, would be far from adequate. Any move forward, on the part of the Russians, would demand swift counteraction; and Cardigan's cavalry patrols operated day and night in the region of the Tchernaya.

"Lord Cardigan", wrote Colonel Hodge of the 4th Dragoon Guards, "is always in front. He is indefatigable." The days were mild and sunny, but after twilight a dew-heavy mist spread over the fields, and the cavalry often had to stay in the saddle, or to stand by their horses all night, because of continual Russian threats.

All this while Lucan and Cardigan persisted in their efforts to deal out pinpricks. Cardigan had an almost spinster-like regard for the maintenance of order, but Lucan managed to find fault with the spacing of the Light Brigade tents. Raglan had replied to Cardigan's complaint written on the night of the Alma, with a severe reminder that Lucan, as commander of the Cavalry Division, could interfere as he thought fit with either of the brigades. He recommended the two generals, since they were possessed of high honour and elevated position, to seek an understanding with each other. Meanwhile the heedless recipients of this good advice were quarrelling over such details as the distribution of forage. Their officers took sides or criticized both as being 'asses', Lucan on account of his invariable caution and Cardigan for being dangerous.

But Lucan was not the only one with whom Cardigan quarrelled. Lord George Paget, according to the notes he kept, had a "turn up" with Cardigan about this time. Paget had been attached to the 2nd Infantry Division under General Sir de Lacy Evans, but Cardigan, who was unaware of this, ordered him to attend a one o'clock parade with the 11th Hussars. Before complying, Paget had to obtain the sanction of the infantry general; and de Lacy Evans, in turn, had first to communicate with the Adjutant-General. The transfer was therefore delayed. Paget, waiting in his tent, could see the Hussars mounted in readiness to move; but he was not free to join them until two o'clock.

Trotting up to the lines he found Cardigan in a very angry state. "Officers commanding regiments" were summoned, and Cardigan, showing displeasure by the way he twisted his moustache, singled out Paget. "Pray, Lord George Paget, I wish to be informed why my brigade order has not been obeyed, and why I have been kept waiting for the last hour."

"If your lordship will allow me to explain," commented Paget, "I think I can satisfy you."

"Proceed, my lord," said Cardigan.

After being told, Cardigan dismissed the affair, and his fellow officer, with another peremptory twist of his moutache. "Quite satisfactory, my lord. Be pleased to join your regiment."

A few days later Cardigan, whose health had been visibly deteriorating, was unable to appear at the usual early morning parade. The Brigade-Major requested Paget to take charge, but within a few minutes of his doing so Cardigan arrived.

"Lord George Paget," he demanded, "why were you to assume that I was not coming to parade?"

Paget explained that he was acting on instructions, whereupon Cardigan "flew off", as Paget expressed it, in a very great temper to the Brigade-Major. The latter passed some very uncomfortable moments.

But Paget had long since made up his mind that he and Cardigan would never seriously quarrel. Cardigan was easily managed, he wrote, "with calmness and firmness, and when one is in the right—which it is not difficult to be with him".

Fanny Duberly had followed, by sea, the army's progress to Balaclava, where she now occupied a cabin on *Star of the South*. She was quite convinced by now that her first impression of Cardigan, influenced by rumour and by his Lordship's imperious bearing, had been wrong. "He has been exceedingly kind to me," she told her sister; and Cardigan found her a sympathetic listener to whom he could relate his cat and dog differences with Lucan. They went riding together, and on one occasion he lent her his chestnut charger, Ronald, who was soon to acquire a deathless name in the animals' Valhalla.

As October wore on the quarrels of the two cavalry generals reached such a pitch that Raglan was forced to separate them. He divided the Light Brigade camp, sending Cardigan, with the 11th Hussars and the 17th Lancers, further up the heights. Paget thought it absurd that the order of the cavalry should be upset because of "two spoilt children", but it was a military necessity. Raglan exhibited similar care in the directions he gave to the cavalry patrols, especially when Cardigan went forward on one occasion to reconnoitre the Sebastopol defences. Raglan emphasized that the chief duties of the Light Cavalry were to ensure the safety of the army from all surprises. On no account should any party engage the enemy without special instructions.

Cardigan's patrol passed off without incident; but some nights later, when he was not on duty, a cavalry outpost sighted a large Russian force on the far right of the British position. The cavalry division formed up and was moving forward when Lucan, obviously intent on following Raglan's instructions, held them back.

Cardigan almost contracted a stroke when he heard of the thwarted operation. To think that his old regiment, the 11th Hussars, had been involved! Their officers, at least, might have been relied on to charge in defiance of orders. They were "a damned set of old women"; but nothing else could be expected when Lucan was in control.

Cardigan's rage was such that Colonel Douglas, an old friend who now commanded the 11th, attempted to calm him down. But Cardigan turned just as fiercely on Douglas, and told him that a lieutenant-colonel must not try to remonstrate with a major-general. Later on Cardigan sent for Douglas and apologized for some of the things he had said. He tried to enlist the support of Paget in condemning Lucan for what he considered a disgraceful affair. "I hope, George Paget, when we go back, that we shall not allow out mouths to be tongue-tied."

But Paget was more philosophical. "You may take it for granted," he said, "that if all ends well, all will be forgotten in the general result, which will be much the best thing."

At a quiet time of day, in Balaclava harbour, Fanny Duberly emerged from her cabin and saw two yachts arrive. She was struck by their "pretty gracefulness" as they dropped anchor amidst the rough vessels of war, "as out of place as a London belle would be". One of the yachts was Lord Cardigan's *Dryad*, which he had lent to his friend Hubert de Burgh. The latter apparently decided to take it out to the Crimea, as one of the armada that was bringing sensation-hungry tourists to the seat of war.

He was not expected, for he landed and went ashore in search of Cardigan, a pleasantly odd figure in frock coat, a flat-brimmed bell topper, and with trousers tightly strapped over patent leather boots. He appears to have been directed by Lord George Paget, who remarked on the visitor's well-shaven chin.

De Burgh came upon Cardigan in his tent, where the latter was seated on a bullock trunk dining off soup served in a jug and boiled salt pork. It was hardly the diet for an invalid, and Cardigan was now plainly ill. He sometimes had to rest for three or four hours during the day. Russell of *The Times* observed, "Lord Cardigan is indisposed and it is understood he will be obliged to go on board ship." Ten days later the far from friendly Paget noted in his diary that Cardigan "looked pale and washed out". Paget continued, perhaps a little hopefully, "I believe he really is ill, and that this will be the end of him."

With the arrival of the *Dryad*, however, Raglan gave Cardigan permission to sleep on the yacht. Cardigan's critics at once seized on this as an instance of favouritism, especially when it was known that among the crew was a French chef. Cardigan was called 'the noble yachtsman', a name that has been repeated by modern writers; but the fact is that had the *Dryad* not arrived, Cardigan was arranging to go on sick leave, which would have meant his being transferred to a vessel in the harbour and the giving up of all military duties.

Colonel Hodge visited Cardigan on his yacht on 22nd October, and found him "very comfortable". "This is the way to make war," Hodge thought enviously.

One of the characters in camp who was to affect the fortunes of Cardigan's Light Brigade was Captain Louis Nolan, of the 15th Hussars, who was serving on Raglan's Staff. Nolan was 35 and of mixed Irish-Italian blood. An outstanding rider and swordsman, he had passed through the Vienna Military College, and was

commissioned in the Austrian cavalry before entering the British
Army.

No ordinary student of military matters, he had written two
books on cavalry training and tactics. Highly intelligent and
educated beyond most of his kind, an ideal hero for a military
romance, and brimful of energy, he lived in a state of fever-heat
that sought an outlet in a traditional cavalry exercise, a dashing
cavalry charge. Light cavalry, he insisted, with the right sort of
leader, could overcome other mounted bodies, break infantry
squares, and capture guns.

The war had promised to provide him with the chance of
proving his theories; but the cavalry, through excessive and mis-
placed prudence, was being held back. Nolan raged against
Raglan, Lucan and Cardigan, though the latter shared something
of Nolan's faith in the use of sabres. But Nolan was too angry to
be just. He was thwarted, caught up in a web of caution that was
spun by a trio of incompetent commanders; and the only operation now pending, against Sebastopol, would be left to the
infantry and the guns.

3

The siege began on the morning of 17th October. Artillery and
naval batteries opened a colossal bombardment, in which the guns
of the fleet joined, throwing thousands of shells upon the town and
its defences. The Russians replied with good effect; and when the
firing ceased, at dusk, the inhabitants of Sebastopol worked till
morning, repairing the damage and bringing up fresh guns and
supplies.

Those first hours established the pattern of the siege which went
on, day after day, dealing out death, confusion, din and blinding
smoke. But the fortress held, and soon the most sanguine among
the besiegers modified their hopes of an early fall. Disillusion set
in, officers blamed each other, and the men lost heart.

Cardigan's comments on the siege show that he appraised the
situation more realistically than did many of the technical Staff.
The orthodox and classic approach, he thought, should have been
set aside in favour of a rapid assault, which might well have led
to the batteries and defences being taken in reverse. Instead, there

was a bombardment that promised nothing, with much of the
army committed to regular and static positions in front of the
town. The operation had started by being a spectacle, with
soldiers not actively engaged, visitors and tourists crowding to
occupy the best observation posts. But now the firing, and moves
to and from the trenches, were taken for granted.

Cardigan, encouraged by the presence of his friend de Burgh,
who was something of an affected *flaneur* about town, openly
ridiculed the conduct of the siege; and on these occasions Cardigan
mimicked the speech and manners of an effeminate type of male
who was then called 'a Molly'. One day the friends met Russell of
The Times who was riding down to Balaclava.

"Haw, haw!" simpered Cardigan, stopping the correspondent.
"Well, Mr. William Russell, what are they doing? What was the
firing for last night? And this morning?"

Russell, uncertain of Cardigan, and thinking it better not to
fall in with such a mood, pretended to be ignorant.

"You hear, Squire?" said Cardigan, addressing his friend.
"This Mr. William Russell knows nothing of the reason for that
firing. I daresay no one does." Before they parted, Cardigan said
more soberly, "I have never in my life seen a siege conducted on
such principles." Russell remained silent. De Burgh, who knew
even less of bombardments, mines and saps than did a cavalier like
Cardigan, readily agreed.

The Russian winter was about to set in, and with most of the
army engaged around Sebastopol the Balaclava defences were left
perilously weak. The vital area was a ridge known as the Causeway Heights, which crossed the plain some 2 miles north of
Balaclava. Two valleys, the north on the far side and the south
valley on the near side, cut across the ridge. Apart from being
their base for stores and shipping, the possession of Balaclava was
essential for the British, since if it fell the siege of Sebastopol
would have to be abandoned; but its defence consisted of little
more than half a dozen earthworks, and a single battalion, the 93rd
Highlanders, detached from Colin Campbell's Highland Brigade.

The earthworks, covering a line about 2 miles long in front of
the Heights, were manned by Turks, some 250 men in each with
a 12-pounder naval gun and a few artillery non-commissioned
officers to provide stiffening.

The night of 24th October closed down under brilliant starlight and a bitter air that swept the plain. It was rumoured that the Russians were massing for attack, and a Turkish spy came in with news of an enemy concentration to the east of Balaclava. General Airey was sufficiently impressed to take the Turk before Raglan, who was in conference with the French Commander-in-Chief, General Canrobert.

But Raglan's sense of chivalry would not allow him to take advantage of tidings, however important, that came through spying. The sight of the Turk (who probably cringed, knowing that his kind was not in favour) was offensive to him, and the patrician Commander returned a bleak "Very well" and dismissed the matter.

In the tents of Cardigan's Light Brigade the frustrated Nolan continued his outbursts against the generals. "The army's in a bad way, I can tell you." An hour before daybreak on Wednesday, 25th October, the Cavalry Division, as usual, turned out on parade; and after being mounted the men, stamping their feet, stood to their horses. Major Willett, commanding the 17th Lancers, froze to death in the saddle. It was pitch dark, the only light coming from dim yellow lanterns that marked out the lines.

Presently a gleam appeared over the Heights, misty, with crimson showing through; and as it broadened, picking out rocks and limestone in the hills, the shadowy forms of Lucan and his Staff rode by to gather reports from the outlying cavalry pickets.

4

They rode at foot pace, for the light was still no more than a lengthening band that reached from the far edge of the valley to Balaclava harbour. As they neared the earthworks they peered through their glasses at a flagstaff that pointed, like a long straight finger, at the vapours floating over the tops and ridges. Two flags were flying from the staff—a signal that the enemy was approaching. The spy had told the truth. A strong Russian cavalry force, under General Liprandi, was advancing up the North Valley towards Balaclava.

Lord George Paget, who was one of the party, set spurs to his horse and galloped back to the Light Brigade. The men had not eaten; the horses had not been fed or watered. But the call, "Boot and Saddle", saw them mounted, then both brigades of the Cavalry Division moved from their bivouac lines across the plain. Lord Cardigan was on the way up from his yacht.

After coming under fire the first three earthworks were attacked and overrun, and as the Russian cavalry crossed the Causeway Heights the Heavy and Light Brigades retired across the plain by alternate regiments. The Light Brigade, drawn up in two lines, faced straight down the North Valley.

A troop of horse artillery, under Captain Shakespear, quickly appeared at the front and went into action. When every round of shot and shell had been exhausted, they were going back to replenish when an angry figure stopped them. It was Cardigan. "Where are you going, Captain Shakespear?" he demanded. "Who gave you leave to retire?"

"We are going for more ammunition, my lord," Shakespear explained.

The sight of Cardigan brought Lucan on the scene. He at once put Cardigan in his place by ordering the horse artillery to fall back. He also drew up the cavalry on the far side of the plain, away from the front of the 93rd Highlanders who now covered the direct approach to Balaclava.

Meanwhile the sun had left the horizon and was well above the plain, dappling the ridges where off-duty officers with their wives and other relatives, tourists and general sightseers, had gathered on hearing the noise of battle. They took their places on the ledges that rose in tiers along the hillside, for all the world like an excited theatre audience anticipating the first act of a drama. The feathered hats worn by Raglan and his Staff, the bright dresses and flowing veils of the ladies, showed up against the patches of green that wavered in the sunlight. Luncheon baskets were opened; the picnic parties drank to the uniformed characters who waited in the slips down in the valley.

Cardigan, at the head of his brigade, was also a spectator. The Russian cavalry advanced at a trot towards the hillock behind which crouched the scanty barrier of the 93rd. They had been ordered to die where they stood, and now they sprang up, form-ing the "thin red line tipped with steel", and poured a volley into the Russian squadrons. Never venturesome, the Russians fell back towards the Heights, crossing the front of the Heavy Brigade as they did so.

Before separating his brigades, Lucan had issued definite instructions to Cardigan. He was to hold the position he occupied, without moving: and an order, once it had been given to Cardigan, was obeyed with Roman-like simplicity. But the sight of the Russians in their light-blue jackets, and the sound of their jingling bits, grated upon his senses like an unanswered challenge, especially when he saw that the Heavy Brigade, led by old Scarlett, with a helmet crammed on his head, was preparing to charge.

Cardigan watched, motionless but fretting, as the Scots Greys and Inniskilling Dragoons wheeled into line and crashed into the Russians who stood, instead of quickening their pace, to meet the attack. He saw the Dragoons disappear as the wings of the Russian mass moved forward and completely enveloped them: then, as if by a miracle, the red coats of the Dragoons broke out from the rear of the enemy, wheeled about, and with arms rising and falling hacked their way to the front, the Russians falling apart as they did so.

Cardigan gnawed his moustache, annoyed that the honours of the first cavalry engagement had gone to the rival brigade. He rode up and down, fuming with impatience. "Damn those Heavies!" he growled. "They'll have the laugh of us today." An attack on the Russian rear and in their flank would have routed them as they streamed back the way they had come: and Captain Morris (who, as senior Captain of the 17th Lancers, had taken over the regiment on Major Willett's death), summoned his trumpeter and ordered "Threes right" in readiness to advance.

Seeing this, Cardigan rode up. "What are you doing, sir?" he demanded coldly. "Front your regiment."

Morris raised his sword and pointed at the retreating Russians. "Look there, my lord."

"Remain where you are, sir, until you get orders," Cardigan told him.

Morris could scarcely believe that such an opportunity, a godsend for eager cavalry, was to be wasted. "My lord, are we not going to charge? They are in disorder."

"We have orders to remain here."

But the other persisted. "Do allow me to charge with the 17th, sir, my lord." His voice was almost frantic with appeal.

"No, no, sir!" Cardigan's hoarse negative was clearly heard by

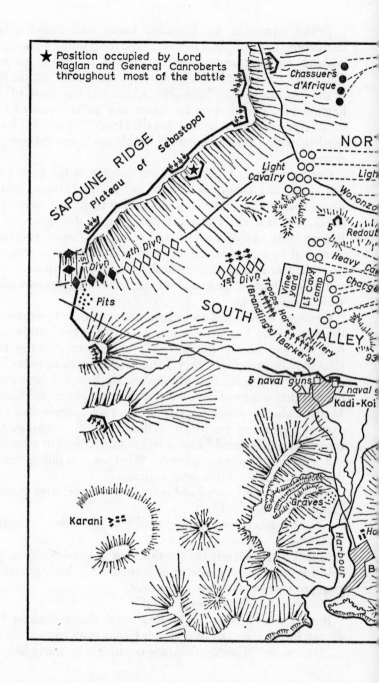

★ Position occupied by Lord
Raglan and General Canroberts
throughout most of the battle

Chassuers
d'Afrique

NOR

SAPOUNE RIDGE of Sebastopol

Plateau

Light
Cavalry

Light

Woronzo

5

Redou

Heavy Ca

4th Divn

1st Divn

Vine-
yard

17 Cav.
camp

Charge

Troops Horse
(Brandlings) (Barker's)
Artillery

Pits

SOUTH

VALLEY

93

5 naval guns

7 naval g

Kadi-Koi

Graves

Karani

Ho

Harbour

B

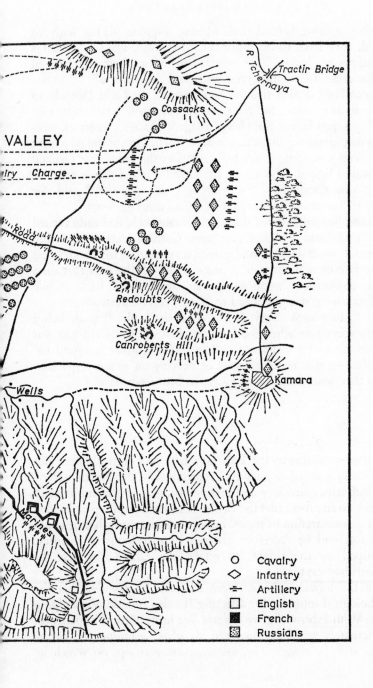

R. Tchernaya

Tractir Bridge

Cossacks

VALLEY

lry Charge

Redd

3

2
Redoubts

1
Canroberts Hill

Kamara

Wells

Marines

VA

○	Cavalry
◇	Infantry
+	Artillery
☐	English
■	French
▦	Russians

the lines waiting behind him. Morris, slapping his leg with his sword, rode back to his regiment. "My God, my God, what a chance we are losing!" He wheeled his horse about and fronted the Lancers. "Gentlemen, you witnessed my request."

Lucan later denied that he had ordered the Light Brigade to maintain its position, and not to charge. According to him he told Cardigan, just before the Heavy Brigade charged, to attack any-thing or everything that came within reach. One of the two must have been mistaken, if not lying; and in the latter case General Sir Evelyn Wood, who was in the Crimea, stated that it was cer-tainly not Cardigan. "For although not popular," said Sir Evelyn, "he was never accused of wilful misstatements."

It must be remembered that Lucan's caution had already earned him the nickname of 'Look on'; while Cardigan, as shown during the march on Balaclava, had gained a reputation for recklessness in the face of odds. It will, moreover, shortly be seen that on a more momentous occasion Lucan again held back, while Cardigan went straight ahead to almost certain destruction.

Cardigan was as angry as Morris at the Light Brigade being merely spectators when the Heavies charged. But Cardigan was responsible to his superior, and he had too great a regard for discipline to risk being accused of defying an order—especially when that order came from his hated brother-in-law.

5

The Russian threat to the Balaclava base had been blunted; but their badly mauled cavalry had regrouped in the North Valley, and with strong artillery and infantry support it was numerically superior to any force that the British could muster. Raglan decided that a demonstration of moral import was the most that he could hope for; and he therefore ordered two divisions of infantry, encamped on the ridges, to retake the earthworks that the Russians had captured.

But the infantry moves were delayed. Raglan felt that the psychological moment for affecting Russian morale was slipping away. With a show of growing and (for him) unusual impatience, he alternately raised and lowered his glass, scanning the earth-works and the ridges. The sole remaining troops on which he could now rely were the two cavalry brigades—the Heavy Brigade, recovered from their recent charge, and Cardigan's Light Brigade, drawn up in two-deep formation on the left of the Heavies.

The men were standing by their horses. No rations had reached them since the previous night; only a few of the more fortunate were provided with hard-boiled eggs or biscuit, while some of the officers had flasks of rum and water. Cardigan sat like a statue on his horse, the perfect horseman, maintaining the easy yet disciplined bearing that distinguished him in the woodland rides and fields of the Midlands. In full front ahead was the glint of Russian guns and the dark masses of enemy troops.

Russell of *The Times*, who had joined the spectators on the Heights, let his glance linger over Cardigan's Light Brigade, the details of their uniforms clearly revealed and the jingling of their horses' bits sounding almost musically through the crisp air. "Little they knew," he wrote, "they were on the eve of being heroes, or of being reckoned among the dead, wounded and missing of a famous fight".

Suddenly a horseman appeared, scrambling down from the Heights and crossing the front of the 17th Lancers. It was Captain Nolan, his eager face glowing under his crimson and gold forage cap, his slung-jacket flying out behind as though reflecting his impatience. He hardly paused as he asked Captain Morris, "Where is Lord Lucan?"

Morris pointed. "There, on the right front." He guessed there was an order for the cavalry commander, and he called after Nolan as he galloped off, "What is it? Are we going to charge?"

"You'll see," Nolan flashed over his shoulder. "You'll see."

A minute or so later Lucan left his post with the Heavy Brigade and rode over to Cardigan. Lucan was tired, cold and hungry. He had been in the saddle since daybreak, and his normally short temper was not improved by the message that reached him from Raglan. The message, which was to raise the curtain on one of the most celebrated epics in history, had been hastily pencilled on a little piece of flimsy paper—"Lord Raglan wishes the cavalry to advance rapidly to the front—follow the enemy and try to prevent the enemy carrying away the guns. Troop Horse Artillery may accompany. French cavalry is on your left. Immediate. (Signed) R. Airey, Quartermaster General."

In so far as one may attempt to read Raglan's mind, it would seem that the front he referred to was along the line of the Causeway Heights, and that the guns were those in the captured earthworks. From his place on the hillside, every part of the immediate landscape was open to Raglan's vision; but Lucan and Cardigan, on the plain, could see only part of the picture. The ridges extending down from the hills screened off the earthworks, which meant that the only guns within sight of the cavalry leaders were those in the menacing North Valley.

The order itself was muddled, ambiguous, and Cardigan saw by their attitudes that an argument developed between Nolan and Lucan when the latter had scanned it. Then he saw Nolan's arm go out. He was pointing, and his gesture was accompanied by a contemptuous phrase that has become almost classical: "There, my lord, there is your enemy, and there the guns."

But to what position had Nolan pointed, and where were the guns? The only guns in sight were those unlimbered in the valley, twelve in front and more pieces on the flanks, with squadrons of Cossacks and Lancers, and riflemen lining the slopes. Approaching this veritable death-trap was an open ride across ploughland, a mile and a half in length, and less than a mile across.

It was quite beyond the power of cavalry to deal with such a situation: but Lucan, after his heated words with Nolan, never paused to consider. He rode over to Cardigan, and ordered him to lead the advance down the North Valley. He (Lucan) would follow with the Heavy Brigade.

Cardigan could scarcely credit the instruction. Some of the most ordinary cavalry precepts, learnt when he was a cornet, flashed through his mind—cavalry must never act without a support . . . infantry should be close at hand when cavalry charge guns. . . .

But there was no artillery or infantry support, and, strict disciplinarian though he was, Cardigan felt that he could not sacrifice his squadrons in a move that promised no military advantage.

But rather than express this to Lucan, he sent an aide-de-camp to frame a remonstrance: and the tension was such that Lucan went over to Cardigan and made the order more positive. But Cardigan was still not satisfied. Bringing his sword down in salute he repeated a summing-up of the situation. He was to charge a battery, a mile and a half away, over ground that was covered by still more batteries and scores of riflemen. "There must be some mistake. I shall never be able to bring a single man back," he concluded.

Lucan could only shrug. They had no choice. He told Cardigan to advance steadily and to keep his brigade well in hand.

Cardigan again saluted. "Very good, sir." As Lucan rode off, Nolan, realizing that the Light Brigade was to lead, came up to seek a place in its lines. The sight of Nolan in the uniform of the 15th Hussars, the regiment from whose command he had been dismissed, cannot have been a pleasant reminder for Cardigan. But he questioned Nolan, asking if the order was correct.

Nolan, fuming at the delay and fearful of being sent back to rejoin the Staff, curled his lip in one of his frequent sneers. "What, is the Light Brigade afraid?"

That was enough. Cardigan's jaw set. He knew there was a flagrant error, somewhere: but now there was an insult to be worked off. He approached Lord George Paget, and told him they were ordered to make an attack, to the front. "You will take command of the second line," Cardigan went on, "and I expect your best support." Cardigan did not like Paget, and he had, besides, been rattled by Nolan's taunt. "Mind, your best support," he repeated.

Paget was always calm when addressing Cardigan, and now, refusing to be irritated by the other's insistence, he replied, "You shall have it, my lord".

The first line of the Light Brigade was formed by the 17th Lancers (where Nolan, without asking Cardigan's permission, had taken place beside his friend Captain Morris), the 13th Light Dragoons and the 11th Hussars. Paget's regiment, the 4th Light Dragoons, was in the second line, with the 8th Hussars. Each regiment was drawn up in line two deep. Their once splendid uniforms were patched and stained, discoloured by the weather: only a few of the lucky ones had some rags, that once had been shirts, next to their skin. They numbered in all 673 sabres and lances, about the strength of a single Russian cavalry regiment.

So far the exchanges between Lucan and Cardigan had been perfectly correct, and without rancour. But at the last moment Lucan intervened to show his authority. He ordered the 11th Hussars, Cardigan's regiment, to fall back behind the 17th

Lancers, his own old regiment, which meant that the Light Brigade was now in three lines: and he gave the order not to Cardigan, who was angered by it, but to the colonel of the 11th. But in this Lucan may have been guided by military considerations, since it meant that the front would now be narrowed and that the first line would have support.

The field officers, fussy to a degree, made a final survey of the lines. All was now in order. The brigade that Cardigan had trained to perfection was about to be tested: and as he took his place, for the last time, at its head, Cardigan appeared more calm and collected than ever he had been on parade. For once there was nothing to correct, no 'dressing down' or rebuke to be delivered. They were about to enter history.

Because of the cold, Cardigan was wearing his heavily braided and furred pelisse like a jacket. His slim youthful figure was topped by the white and crimson plume of his brown busby. His long cherry-coloured overalls, and crimson sabretache, made streaks of colour against the smooth chestnut gloss of his charger, Ronald. He advanced to the regulation pace of two horses' length in front of his Staff (Captains Fitz Maxse and Lockwood, and Lieutenant Wombwell) and five paces length from the centre of the leading line. It was one of those moments when men make light of individual feelings and shed their malevolence, so that even those who had fallen foul of Cardigan in the past were impressed by the air of responsibility and control that was radiated by that lonely figure in front of doomed squadrons. He was, as one noted, "stately, square, erect, master of himself, his Brigade, his noble charger".

Those men who deny all mystery in human affairs have never known the moment of unearthly, almost sinister silence that precedes a battle. It settled now over the heights and valley of Balaclava as the Light Brigade, rigid in their last alignment, held rein and kept spur ready for the move forward. Watchers on the hillside, who lived to be old, remembered that silence: and whenever they did so the years fell away till they were back in the pale sunlight of that October day, 1854, with their gaze divided between the motionless horsemen and the dark concentration at the end of the valley.

As Cardigan rode into place his normally hoarse voice was heard, in not much more than a murmur, "Here goes the last of the Brudenells!" Then, without turning, he gave the fatal order, "The Brigade will advance. First squadron of the 17th Lancers will direct." His brigade trumpeter, Britten, sounded "Walk", and the horses of the front line, ready as the men to obey the well-known cavalry call, and as though taking their time from Ronald's two white stockings, went forward tossing their heads with jingle of collar chain, harness bit and bridle.

The regimental trumpeters repeated the call, and when the front line had made an interval of 100 yards between itself and the second line, the 11th Hussars followed. At a similar distance, and directed by the 4th Light Dragoons, Paget's command fell into line behind them.

The sun by now was high above the valley, and as it broke free or was lost behind a covering of cloud the parade of death appeared to be moving over waves of shadow. The order was still "Walk". The eyes of posterity were preparing to focus on the men and the horses and the solitary figure in the van. Russell of *The Times*, who was among the spectators on the hills, glanced at his watch; it was twenty minutes past eleven.

6

From the moment that Trumpeter Britten sounded "Walk", Cardigan, whom nothing had escaped in the past, never turned his head to note the progress of his brigade. For no one knew better than he what was required of a cavalry leader. His bearing, his carriage at the head of his men, was to be their model. The slightest move away from the object in view could run like a rift along the lines that were following down the valley; and to preserve those lines there must be no flaw in the rigid way he rode, some yards ahead of the foremost squadron, straight towards the green-painted guns that for some moments more were part of the overhanging silence.

Those near to Cardigan, on that last ride, noted the unyielding stiffness of his back and the set of his shoulders. Some remembered having seen him, unconcerned as now he appeared to be, passing up and down the Row. One of his Staff, in a flash of friendly enthusiasm, saw him as "the very incarnation of bravery". Another said he was "steady as a church". The historian Kinglake soberly recorded that "from the moment in which he learnt the nature of the task imposed upon him to the one when he bowed to authority and composedly accepted his martyrdom, Lord Cardigan's demeanour was faultless". But the praise that Cardigan must have relished most came from the far from partisan Captain Morris, who said that he "led like a gentleman".

At a sign from Cardigan the trumpeter sounded "Trot", and the pace quickened. They were heading straight down the valley, towards the guns. It was now that Captain Nolan, riding with the 17th Lancers, broke the order of the brigade by inexplicably setting spur to his horse and pressing forward, right across the front of the leading line, to where the solitary figure in crimson overalls was setting the pace and marking the direction.

Captain Morris shouted after his friend, "No, no. That won't do. We have a long way to go and must be steady." But Nolan was wildly excited and waving his sword—was he using it to point at the Causeway Heights? Some claimed to have heard him shouting "Threes right!" and indicating a wheeling motion that would turn them aside from their headlong course. Cardigan, still rigid in the saddle and without moving a muscle, though the blood was pounding at his brain because of the aide-de-camp's effrontery, called on him to halt.

But at that moment a report and a burst of smoke, from the end of the valley, showed that the first of the Russian artillerymen to recover from their initial surprise had brought a gun into action. Nolan dropped back from Cardigan's line of vision with a splinter of shell in his chest and his torn tunic mixed with the bloody pulp, the perfect rider for once sagging and huddled though his sword arm was still in the air and his knees and thighs instinctively gripped the saddle, while a last twitch of his bridle-arm caused his charger to turn and gallop back, through an interval in the lines, the way they had come.

Cardigan heard the cry—some thought it must have issued from Nolan's corpse—that floated over the doomed brigade and echoed to the nearest of the breathless watchers on the hills. But beyond registering, in his mind, some future punishment for "that devil of a Nolan", Cardigan's sense of responsibility was momently heightened as he neared the Russian guns. It was for him to hold the brigade together, to keep them steady so that the shock of contact (meagre enough, the weight of five greatly diminished regiments) might be as great as possible. He was their guide, their focus, going forward at a steady canter that was beaten out by the motion of Ronald's white stockings.

Again he motioned to Trumpeter Britten, and the "Trot" gave way to the "Gallop". It was heavier, faster going now, and the feeling of exaltation in which a man forgets that he is mortal spread through and over the advancing lines. The Lancers in the front of the brigade surged forward at an impetuous pace that brought them nearer to Cardigan; and still without a turn of the head his hoarse voice ordered them back. "Steady, steady the 17th. Steady, Captain Morris!" Cardigan, though icy calm outside, was still seething inwardly at the enormity of Nolan's offence; they were riding into the very mouth of the guns; the Russian artillerymen were loading their pieces. But always it was, "Steady!" Their leader checked and restrained them by an authority built up over the years.

But by now a feeling of madness was threatening the order of the brigade, and the inner or directing squadron of the Lancers, under Captain White, went forging ahead, a little to the rear of Cardigan's right. Still without turning, Cardigan's sword arm went out and his blade extended across the Captain's chest, a calm reminder even then that it was not for White to force the pace nor to ride level with his commander. The hoof-beats pounded on: those close behind Cardigan remembered seeing his sword go back to the slope, and hearing his voice giving the same order, but now for the last time, to the brigade he was leading so well, "Steady! Close in. Steady!"

The surprised Russian gunners had by this time loaded and fired their first salvo. Flashes and clouds of smoke filled the end of the valley as the guns hurled their shot and shell full in the face of the Light Dragoons and Lancers forming the first line who, heads down, leaning forward, boot to boot and knee to knee, filled with battle lust, crashed cheering and yelling through the iron curb imposed by the presence of Cardigan and raced for the guns. A young lieutenant who caught a fleeting glimpse of his men before they were swept down, thought it "a fine sight". "Every man", said a hussar, "was seized with a cannibal hunger and could have eaten a squadron without salt."

Between the showers of grape and round shot, the flash and flame of the guns, Cardigan thought he was riding into certain death. "But I led straight," he was to say later, "and no man flinched."

It is commonly asserted that the "Charge" was not sounded at Balaclava. These denials are founded on negative evidence from those who, such was the din of thundering hoofs and the roaring of gunfire, might not have heard it in any case. But it is unlikely that the meticulous and collected Cardigan, with Britten close at hand (though the trumpeter soon fell mortally wounded) neglected to give the order that followed naturally on "Gallop". One of the 8th Hussars, forming the third line, was to make a positive statement: "A trumpet sounded the 'Charge' and we were off."

Cardigan's well-trained horse shied only a little as it was blown sideways by the roar of the battery so that it needed but a jerk of the rider's hand, and the pressure of his heel, to restore their balance. For a moment Cardigan thought that his leg had been taken off—they were barely 100 yards from the smoke-clouded guns—and apparently isolated. In the moment of righting himself his mind worked quickly and clearly. He had noted, by their flashes, the position of the two nearest guns, and letting Ronald out at full gallop he made for the space between them. A hussar who was nearing the front of the battery said that Cardigan "went in a regular buster". He narrowly escaped being crushed against a wheel as he went by the foremost gun and its carriage, yet he was still sufficiently master of himself to be aware of tidy compact thoughts—what, if anything, was a man's sensation likely to be on being cut in half by a cannon ball? . . . he must have been riding at a full 17 miles an hour when he plunged through the smoke . . . he would make things uncomfortable for Nolan—then he was out beyond the guns and face to face with the Cossacks and lancers massed in their rear.

He noticed that their teeth and their features were working, and he put it down to a frenzy of greed produced by the sight of his splendid uniform, the lace, braid and fur, and the arrogant plume; while for his part, and even in those moments, Cardigan viewed the Russian riders, and especially their mounts, with the utmost contempt. Not a nag among them standing more than 14½ hands high, with plain bridles and clumsy-looking saddles! A group of Cossacks edged towards him, not greatly menacing but still grinding their teeth; for one of their officers, Prince Radzivill,

The British encampment near Sebastopol

The Redan at Sebastopol

Sant's painting of Lord Cardigan telling the story of the Charge to the Royal Family. Left to right: Prince Alfred, the Prince of Wales, Lord Cardigan, the Prince Consort, Princess Helena, Princess Louise, Prince Arthur, the Princess Royal, Princess Alice, the Duchess of Wellington and Lord Rivers. Queen Victoria had herself painted out of the picture recognized Cardigan whom he had met, socially, when visiting London. Radzivill thought it would be amusing to capture the Earl and recall the incident, as part of the polite dealing that was still current, even in battle, in those days.

But Cardigan held his ground and kept his sword at the slope. He might have used his revolver, had it not been left in camp or on his yacht for the first time that morning, though it was an article of his military faith that it was not a general's duty "to fight the enemy among private soldiers". The Cossacks, not knowing what to make of the solitary and stationary figure, lowered their lances and prodded through his overalls, but half-heartedly, as the Prince had told them to take him alive. Cardigan sat on while a point inflicted a flesh wound near his thigh; then, not being halted or surrounded—the Russians throughout were strangely uncertain—he wheeled about, thinking to rejoin what was left of the brigade that had followed him down the valley.

Behind him were the dead, dying and wounded of the five regiments, men and horses together. Some survivors were crawling and staggering along the slopes. Apart from these vestiges of destruction, quiet, writhing, or horribly maimed, he might have been alone. Since he had never looked back, he realized now that he was far from sure that he had led the full strength of his brigade. Perhaps the second and third lines had been held back by Lucan, who had, in fact, called off the Heavies when they were half-way down the valley.

There they had come under fire. Lucan was hit in the leg. One of his Staff was killed, another had his cap shot away; and on seeing the Light Brigade disappear into the smoke, Lucan took a decision that required its own brand of independent courage. He determined that the Greys, the Royals and Inniskillings should not be sacrificed as their fellow brigade had been, and led them back out of range in columns of squadrons.

Cardigan's front line had vanished. There were no supports, and through rifts in the smoke nothing active was visible on either side. The second and third lines of the brigade had crashed into the battery, cutting down the gunners and somehow breaking through to the end of the valley. There they rallied in small groups, with Russian cavalry forming like "a thick set hedge" to bar their retreat.

Nothing of this was apparent to Cardigan, a solitary figure

12

menaced by lancers in his rear, and a perfect target for riflemen on either flank. He could only go back, along with the dazed survivors, or be taken by the Russians. Already their general was wondering who was the English officer on the chestnut horse with the white heels? Cossacks were fanning out from the end of the valley, searching for arms or dragging off the wounded as prisoners. The main fight was over, though groups that had rallied behind the guns were having to fight clear. How they did so, as an officer confessed, was a mystery. "There is one explanation, and one only; the hand of God was upon us." But Cardigan, with a partly wrecked battery, clouds of smoke and a sense of disastrous confusion between him and the remnants of his brigade, saw nothing of this.

He had carried out orders: he had acted in defiance of his judgment and lived up to the letter of his command: now he could do no more than ride back. He set a slow, steady pace: he was too proud to hurry.

Little groups of wounded or horseless men were making their way as best they could in the same direction, and Cardigan fell in with these, asking, "Has anyone seen my regiment?" On being answered in the negative he turned back towards the Russian position, and when level with number two redoubt he was joined by more survivors of his shattered brigade. The extent and meaning of the tragedy had not yet begun to weigh upon Cardigan's conscience. His mind could still function at a practical, even casual level. He came upon a sergeant of Light Dragoons, who was mentally blinded by shock.

Cardigan paused to ask, "Where is your horse?"

The sergeant stared, pulled himself together. "Killed, my lord." He was grieving for the animal.

"Then you had better make your way back as fast as you can, or you will be taken prisoner." Cardigan's tone and meaning were precise. He knew that the Cossacks were behind him: but he could afford to be disdainful of them in a manner unknown to the sergeant. He went on, still at a walk, and some of those near him heard him mutter as though to himself. Cardigan was not usually flippant: but the urge to be so, as a means of shutting out the events of the morning, was now apparent in his over-wrought mind. He returned his sword, and with his free hand adjusted part of his underclothing under his tunic and pelisse, saying as he did so that the Russian instruments were blunt and tickled up one's ribs.

A little further on he encountered Captain Shakespear who, with his horse gunners, had followed the Heavy Brigade on its partial progress down the valley.

Cardigan showed Captain Shakespear the tear in his overalls made by the probing Cossack lance. "Damn nice thing," he grumbled, "and I haven't anything to keep the cold out."

Shakespear beckoned to one of his men, who produced a flask. "The artillery are always prepared for an emergency." Cardigan drank and went on his way to where General Scarlett, fiercely embattled behind his white moustache and ruddy complexion, as though waiting for a word to restore order out of the prevailing chaos, sat bolt upright in the saddle at the head of his dragoons.

By then, and perhaps thawed by the drink, Cardigan was running over the happenings of the past hour, and at once his resentment lighted upon Captain Nolan who had made a show of daring to cross his front. "What do you think of Nolan," he asked General Scarlett, "screaming like a woman when he was hit?"

Old Scarlett had known the meaning of the aide-de-camp's cry. He had, moreover, passed close to the earthwork on the last of the miniature hills that rose into the ridge, where Nolan had fallen. "Say no more, my lord," he told Cardigan. "I have just ridden over Captain Nolan's dead body." As Cardigan passed the Heavy Dragoons they cheered the leader of the rival brigade who had covered himself with glory, and Cardigan raised his hand in salute.

Lord George Paget, who had rallied one of the groups that had somehow broken through the Russian wall, caught up with Cardigan for part of the way back. Paget was still smarting from Cardigan's requests for his "best support", and now he attempted a piece of superfluous raillery. "Hallo, Lord Cardigan, were you there?"

Cardigan replied in the same vein. "Wasn't I, though!" and turned to Captain Jenyns of the 13th Light Dragoons. "Did you not see me at the guns?" Jenyns had been in the first line and so had had a clear view of Cardigan as he rode into the battery.

Paget made no attempt to hide his feelings. "God alone knows what has happened to my poor regiment!" Cardigan struck him as being cool and composed, abnormally master of himself. But a little later—the sun had already passed its pitch and was beginning to pale—Cardigan fell in with General Cathcart who had ridden down with his 4th Division: and Cardigan, now forgetful of Nolan's insolence and the ignominious thrust of a Cossack lance, at last made mention of the catastrophe that was upon him—"I have lost my brigade!"

While he spoke more survivors of that brigade were straggling past him, singly or in little groups, some still in the saddle or leading their horses, dishevelled, covered with blood and grime, limping or staggering like men in search of sleep, some clutching the now useless weapons that discipline forbade them to cast aside: and still bound by discipline they formed up on a slope overlooking Balaclava, and there Cardigan faced them.

The reaction that spreads a mutual awareness of human weakness was setting in. Men clasped each other by the hand: each knew that the other shared his confused sense in which pride, in what they had done, struggled with resentment and grief for the wreckage left behind in the valley. The horses—men kissed their patient noses or hugged their necks—came in for gratitude. Some were lamented. "Malta carried me after a ball had passed through her neck near the windpipe." "Poor old Moses!" A hardened non-commissioned officer said through his tears, "She was a light bay, nearly thoroughbred. I became her master three years ago." Cardigan's husky voice broke in. "Men, it was a hare-brained trick, but it was no fault of mine": and the answer, coming at such a time, from an unknown man in the ranks, showed how Cardigan's iron justice was esteemed by those it had moulded— "Never mind, my lord, we're ready to do it again." Cardigan's reply was addressed to them all, "No, no, men, you've done enough."

One of the Light Brigade Staff, Captain Lockwood, who had lost sight of Cardigan in the valley, approached Lucan who was making his way to where the survivors, the headquarter's Staff, and those who had watched the charge, were assembling. Lockwood asked if Cardigan had been seen, and Lucan replied that he had passed some little while ago. The Captain must have misunderstood what was said, for he wheeled about, rode slowly back into the valley, and no one set eyes on him again.

Grey autumn clouds were blowing in from the sea. A cold mist

was settling in the hollows between the hills. It promised to be a
cold night. Two hundred and forty-five men, the killed and the
badly wounded, failed to answer when they were summoned to
parade, a few scanty lines, for the roll call, which was conducted
by the brigade major, Lieutenant-Colonel Mayow. The survivors were left to stand about in aimless groups, without fire or
food, while senior officers struggled to collect their shocked or
outraged feelings.

Russell of *The Times* was standing by when Raglan, his nervously fine face set and grim, was approached by Cardigan.
"What do you mean, sir," demanded Raglan, the pulse in his
half-empty sleeve betraying his emotion, "what do you mean by
attacking a battery in front?"

Cardigan's answer was smooth, direct and confident. He had
not broken a rule of war, nor gone against the customs of the
service. "My lord, I hope you will not blame me: for I received
the order to attack from my superior officer in front of the
troops."

No soldier could say more, neither could any commander find
fault with such an explanation: and Russell noted that when
Cardigan went back to join the survivors (there was no *immediate*
return to his yacht, where he straightway and selfishly enjoyed
the luxuries of champagne and a hot bath while his famished men
shivered on the slopes) he seemed in no way depressed. Cardigan
then, in spite of his weariness, made a point of seeking out the
French General d'Allonville, and thanking him for a charge,
carried out by the 4th Chasseurs d'Afrique, which had silenced
some of the Russian guns.

One must repeat—Cardigan did, of course, go back to the
Dryad, where he had been given permission to stay, being sick,
before the events at Balaclava. But he was not so callously indif-
ferent to the fate of his brigade as to turn his back almost as soon
as it had been shattered: neither was he anxiously concerned, as
Lucan was, to exempt himself from blame for the disaster. Raglan
had turned coldly on Lucan. "You have lost the Light Brigade";
and Lucan's indignation boiled over. He was outraged, and sat in
his tent for most of the night, ankle-deep in the muddy earth and
sweepings of the camp, and with the canvas yielding in places to
the bitter wind, penning the first of several explanations that were
intended to put the blame on Cardigan, on Raglan's fatal order,

and on the dead Nolan who had delivered it, on anyone but himself, the deeply injured leader of the Cavalry Division. The angry
man might well be pitied. His own splendid regiment, the 17th
Lancers, now numbered but thirty-seven privates.

Russell was also busy in his tent. Using a saddle for a chair and
by the light of a candle-end stuck in a bottle, he was writing the
story of the day, prompted by men, who were too exhausted to
sleep, to jot down this or that detail of the charge, how sword
crossed lance, some almost miraculous escape that would surely
bring wonder to the faces of people at home . . . "Remember to
say this . . .". The ink seemed to boil from his pen as he went on
writing till the candle guttered out.

The night was starry. A few fires were lighted, but only in sheltered spots for fear of a Cossack raid. Figures moved listlessly
about, or sat in the ruddy glow nursing their wounds. Cardigan
joined one of the groups. Those who had lost their horses were
without cloak or blanket, but Cardigan had stayed mounted
throughout and so retained his cloak. One who came across him
as the dreary evening dragged on into darkness, Lieutenant Earle
of the 57th Foot, said that "he had never seen a man so grieved".
After a time Cardigan, wrapped in his cloak, fell asleep on the
ground. So much is vouched for (to contradict the hearsay of later
writers) by Captain Fitz Maxse, who, as one of Cardigan's aides,
was on the spot during and immediately after the charge.

It was only a matter of hours before the two earls were again
tangled in argument. Lucan declared that he had merely carried out
the order to charge, given in writing by Raglan and verbally by
his messenger, Nolan. He considered that he had acted under "a
most imperious necessity", and refused to bear the smallest
particle of blame.

Raglan thought otherwise, and said that Lucan had misunderstood the instruction. In that respect two points may be debated,
as they have been over the years, without hope of settlement—
was the order clear and unmistakable in pointing the direction of
the advance, and how far could Lucan have exercised his own discretion on being told (as he certainly was at the time) that the
cavalry was to attack?

The one thing that clearly emerges, beyond all argument, is that
Cardigan stands acquitted of all responsibility for the blunder. He

first of all questioned the order to advance. That order was repeated to him; but even so he protested, and that same order, without proviso or modification, was again repeated. He went as far as the observance of discipline permitted; and after that, barring mutinous refusal, he could only obey. He always contended that the loss of the Light Brigade was caused by Lucan's lack of moral courage in failing to insist on clarification of the order.

It seems, by his subsequent behaviour, that Lucan's conscience was none too easy on that score. Nothing would satisfy him but a thorough and complete vindication, and since that was not forthcoming he pestered the authorities and started another exchange of letters with Cardigan over details that properly belonged to regimental officers.

Cardigan, as always, was only too ready to retaliate, and he purposely delayed the replies and returns that Lucan demanded. In addition, Cardigan compiled a long list of Lucan's attempts to interfere with the ordinary discharge of daily duties, and sent this to Raglan.

Lucan, aware that his rival was now in better odour than himself, struck out blindly. He let it be known that he was applying to the Secretary for War, the Duke of Newcastle, asking that he be exonerated from all blame for the brigade calamity. Raglan warned him to hold his hand, but Lucan was deaf and blind to reason. His appeal went to London, but instead of being cleared Lucan was requested to give up his command and to return home.

A sadly disappointed and, as he thought, badly treated man, he spent much of his future in trying to obtain a court martial, or at least a hearing, in the hope of bringing judgment to bear upon Cardigan. But the authorities knew better than to allow the two angry earls to confront each other on an official army platform; and Lucan and Cardigan had to be content with thrashing the matter out in a series of somewhat repetitive letters in the columns of the Press.

Cardigan certainly came off best in the matter of reputation: he could, moreover, congratulate himself on the magnificent bearing of the brigade he had trained when, in fulfilment of an error, it rode to its palpable doom. For that he had incurred the charge of being a tyrant; he had set the public by the ears, and proved himself a thorn in the side of the Horse Guards: but his code and conduct had been fully justified by a superb example of military devotion and courage.

He had more personal grounds for gratification. His bearing and self-esteem, which always tended to make him appear as a hero in the making, had proved itself to be the outcome, not of fraud or of conceit, as many supposed, but of a genuine dauntless spirit. Even Lucan, in a first natural flush of enthusiasm for the charge, and before his anger got out of hand, reported to Raglan that "Major-General the Earl of Cardigan led this attack in the most gallant and intrepid manner." Raglan endorsed this by saying that Cardigan "acted throughout with the greatest steadiness and gallantry, as well as perseverance". The Commander-in-Chief was the first to acknowledge the moral effect of the charge in that it left the Russians, from then on, unwilling to try conclusions with what was left of the British cavalry.

The Russians were convinced that Cardigan's men, to have come on in such a fashion, were mad with drink. Their General Liprandi said, "I never saw anything like it," while Russian prisoners confessed to having been bewildered by the daring of the charge.

Cardigan was quite at home in the atmosphere of glory. He was ever ready to bring attention to bear upon some detail connected with his greatest day, as when he sent an aide to remind Raglan, superfluously enough, that his men had cut down all the Russians who stood to their pieces. He wanted to know if anyone had ever heard of cavalry attacking batteries in front and a colonel told him "Yes, at Aliwal, in the Sikh campaign of 1846," when the 16th Lancers had routed an army of 24,000 and captured all the gunners on the field. Cardigan's cloak, carried rolled up in front of his saddle, had been rent by the half-hearted Cossack thrusts that tore his overalls: and he would lift the sheepskin and exhibit the cloak to anyone showing interest. "Here's the result of charging batteries in front."

When Lucan went home it was whispered, with varying degrees of apprehension, that Cardigan would replace him as commander of the Cavalry Division, the Heavy as well as the greatly attenuated Light Brigade: but it was no more than a camp rumour.

Between these whiles of being his confident, flamboyant self, full of flourish, Cardigan was revealing another side of his nature that seldom appears in the popular estimates. Trumpeter Britten, who sounded the calls directing the motion of the charge, was dying of wounds in a Balaclava hospital: and Cardigan provided whatever comforts could be had in those surroundings, and sat for hours at Britten's bedside.

The news of the charge electrified and newly inspired the people at home. But for those at the front the excitement it caused soon died down in the bitter disillusion that was now the general mood of the army besieging Sebastopol. The fortress was still holding out: there was no sign of it weakening, still less falling: and the British and French commanders, the latter especially, anxiously reviewed their positions.

General Canrobert feared that the recent Russian move towards Balaclava heralded a sortie from the fortress. This could menace the French siege works that were in the rear of the British: and Canrobert requested Raglan to post the remnant of Cardigan's brigade closer to the French rear and centre, to the right of a windmill on the heights of Inkerman, a good 7 miles from Balaclava.

Raglan's delicate mind was scarcely able to sustain his better judgment at tough military councils, and he gave way over an issue that was later to bear upon Cardigan's reputation as a cavalry leader. Cardigan pointed out at the time that if, as was possible, the one road to Balaclava became impassable, supplies of forage for horses in the new position would soon be exhausted.

But Canrobert insisted, and Cardigan, with Raglan's compliance, was overruled. Each day a number of horses travelled the distance between Inkerman and the base to bring back hay and barley. This imposed an additional strain on horses that were in pretty poor shape to begin with. Yet so far it was possible, for the weather held and the road to Balaclava remained open. But every day brought a chilly reminder that the Russian winter was closing in on the Crimea. In place of the tinted sky there was now a low canopy of leaden cloud: and on 30th October the first snow appeared on the hills.

7

For some days after the Balaclava actions there was only the intermittent rumble of siege guns to tell that the war was still going on. It was being borne in upon the ragged British Army, cut off on the heights and the plateau overlooking Sebastopol, that there was little if any hope of equipment or supplies, that were fast running out, reaching them for the dreary days ahead. A mood of hopelessness replaced the resignation that had already set in. Cardigan, whose health was visibly declining, rode up from the harbour to the cavalry camp once or twice daily. He had never, even in England, stood up well to the cold: and now he habitually appeared wearing the woollen garment that, by being called after him, has popularized his name even among those who seldom, if indeed ever, recall the Six Hundred.

With the trenches and the siege works to man, the British lines on the Inkerman ridge were pitifully thin. The early days of November brought chilling fog and heavy rain that left the earth sodden while the thick undergrowth and trees dripped gloom upon the camp; and early on the morning of the 5th, a Sunday, the Russians made their most determined effort of the campaign.

Some 60,000 infantry, prepared to strike home with the bayonet, swarmed up the slopes. The heavily outnumbered British were forced back, leaving their dead along each yard of the way. Bursts of yellow sunlight followed the rain, and men tore off their greatcoats, the better to use their rifle butts or even bare fists, when the dense columns with flat impassive faces that matched their muffin-like caps, were too close for the use of steel.

The cry "Keep firm on the Colours!" was heard as a mere handful of Guards swayed to and fro against the rampart of bodies. Between the sunlight, folds of fog drifted in, so that men struggled on blindly and seemed to be sustaining the battle single-handed. Some shouted their names or the number of their regiment in the hope of hearing the assurance of a friendly answer.

The early sound of bugles shrilling the "Alarm" had not penetrated to Balaclava harbour where Cardigan stayed late on his yacht. There was no place for the British cavalry at Inkerman, even if it had been strong enough to prove effective: but Lord George Paget, shortly before nine o'clock, mustered the remnant of Cardigan's brigade and held it in reserve. They were on elevated ground, and in spite of the mist the Russian gunners soon picked them out, inflicting some casualties.

When Cardigan arrived, the fate of the army was still being decided by the straggling fights that he could hear going on in the foggy hollows and ravines. But his sense of discipline was stronger than whatever concern he felt over the issue. He found fault with Paget who, in the flurry of excitement caused by the rattle of musketry in the darkness, had not mounted a full guard before leaving camp, and with the brigade major for not having had the morning returns made out and signed.

Meanwhile the British infantry, decimated and worn down, held doggedly on to a front that yielded ground here and there without being definitely broken. Relief came in the form of a brilliant charge by French Zouaves and Algerians, the 'children of fire' whose dash drove the Russians from the field. But though Inkerman ended the Russian hopes of ending the war, it was a 'victory' that drained the life-blood of the British: and a few days later the elements took a hand.

The camps were literally devastated, blown away by a terrific hurricane. Twenty-one vessels with the last of the stores, winter clothing and forage, were wrecked in Balaclava harbour. Then came rain, snow and ice to complete the ruin of an army that was starved, threadbare, shoeless and without shelter. One man out of every two fell sick or died. The survivors barely existed on mouldy biscuit and frozen meat that, since all wood in the district was speedily used up, could not be cooked. Not many could summon strength to hack out graves in the frozen ground.

The remaining horses of Cardigan's command, positioned some miles from the Balaclava base because Canrobert wished it, were starving to death. There was no hay or straw. The restricted daily allowance of 3 pounds of barley for each horse was soon further cut down, so that anything that came within reach— saddles, blankets, ropes, picket-pegs, the spokes of wheels, even the frozen hair on the faces of the men—was gnawed or seized on by the famished creatures.

The horses sent to the base to bring back barley sank under their burdens, being too weak to stagger through mud that was often knee-deep. Finally the few near-skeletons of the once magnificent chargers were ordered back to their old quarters near Kadikoi. Seventeen perished on the way. "The cavalry", wrote Colonel Hodge, "are utterly done for."

With first the men lost (many survivors of the charge had since

died) and now most of the horses, Cardigan's command had virtually ceased to exist. There were now no field days to order, no
careless officer to reprimand on his daily round of the camp. He
took on a quieter, more tractable mood, as Lord George Paget
discovered when he criticized some of the arrangements that
Cardigan made at Kadikoi. The horses, Paget pointed out, were
exposed with their front unprotected. They needed to be in what
is known as an 'inside' position, where, in the event of a night
attack, help could reach them.

Cardigan listened. There was no resentment, no sarcastic reply;
and a little later, with a suggestion of weariness in his voice and
manner, he approached Paget. "Here, Lord George, you seem to
know about these things. Be good enough to picket the horses
according to your ideas." Paget thought to himself that Cardigan
was an odd man.

On 16th November, after a visit to the camp, Cardigan wrote
to the assistant adjutant-general asking that something be done for
those of the Light Brigade who were still in hospital. "I am bound
to say that every measure to relieve the discomforts and sufferings
of those men is necessary at the earliest moment. There are several
men of every regiment, lying without socks and most of the sick
in boots saturated with wet: men labouring under dysentery,
diarrhoea, fevers and rheumatism: complaints all requiring
warmth and comfort. I earnestly, therefore, press upon the attention of the Lieutenant-General commanding the division the
expediency of prompt measures being carried into effect for the
removal of all worst cases selected by the Staff surgeon on board
ship." On the day when he wrote this, Cardigan was confined to
his yacht with sickness.

His friend Fanny Duberly, who lasted out the campaign, was
at Balaclava, and Cardigan was again drawn to speak freely to her.
She found him now a man in eclipse, with much of his old
swagger gone, as hungry for sympathy and comfort as once he
had been for glory. "I have no brigade," he told her. "My
brigade is gone. My heart and health are broken. I must go
home."

On 21st November Russell of *The Times* noted, "Lord Cardigan
is almost unable to leave his yacht owing to his indisposition": and
on 2nd, 20th and 22nd December Cardigan was too ill to go
ashore. The Russian winter with its full volume of snow, ice and

freezing winds was upon them. The war, with no decisive victory since the Alma to compensate for the suffering it caused, had apparently come to a standstill. There was no good reason, except the reduction of Sebastopol, for firing another shot: and Sebastopol had so far withstood the siege.

All things necessary for prolonging the deadlock (and personal enthusiasm was no less vital than supplies) were now wholly lacking, and officers who could reasonably do so on account of wounds, sickness or fatigue, were starting to go home. The Duke of Cambridge, and hardened old warriors such as General George Brown and General de Lacy Evans, who were unfit for further service, were among those to go.

The news that some "lucky devils" were leaving was greeted with greater tolerance by men in the field than it was by many civilians at home. When it was announced that a certain noble lord would soon be returning it was generally thought to mean Cardigan; but it proved to be Paget. The latter, unlike Cardigan, had never been intent on becoming a soldier. Shortly before the outbreak of war he had sent in his papers; but he stayed on rather than leave his regiment when it was ordered abroad.

The sudden change in Cardigan's nature revealed itself when Paget told him that Raglan had consented to his going home. He congratulated Paget, saying that his case "was different from that of the others". "I think you are quite right," continued Cardigan (who had always put duty before all personal considerations), "and were I in your position I would do the same."

But when Paget reached home—he sailed on 11th November— he soon found that Cardigan's lenient view was not shared by many of those (inveterate club-men for the most part) whose experience of the war had been limited to perusing the papers. Outlooks and judgments were sterner then, there were no psychological explanations to vindicate one who appeared to have turned his back upon danger; and Paget, in spite of being a home-loving man and devoted to his wife, returned to the Crimea in the last week of February 1855.

During his absence Cardigan applied to Raglan for leave to go home. He explained that his health, far from improving, was worsening every day. Had it not been for that, he assured Raglan, "I should have no wish to go, for you know you have no keener soldier in your army." There was little he could do by staying on.

His brigade was reduced to some 270 or 280 horses in the field: others were dying daily of starvation and weakness. He thought of residing for a time in a warm climate. He had Naples in mind. "But I will follow your wishes and advice, even to the detriment of my health."

A few days later, on Raglan's instructions, the members of a medical board examined Cardigan on his yacht. They reported that "Lord Cardigan is much reduced in strength, and the Board, considering the serious nature of his complaints, recommend that he may be allowed to proceed to England for the recovery of his health." He was suffering from dysenteric diarrhoea, and had difficulty in passing his urine.

Cardigan observed the formality of resigning his command, and said farewell to Raglan, who showed him a letter, from the Secretary for War, informing him that the Queen was deeply sensible of the gallant services he had rendered. With that to cheer him, and to reawaken his old confidence, he boarded the *Caradoc* and left the Crimea on 8th December. His brigade major, Mayow, was delighted to see him go.

Then followed a short stay at Constantinople, where Cardigan attended the New Year's ball given by the British ambassador to Turkey, Lord Stratford de Redcliffe. Here he encountered his old world of brilliance and beauty that made the miseries of life on the ridges of the Crimea, and in Florence Nightingale's hospital at Scutari (the latter quite near at hand) seem very far away.

Sir Colin Campbell, Lord William Paulet, Omar Pasha, several Sardinian officers, and fat and fierce General Pelissier, represented the Allied military commanders; diplomats and their wives lent a somewhat quieter tone; Lady George Paget, with Lady Stratford de Redcliffe a good second, upheld the charm, grace and dignity of English womanhood; the plump necks and fingers of Armenian ladies glistened with diamonds.

As the playing of "God Save the Queen" announced the entry of the principal guests, Cardigan came face to face with his old enemy Lucan. The evening was blemished for them both, and they processed in, as a young lady observed, looking "very grumpy".

When it came to dancing, Cardigan quite outshone his brother-in-law. He was especially light and polished in the quadrille, though his breath and whiskers discharged whiffs of wine into the averted faces of his partners—but much could now be forgiven the man who had led an immortal ride.

The sight of Lucan, however, reminded Cardigan that he had still many wrongs to redress; and although he was going home, and should have experienced nothing but relief at heading for the familiar white cliffs, he devoted some time to drawing up another long list of complaints, touching Lucan's rude and offensive behaviour, and despatched it to Raglan.

He landed at Marseilles, where he slept in a house "for the first time in many months" (one may assume that he lived on board the *Caradoc* when at Constantinople). Here a communication from Raglan caught up with him, in which was expressed the thanks of both Houses of Parliament for his distinguished conduct in the Crimea. Cardigan had no doubts as to the popular reception that awaited him in England, and now officialdom was moving in his favour. Those twenty minutes at Balaclava had surely achieved his redemption. But he underestimated the venom of the Press, which partly subsists on the naming and the maiming of victims. During Cardigan's journey home it was singling out Raglan for attack, crushing first his spirit and then his body.

On the way to Boulogne Cardigan stopped at Paris and called on the Emperor Napoleon. But he had to forego the pleasure of dining at the Tuileries and again kissing the Empress's hand since, as one of the minor complaints resulting from his illness, his feet were badly swollen and could not be pressed into his dress shoes.

8

A tall broad-shouldered man was pacing the drawing-room of a house called Farringford, on the Isle of Wight. It was a red room, furnished in dark, rather ponderous style, and with heavy curtains. The candles had not been lighted although it was a dim grey morning in mid-November, and the pacing figure moved in the reflection of a wood fire flaming on the hearth. The windows admitted a view over grassland, where chestnut leaves rustled in a sharp wind that carried a tang of the sea from Freshwater Bay.

From time to time Alfred Tennyson (for the dark features were those of the Poet-Laureate) murmured some words that had come into his head after reading a recent copy of *The Times*, which contained Russell's leader on the Charge of the Light Brigade.

In writing it, Russell had dipped his pen into something more ardent and creative than normal journalistic ink. "They swept proudly past, glittering in the morning sun in all the pride and splendour of war. We could scarcely believe the evidence of our senses! Surely that handful of men are not going to charge an army in position? Alas, it was but too true. . . . With a halo of flashing steel above their heads, and with a cheer that was many a noble fellow's death-cry, they flew into the smoke of the batteries, but ere they were lost from view the ground was strewed with their bodies. . . .

"Through the clouds of smoke we could see the sabres flashing as they rode up to the guns. . . ."

The pacing figure stopped, muttered words that seemed lost in his beard, then seized a pen and dashed off lines that embodied his vision of the charge:

> Half a league, half a league,
> Half a league onward,
> All in the valley of Death
> Rode the Six Hundred.

The ballad entered into and became a part of the spirit of Victorian England. It called up tears, pride, grief, admiration. It invaded homes, school-rooms, and entertainment platforms throughout the country. It marked one of those rare occasions when a poet speaks direct to the people, in a language they understand, and when the people respond. Even prigs, purists and pedants cannot avoid knowing some of the lines, that have firmly established themselves among the best-known quotations in the world.

The public first read the ballad on 9th December, in *The Examiner*: copies soon reached the Crimea: and survivors of the charge who were still in hospital, or perishing of cold and misery on the desolate heights overlooking the scene of their epic, felt ready, as one of their number had called out to Cardigan at the time, "to do it again".

A chaplain in the Scutari hospital was astonished to note the effect it had upon the men to whom he read it, and he wrote home asking that copies might be printed and sent to the front. It would

(*Above*) The Crimean
Enquiry: the
examination of the
Earl of Lucan. (*Right*)
Lord Cardigan in later
life

The second Lady Cardigan in later life

be, he said, the greatest service that could be done at the moment. "Half are singing it, and all want to have it in black and white." And before the end of August 2,000 slips bearing the laureate's words had reached him for distribution.

A doctor in the same hospital had given up one of his patients who was suffering from extreme shock after the charge. Nothing could rouse him from the state of complete inertia in which he existed. In desperation, the doctor took a copy of the verses to the man's bedside, and read them aloud. Within a few minutes the soldier appeared to be listening: his expression of stupor disappeared, and before many hours had passed he was thoroughly restored and supplementing the poet's lines by his own first-hand version of Balaclava.

The first anniversary of the charge was celebrated, at the front, in a store hut near the valley. Seats were found for as many as could be fitted in, the boards serving as tables were covered with bran sacks; and, standing by one of these tables, a sergeant of dragoons recited the ballad. Men who could say they had ridden with Cardigan felt their spirits revive as they re-lived that October morning when the General's voice had initiated their great twenty minutes: "The brigade will advance."

It was being borne out, as someone on the spot wrote to Tennyson, that "the poet can now make heroes, just as in days of yore, if he will". The charge marked the St. Crispin's day of the cavalry, when the lance and sabre became invested with the magic of the bows that were drawn at Agincourt: and twenty years later, in London, when a dinner was arranged for survivors of the Light Brigade (by then a mere handful) some 750 old soldiers turned up and claimed to have belonged to the original 673 who had gone down the valley.

PART FIVE

The Conquering Hero

I

The strains of Handel's triumphal chorus were heard time and again during the early weeks of 1855. They were played by a brass band when, on 13th January, Cardigan came ashore at Folkestone, where the crowd on the pier gave three cheers for 'the hero of Balaclava'; and they were to follow him on his progress through the provincial towns where he was greeted with civic honours.

But his arrival in London, at 10.30 on the morning of the same day, was surprisingly quiet. He was apparently unexpected, and went straight to the house of his friend de Burgh, in Grosvenor Crescent. In the afternoon he called on Lord Hardinge, who was then Commander-in-Chief; and again with de Burgh he attended an evening concert at Covent Garden.

The programme included Rossini's "Stabat Mater", the Larghetto from Beethoven's Symphony in D, and a specially arranged Grand Allied Armies Quadrille, in which the three Guards bands took part. The conductor was the fiercely excited Monsieur Jullien, who had wielded the baton before an audience that, fifteen years earlier, had greeted the appearance of Cardigan with boos and hisses.

But wherever he went now there were outbursts of a totally different kind. He had become a popular idol, a hero whose calm acceptance of a forlorn mission reminded the Victorians that they were still a military people whose glory was not only in the past. The disaster in which he had figured acquired the reputation of a resounding victory, one that was all the greater for having been achieved against terrific odds: and Cardigan was admirably fitted by nature to play the part demanded of a national figure.

It might be said that all his life he had been prepared for this period of adulation. He had never doubted that his hour would strike, or that his character would stand the test. In the past, and in the face of continual opposition, he had been proved right (if only to his own satisfaction) on several notable occasions. Now the whole country was united in paying him homage.

His ordeal in the Russian valley was the topic of the day. His picture, sometimes the centre-piece of a colourful patriotic display, appeared in shop windows and was sold in the streets. Prints depicted him mounted on Ronald, leaping over a gun and spitting a Russian while his sword was poised in the air. A species of woollen jacket was called after him, and hardy mortals who had braved colder winters without such a garment now wore one as a token of respect: and it was matter for news when the steamship *Cambria* arrived in the Mersey and the principal passenger to go ashore was the powerful chestnut charger, Ronald, "which had carried the Earl so gallantly through the memorable day at Balaclava".

Even the Queen came round and responded to the popular fervour. Although conceding that "Lord Cardigan's personal character does not stand very high in the country", she was now ready to admit him to the company of Albert and herself, and she invited the gilded reprobate to Windsor Castle.

His tall trim figure was recognized at evening service in St. James's Chapel on Sunday the 14th. On the following morning he kept an appointment with the Duke of Newcastle, Secretary for War, where, it may be safely assumed, the part Lucan had played in the Crimea was painted in far from glowing colours. His diary for 15th January contains a brief statement: "Dined with Mr. de Horsey, a small party." Judging by this, Adeline's father was one of the many who had reversed their earlier and unfavourable estimate of Cardigan; and whether or not Adeline was one of the party, it was now permissible for her to experience a wave of devotion that sprang (like that of Desdemona towards Othello) from a telling and re-telling of the dangers through which Cardigan had passed.

His diary for the 16th records that he "went down to Windsor by the half past five train". The Queen reflected the changed attitude of the nation towards him by receiving Cardigan most graciously, while registering in her mind that he looked older and thinner. He sat by her side at dinner, where the guests included the Duchess of Kent and the French ambassador, Count Walewski, and his wife. The Queen was not one of those women who think it feminine to show a marked aversion to military details. She was able to hold her own in discussing the campaign, and she further delighted Cardigan by showing appreciation of his conduct at Balaclava.

Cardigan was not slow in adding to her impressions. He blamed Lucan for ordering the direction of the charge, and said that the death of Captain Nolan at its commencement "was one of the strangest things he knew". He found the Queen a most attentive listener. Others leaned forward as Cardigan's voice went on. The band of the Royal Buckinghamshire Militia provided a suitable background. The Light Brigade spurred forward again in the imaginations of those gathered about the long table: and it was arranged for Cardigan to continue his story on the following day.

The painter George Sant had been commanded to be present when Cardigan's audience, including the Queen and the Prince Consort, Prince Albert Edward (the future Edward VII) and Prince Arthur (afterwards the Duke of Connaught) gathered in the Long Gallery. This time Cardigan reinforced his account by exhibiting a water-colour of the charge by William Simpson, an artist who had also been a war correspondent: and once again his listeners, the children especially, were enthralled. The Queen found Cardigan's description very simple and graphic, and very modest, when it came to his own part, though she noted that he spoke of this "with evident and very natural satisfaction".

Sant made preliminary sketches during the narration, and the group in the Long Gallery, waiting on the words of Cardigan who stood next to the Queen, became the subject of a large impressive canvas. That picture is now at Deene Park, but (as will be remarked on later) one of the principal figures has been blotted out by layers of self-righteousness and paint.

On the way back from Windsor, still by train, Cardigan stopped at Richmond where he called on the Duchess of Cambridge and her daughter, Princess Mary. Then came a second visit to the Commander-in-Chief, Lord Hardinge, who informed Cardigan that he was to be appointed Inspector-General of Cavalry.

He took full advantage of the Lord Mayor's banquet on 6th February, in the Egyptian Hall of the Mansion House, where he was guest of honour. The large crowd gathered outside gave a cheer of delight when Cardigan arrived, mounted on Ronald, and wearing the blue and crimson uniform of Balaclava. On their way to the entrance people pressed forward to pluck a hair from the tail of Ronald, as once their medieval forbears had clamoured to snatch a relic from the person of a saint. In his speech Cardigan, with somewhat excessive use of the ego, gave detailed accounts of his experiences in the Balkans, where he had carried out the 'Soreback Reconnaissance', and in the Crimea. His main point was, of course, to clarify the circumstances in which he had been given the order to charge.

"I received that order, my Lord Mayor, and I obeyed it. I delivered that order myself to the brigade under my command. I ordered them to march, I ordered them to advance. I ordered them to attack the Russians in the valley. But, my lord, I must say this, that on that occasion, it being my duty to give the order to my men, I did give it, though I deeply regretted it at the time, and I am sure I should have much more regretted it if anything had prevented my performing the rest of my duty, which was to share the dangers that those brave men so boldly faced." At this point his voice faltered. . . . More than once, during the coming weeks, Cardigan was to choke back tears when he spoke of "that morning".

His old enemy, The Times, soon shook off the effects of Cardigan's sudden accession to glory: and next day, influenced by his having been in uniform, on horseback, and perhaps not least by the idolatrous assaults on Ronald's tail, a leader-writer found something "suggestive of Madame Tussaud" in his appearance at the Mansion House. But even this critic was compelled to admit that Cardigan "did his part with perfect good taste". Lord George Paget, who was then in London, having not yet bowed to the increasingly hostile remarks that would soon make him glad to return to the more friendly atmosphere of the Crimea, observed with a touch of occasional sourness, "Lord Cardigan was a vain as well as an ambitious man, and his vanity led him astray when he came in contact with the admiring mob of London."

But the 'Cardigan fever' extended beyond London. The strains of "See the Conquering Hero" greeted his appearance in several parts of the provinces, wherever there was a banquet, a presentation, or some military affair to mark the closing stages of a war that was long since bare of purpose.

His appointment as Inspector-General of Cavalry came into effect on 1st February. The office entailed the building up of cavalry regiments weakened by the war, and the preparation of remounts and recruits. It was a task that called upon Cardigan's high standard of efficiency, his obsession with detail; and in performing it he soon made his presence felt.

When he arrived to inspect a regiment he insisted on being met by an officer and a sergeant (the latter acting as orderly), both in full dress. Senior officers were made to realize that their experience counted for little, while newly gazetted cornets and young lieutenants felt weak at the knees as the inspection proceeded. The smallest button was noticed, every strap and buckle was checked. Sudden questions were fired as to the use and maintenance of equipment, the age of each horse and its place of origin.

The riding and methods employed in the school were invariably criticized. The wearing of leathered overalls at foot parades was forbidden. The ranks, made nervous by all they knew was expected of them, were apt to fall into confusion, so that after an inspection Cardigan often had cause to complain of their lack of order and faulty dressing: and when the mounted parade, the stables and the riding school were relieved from scrutiny, the Inspector-General proceeded to pass a severely critical eye over Messing arrangements. Such routine inquisitions came to be rated among the most difficult and unpleasant duties in the round of cavalry regiments quartered in Britain, though a letter written by Cardigan about this time, after the 4th Dragoon Guards had passed under review, suggests that even the uncompromising Inspector-General could temper reproof with a touch of personal consideration.

The letter, addressed to Colonel Hodge who commanded the regiment, followed a customary course by stating that the riding "was not as perfect as it should be". It then proceeded, "A friend of mine, Hubert de Burgh, is interested about Miss Reynolds, one of the principal actresses at the Haymarket Theatre, and who is going to act immediately at the Manchester Theatre, and he has requested me to ask you and your officers to patronize her." One wonders how Colonel Hodge, who was on the staid side, and those of his officers who were not so staid, interpreted that request.

Meanwhile the campaign between Cardigan and Lucan, in the columns of the Press, continued at full blast. Neither showed any sign of yielding a single point. The main argument raged about responsibility for the interpretation of Raglan's order. In that, of course, the advantage was clearly with Cardigan, who could rightfully claim to have carried out Lucan's instruction, given to him verbally in front of the troops.

But when thwarted there, Lucan shifted his attack to the Light Brigade's failure to execute a flank move against the Russians after the Heavies had charged. To this, Cardigan replied that Lucan had ordered him to stand firm—and here, it must be remembered, Cardigan was a life-long believer in going forward, whereas Lucan was habitually more restrained.

But Lucan denied that he had given any such order. Cardigan went on repeating that he had received it. Both men continued to hurl forth affirmations and denials. The papers received and made use of a lot of free copy: and people who found entertainment in reading it professed to be shocked by the spectacle of brother earls airing such rancour and bitterness in public.

2

There was renewed cheering, mingled with the brassy strains of Handel's chorus, when a train from London drew into Northampton station shortly after noon on 8th February. The whole of that month was exceptionally cold. The roofs were covered with snow, which was quite deep in the streets. But crowds had assembled, with many from nearby parts of the county, to welcome the hero of Balaclava, who was to be the honoured guest at a reception in the George Assembly Room.

The approaches to the station were jammed, and waves of cheering were carried back, to be repeated by those on the outskirts of the throng, as Cardigan stepped out on the platform. He was approached by the leader of a team who had drawn, by ropes, an empty carriage that was meant to convey Cardigan to his reception. But he let it be known that he preferred his own carriage, which had travelled with him on the train: and the ropes were transferred from the more humble vehicle to the suitably embellished conveyance that willing hands, not without difficulty, pulled through the streets.

Every inch of the way, every improvised stand and balcony was crowded; buildings were hung with flags and laurelled decorations; church bells rang as the procession made its way, almost by inches, over the trampled snow. In places where the pressure was greatest the cheers and the brass band drowned the cries of people who fell and the crash of broken windows.

There were more scenes of enthusiasm in the Assembly Room, where the mayor and local dignitaries were gathered about a platform where Cardigan, once silence had been obtained, stood to address them.

He began by accounting for his presence there and his reasons for leaving the Crimea. Bad health, over which he had no control, was partly responsible, together with the fact that he had nothing left to command. He enlarged on the sorry condition of the horses. The Commissariat had failed to provide forage: at the time of his leaving the army the horses of his brigade had existed on "a very small portion of barley". They had been without hay for eighteen days (cries of "shame!" greeted this); consequently the horses died in great numbers.

He then turned to the controversy that was exercising his mind —the order he received at Balaclava. It was a matter of deep regret that the order to charge was given. He differed in opinion as to the propriety of the order (there was no actual reference to Lucan), but having received it he placed himself at the head of his brigade, and gave the word of command.

"Whatever gallantry you may attribute to me," he continued, "was equalled by every man in that brigade. I never witnessed anything done with more spirit or with lighter hearts." In speaking of the vital moments of the charge—riding to within 30 yards of the Russian guns where they were encircled and surrounded by a blaze of fire—his voice faltered. Several women among the listeners were already in tears. Men cleared their throats. It was some little time before Cardigan could choke back emotion and continue his speech.

The snow was again falling, but a crowd still waited outside the 'George' for a sight of Cardigan. By the time the reception was over the snow had given way to driving sleet, but Cardigan showed himself on the balcony and addressed some "kindly words" to those standing below. At the end of his visit the mayor, aldermen and citizens of Northampton presented him with a remarkable testimonial—a roll more than 40 yards long composed of sheets pasted together and bearing between 4,000 and 5,000 signatures, nearly all written in the legible Victorian hand. Leicestershire, another county with which the Brudenells were associated, gave him an illuminated address.

The details of the charge at Balaclava were by now almost as well known to his audiences as they were to Cardigan himself. He was to repeat them, with slight variations, throughout the weeks of his triumph, and always with the same accompaniment of cheers, mingled with tears, that marked his progress.

3

Soldiers home from the war, some of whom had carried out but day-to-day duties, were being rewarded. The Queen, at a ceremony on the Horse Guards Parade where Cardigan was in attendance, distributed the first batch of a new decoration, the Crimean Medal, to officers and men who had served under Raglan. Not all those entitled to it coveted the medal, which some described as a vulgar-looking thing with clasps like gin-labels.

In the summer of 1855 Cardigan received the K.C.B. The Legion of Honour followed, then the Knighthood of the Second Class of the Turkish order of Medjidie. But in spite of his eminence, private and official opinion in England was still undecided about him.

Lord Aberdeen, the pedestrian middle-of-the-road Prime Minister who headed a coalition of Whigs and Peelites, told the Queen: "From his rank and station, Lord Cardigan might fairly pretend to the Garter, but his violent Party politics would make it impossible for Lord Aberdeen, under ordinary circumstances, to submit his name to Your Majesty for that purpose."

For a specimen of the popular outcry against Cardigan that never, even in the days of his triumph, quite died down, we need only look at a booklet, *Was Lord Cardigan a Hero at Balaclava?* produced by a journalist, George Ryan. When it was announced

that Cardigan was receiving the K.C.B., Ryan appealed to the
Queen expressing his regret in these terms:

"Oh, Majesty of England! Insulted chivalry cries out against an
outrage on its sanctity. Graves open up at Balaclava! Heroes in the
blood-soaked winding-sheets stand forth! Behold the mangled
bodies of your brave! Russian swords and Russian shells have
lashed and crushed them into worm's meat. See, they point to
their glorious wounds and weep. Oh, Majesty of England, slay
them not again, stay that chaste hand! Rob not these gods of
their immortal fame—the greatness of Balaclava is theirs. It is not
his. Withhold that insignia—it was made for a Knight Commander, and should not bedeck the person of a braggadocio. But
it is done. True heroism is cheated, and six foot of imposture is
triumphant!"

Events in the Crimea were threatening to drag to a disappointing
stalemate: but England's military pulse, in so far as its home beats
were concerned, was still strong. Reviews, parades and sham
fights assumed the character of popular spectacles rather than
exercises, especially when Cardigan was in charge. He commanded a review of the two Household Cavalry regiments, and
the 6th Dragoon Guards, in Hyde Park. Napoleon and his
empress were then in London, and the Queen and Eugénie, in an
open carriage, were attended by the entire Court. The review
ended with a drawing of swords and a mock charge, after which
Napoleon rode up to Cardigan and expressed himself "highly
satisfied". The diarist Greville thought he was being polite, as the
affair, judged by numbers, "was a mere toy compared with what
the French are accustomed to see".

At the end of June, on the dreary heights of the Crimea, surrounded by the graves of his army, Cardigan's old commander,
Lord Raglan, died of a broken heart. It was the one thing left for
him to do. "I could never return to England," he had said, "they
would stone me to death." A few weeks later the Russians
silently evacuated the fortress of Sebastopol, the pivot of the war:
and on 30th March 1856 the Treaty of Paris was signed. Prince
Albert wrote that the news was received "with moderate
satisfaction: in Paris with exultation".

Throughout those months Cardigan divided his time between
Deene Park, London and the Isle of Wight. He knew that his wife

was seriously ill, perhaps dying. But so far he had made no effort to see her, and she had not requested a meeting. For the time being, at least, he was faithful to Adeline. He concerned himself with the business of the Royal Southern Yacht Club, Southampton, and when not living on the *Dryad* he occupied a house at the village of Shalfleet, near Yarmouth, on the Isle of Wight.

The master of the yacht, William Slater, saw to the vessel being laid up for the winter, and their correspondence shows that Slater sometimes carried out the duties of manservant. He writes that he had forwarded on some shooting clothes. "I hope, my lord, that I have not done wrong by sending these things." But he was unable to find any slippers. "I hope they will be found in some of the cases." And what should he do with the coat? "Shall I, my lord, put your Lordship's watch in the pocket of the coat? It will be quite safe there, being well covered up with something soft."

But apart from the care of his yacht, and the handling of his clothes, there were more troublesome matters building up for Cardigan.

The war was behind him now, but angry voices were still being raised concerning the way in which it had been conducted. The leaders, following a report that led to a Board of Inquiry being set up, were coming in for censure: and since one of the subjects to be examined was the state of the horses, the name of Cardigan (who still had more enemies, perhaps, than any man in England) figured high on the list of those to be summoned.

4

The report originated in February 1855, when the desperate plight of the army in the Crimea had become common knowledge. It was drawn up by Sir John McNeill, a former diplomat who became chairman of the Scottish Poor Law Board, and Colonel Alexander Tulloch. Both these commissioners visited the Crimea, and drew up a detailed survey of supply and distribution arrangements, their inadequacy from the start, and why they had further broken down.

This *Inquiry into the Supplies of the British Army in the Crimea* was presented to both Houses of Parliament. It was soon made known that it named certain officers who in some degree could be held responsible for the issue of stores, and the running of the Commissariat. The Press and public took this up, demanding that measures should be taken against them: and when it was announced that generals Airey, Lucan and Cardigan were among those named, the demand became overwhelming.

More responsible quarters regretted that the report had been sent to Parliament, instead of to the military authorities whose business it was to deal with the officers concerned. The Queen, rightly interpreting the move as part of a political plan to remove control of the army from the Crown to the Commons, expressed her opinion in a letter that was read before the Cabinet.

She regretted that the Press, being the sworn enemy of the officers named in the report, and being determined to effect their ruin (for which it possessed "unlimited means"), should be allowed to influence opinion against them. The Press had already condemned those officers in advance, whereas judgment should properly be left to those who could feel "the weight of their responsibility".

The Queen had not spoken without cause. *The Times* was already leading the attack with sneers directed at Cardigan and Lucan—"those gentlemen" who were now "strutting about our streets with the halo of heroism about their heads"; and for once the two earls acted together, rushing into print to defend themselves, but sometimes yielding to custom and thrusting, not at the report or at the Press, but at each other when their indignation boiled over.

Cardigan challenged the accuracy of the report, and demanded that the charges levelled against him should be investigated. It was finally announced that a board of inquiry was being set up, to look into the conduct of certain officers named by the commissioners: and since one of those officers was Cardigan, whose notoriety, now mixed with more legitimate fame, was fresh as ever, the public looked forward to being entertained by a controversy that could involve the blackening of military reputations.

The board, consisting of officers who had reached the rank of general without having figured in any outstanding operation, met in the Great Hall of Chelsea Hospital on 3rd April 1856. The hall was specially fitted out for an occasion that was concerned with preliminaries for more than a week, and that finally got down to business on 12th April. One of the commissioners, Sir John McNeill, refused to attend, pleading that to do so would be out of place in one who, in making the report, was acting under the Crown. Colonel Tulloch announced that he was ready to stand by his statements and to undergo interrogation.

It was an occasion that, judging by his several similar experiences in the past, was not likely to find Cardigan wanting: and anticipating this a large proportion of the spectators present, who on each of the early days of the hearing numbered about two thousand, was made up of ladies. A newspaper commented on the varied hues of their costumes and hats, and the uniforms of the military, which provided a colourful contrast to the mellow panelling of the hall.

The main charges were brought against General Airey, who, as Quartermaster-General, had been more concerned with the handling of supplies than had either Lucan or Cardigan. But the fatal shortcomings in Airey's department could be attributed to lack of transport, which prevented any adequate distribution of clothing and other necessities that were sent, however belatedly, to the Crimea. Lucan and Cardigan were blamed for failing to bring up fodder to the cavalry camp, and for not having had the horses hutted and stabled until the winter was well advanced.

Lucan did not shine as a witness. He came near losing control of himself when under examination, and the papers were delighted to comment on his obvious bad temper. But Cardigan, whose habitual self-confidence seemed to increase when he faced opposition, was cool and collected, ready with plausible answers that were borne out by other parts of the evidence, as they were later to be by a former member of the Staff who, far from being friendly, was ready to injure Cardigan whenever he could.

Cardigan appeared before the Board on 30th April. He was undoubtedly the principal character in the affair, the man whom most of the spectators present had come to see. A witness observed that he faced his questioners "cheerfully"; and certainly the core of his defence was of the kind that no soldier could challenge, since it was based on orders received from superior authority.

As in Airey's case, the actual cause of failing to bring up fodder for the horses was lack of transport. In spite of losses through the hurricane and the breakdown of commissariat arrangements, there was fodder at the Balaclava base. But, said Cardigan, a good many horses, more than a hundred, would have had to go down daily to bring it to the camp: and their being detached from the small cavalry force then existing would have rendered that force ineffective if the Russian thrust, feared by Canrobert, had materialized.

This would have defeated the very purpose that Canrobert had in mind when, against Raglan's wishes, he insisted that the cavalry be moved to the position it came to occupy near Inkerman. Cardigan had represented to Raglan the folly of keeping the cavalry there, but Canrobert's will had prevailed; and Cardigan's statement was in keeping with the testimony of Major Calthorpe, who on another occasion was to say that the positioning of the Light Brigade had been brought about "chiefly by the desire of General Canrobert".

Cardigan thus easily disposed of the charge he was called upon to face, venturing to hope, as he did so, that such a charge "was inconsistent with his whole professional career". The audience broke into applause when he concluded; and since even *The Times* could not seriously impugn the vital fact by which he was exonerated, it had to be content with observing that Cardigan's defence was couched "in the usual style of circuitous crimination of which the country has latterly seen so much"—meaning, of course, his exchange of angry letters with Lucan.

The proceedings lasted into the first week of July, and altogether some forty meetings were held. The same questions were repeated, and the same answers given. Colonel Tulloch, who was constantly under fire from the board and from the various witnesses, finally had a physical breakdown. When it became clear that any forthcoming blame was going to be levelled at 'the system' (meaning impersonal elements such as supply and commissariat departments) and that no individual was likely to be humiliated or disgraced, public interest flagged, though some of the more sanguine ladies sat on and applied themselves (while keeping one ear at the ready for any suggestion of scandal) to their knitting and sewing. Their needles moved so industriously that before the board broke up "various elaborate patterns in fancy work and ingenious devices for consuming silk, patience and time were advanced a stage".

'The system' was condemned for having proved incapable of

coping with the exigencies of the Crimean campaign. The army, serving far away and in the grip of a terrible winter, had no reserves, no transport, no organization for supply. The resulting disasters were beyond the power of any individual to control. Each had done his best in the face of exceptional difficulties and hardship—though the board implied that transport to and from the base might have continued possible if the horses had been moved to a less unfavourable position than that which had been recommended by Canrobert and reluctantly assented to by Raglan.

Such a move might have been attempted if Lucan and Cardigan had worked together to obtain the necessary sanction, but, the board summed up, "there is too much reason to fear, from the official correspondence of these noblemen, that there had not been between them that cordiality of feeling which is essential to effective co-operation in the field".

Those sections of the Press which had hoped to be presented with a scapegoat, preferably in the person of Cardigan or Lucan, were disappointed by the luke-warm or negative conclusions arrived at by the 'White-washing Board', as they now called it. Were those incompetent officers, who between them 'had destroyed one-third of the Army committed to their care", to be acquitted? Readers were reminded that the blood of ten thousand gallant veterans was crying from the ground for vengeance.

But the troops who had suffered seldom spoke with anything like the virulence of those civilian voices that demanded retribution as strongly as once they had advocated war: while Cardigan, for his part, felt as free from blame in the matter as he did from responsibility for the Balaclava charge.

5

The sudden appearance of Lord Cardigan at a West Country wedding, in the spring of 1856, caused some annoyance. For one thing, he was not expected: for another, the bridegroom was Captain Robert Portal of the 4th Light Dragoons, one of Cardigan's brigade who entertained far from friendly feelings towards his commanding officer. Lord George Paget was best man, while also present was Captain Morris of the 17th Lancers, whose wife, Amelia, was a sister of the bride. Both Paget and Morris shared Portal's opinion of Cardigan.

The bride was Miss Eliza Taylor, a daughter of Major-General Thomas William Taylor, who had served in India and at Waterloo before becoming lieutenant-governor of the Royal Military College, Sandhurst. Eliza's brother-in-law was Sir Walter Carew, a full-blooded Victorian squire who overcame everyone by the sheer weight of his tongue, a propensity which was inherited, though in somewhat lesser degree, by his daughter Bessie. Lord Palmerston, who was then Prime Minister, was among the guests, while also included were Sir Colin Campbell and Admiral Lyons.

This wedding at the village of West Ogwell, near Newton Abbot, might have been regarded as a Crimean occasion, though it was blemished by the arrival of Cardigan who, as Bessie wrote in her diary, "no one particularly wanted to see". She observed him closely during the wedding breakfast. The one person he obviously got on with was her formidable father, perhaps because Sir Walter, like Cardigan, never disguised the fact that he put his own feelings first, but also because, as Miss Bessie noted, "they both liked champagne".

In a speech after the breakfast Palmerston, in paying tribute to the bride, remarked on the good fortune that had come her way in choosing one of the heroes of the Light Brigade, "of whom England was so proud". At this point Cardigan, who had been steadily regaling himself with the queen of wines, interjected a vigorous "Hear, hear!" which surprised them all and added to Miss Bessie's annoyance. "As if Lord Palmerston", she afterwards confided to her diary, "was including him!"

There were several occasions throughout the summer that enabled Cardigan to appear before the public, still wearing the "halo of heroism" that, unlike the sarcastic columnist who penned the phrase, many people were only too ready to accord him. He was present, again mounted on Ronald, in Hyde Park, when the Guards under the Duke of Cambridge were reviewed by the Queen and Prince Albert on 9th July.

It was lovely weather, one of 'the Queen's days'. Church bells pealed, the fronts of public buildings were hung with red cloth, excited ladies showered branches of laurel on the bronzed and bearded veterans and on their Colours bearing the tatters made by

Russian shot at the Alma and in the shambles of Inkerman. At the end of the ceremony, when the Guards formed in square behind a cordon of Household Cavalry and Light Dragoons, the enthusiasm rose to such heights that the people broke through: and Cardigan, although of course not a Guardsman, responded to and formally acknowledged the cheers with the gesture, made popular by the Duke, of fingers raised to his hat.

The strains of "The Conquering Hero" were heard at Sheffield in July when the city entertained Cardigan at a banquet at the Royal Hotel, "where the wines were choice and abundant" And the chorus greeted him at Leeds, at the end of August, when a public dinner was held in his honour at the Stock Exchange Hall. Here he was presented with a Mameluke-pattern sabre, richly chased, with a double scabbard of silver gilt, purchased for a sum of 250 guineas raised by public subscription.

The chairman of the reception committee, a Mr. Beecroft, referred to Cardigan's gallantry at Balaclava, the name of which valley had become "a password in the soldier's mouth". Then came a tribute to their guest's sense of duty. Although in possession of great wealth and high honours at home, he had cheerfully responded to the call of Queen and country at the start of the struggle, "and hastened to the scene of war, desolation and death, with alacrity and devotion". That high regard for duty had been uppermost in Cardigan's mind when he received the fatal order to charge at Balaclava: for although he was a British peer, concluded Mr. Beecroft, he was ready to obey the commands of his superior officer "let the consequences be what they might".

When Cardigan rose, he announced that he intended to say but a very few words in reply. But he soon got into his stride, and launched into a description of events leading up to Balaclava. He was probably aware of a new whispering campaign that was starting against him, for he proceeded to outline the duties of a cavalry general who leads a cavalry brigade into action, about which, he stated, one or two fallacies were being entertained.

> One would suppose, from what has been said, that when a charge of cavalry is ordered, the general officer commanding a brigade has nothing to do but to wave his sword and gallop off, his men following him, and come into personal contact with the enemy troops.
> Gentlemen, no such thing is the case. The duties of a cavalry

general, in leading a charge, are very important. In the first place, it is his duty to keep the regiments together: secondly, it is his duty to lead them at such a regular pace, under any fire to which they may be exposed, that when they come into contact with the enemy, they may attack him with a proper and full impetus. Further, it is necessary that, under any fire to which they may be exposed during the advance, the general officer should keep the adjustment of his regiments.

I believe there is no person who was present, and there are many persons who were spectators (for the hills on all sides were covered with our own troops and those of our Allies) who will deny that the leading of the regiments of the Light Brigade into the battery on the day of Balaclava was a firm, satisfactory and compact one, well and gallantly supported by the three other regiments belonging to the Brigade, which came on in succession under their respective commanding officers.

Cardigan emphasized that it was not the duty of a general officer commanding cavalry to fight the enemy, with and among private soldiers, on contact. He quoted the example of "that noble Hussar, Lord Anglesey, who frequently commanded cavalry", and instances of the Peninsular War and Waterloo, where generals did not raise a sword against the enemy.

In all this Cardigan was strictly correct, speaking with a professional soldier's knowledge of the responsibility in which he had been trained. His speech should have been accepted as a sober admonition intended for newspaper critics who were always at his heels, and who even now refused to be silent. For a few days later the *Daily News* returned to the offensive by complaining that "the first thing you see on opening a newspaper is the account of some banquet to some Crimean hero, at which he is generally presented with a magnificent sword. . . . Let after dinner orators applaud the bulldog courage of the soldiers to the very echo, but keep silent on the achievements of most of the general officers."

The *Daily News* attack was pressed home some time later at a dinner given to Captain Morris, of the 17th Lancers, at Torrington, Devon. The principal speaker was Colonel Buck, Tory M.P. for Barnstaple, who compared Cardigan's attitude in explaining his tactics at Balaclava with that of Captain Morris. There was nothing in the conduct of their gallant guest, said Colonel Buck, "so equivocal as to require such an explanation about the duties of cavalry officers as that made by the Earl of

Cardigan at Leeds". As a further disparagement, Colonel Buck repeated the story that Cardigan had paid £40,000 for his position in the army.

A report of the speech appeared in the *Daily News*, and Cardigan took up the challenge by writing to Colonel Buck. The latter had, of course, been at fault, as Cardigan's exposition of cavalry duties applied only to generals when leading a brigade in a charge. They could not possibly apply to Morris, who was only a captain. The forced comparison attempted by Colonel Buck was therefore without point, and his case was further weakened when he explained to Cardigan that the *Daily News* had credited him with words that he never said.

Cardigan followed up by telling the Colonel that nothing could be more unsatisfactory, unstraightforward and evasive than his reply. He (Cardigan) was the victim of anonymous libellers, and Buck's insinuations made at Torrington "were probably founded upon the calumnious statements of some anonymous publication, which the respectable parts of the Press were too generous to encourage by any notice"; and besides saying this Cardigan availed himself of the opportunity to present the Colonel with another precise summary of the charge and his own part in it.

One of the several military occasions at which Cardigan figured was the distribution of the first Victoria Crosses in Hyde Park on 26th June 1857. Crowds were arriving in the Park by seven o'clock in the morning. A mellow midsummer mist enveloped the scene, with the bronze figure of Achilles (then recently erected) towering in the foreground. By the time the Queen arrived, wearing a red tunic with purple skirt, a hat with a red and white plume, and a general's sash, a broiling sun was beating down to make the day the hottest known in London for forty years. The Royal Standard marking the centre of the ceremony drooped in a breathless air. With the Queen were the members of her family, with Prince William Frederick of Prussia, and a group of general officers including Cardigan, who was to lead his old regiment, the 11th Hussars, in a review when the crosses had been given out.

Most of the people were packed forty deep in the public parts, their view entirely shut off by a thick wedge of police and mounted troops. Stands of sloping boards were provided for the

privileged spectators. But most of the front places were occupied
by officers whose shakos and helmets obstructed the view of those
behind. There were cries of "hats off" and even some swearing,
this last being uttered (as one paper reported) "in a more audible
tone than is generally allowed to good society in public". But even
so, the paper went on, "aged persons, delicate ladies and others of
low stature saw no more of the glorious transactions of the day
than the vendors of lemonade and ginger beer".

The gunfire salute that greeted the Queen's arrival was the
loudest so far to be heard in London. Sweeps who were busy at
their task in tall West End chimneys felt their bricked-in world
rocking about them and feared they were going to be blown out.
More than sixty soldiers and sailors came forward to receive the
illustrious decoration from the hands of the Queen: and afterwards Cardigan, in full uniform and mounted on Ronald, led the
11th in a slow march past the saluting base to the tune of
"Coburg".

6

It was the summer of 1858. A dawn light was breaking over the
roofs of Mayfair. The streets were deserted save for the figure of
a man who was knocking on the door of a house in Norfolk
Street. Because of the early hour the knocking continued, rousing
first a servant then the lady occupant of the house, who was
Adeline de Horsey. She started from bed and flung on a dressing-
gown as the bolts were being drawn. She heard someone rushing up-
stairs and seconds later Cardigan, throwing open the door, caught
her in his arms before she could recover from her initial surprise.

"My dearest," he exclaimed. "She's dead!"

There was no need for Adeline to ask his meaning, especially as
Cardigan continued, "Let's get married at once."

He had come directly from the death-bed of his wife, Elizabeth,
who had been ill for some time. Her death, apart from a feeling
of relief, made no impression upon him. It was thirty years since
her fragile figure, her eyes limpid with appeal, her delicate mouth
and cloud of hair, had caused him to hurry to Ham House with
the eagerness he now showed in hastening to Norfolk Street. He
carried with him now a brief memory of a pitifully wasted body,

lustreless hair, and a mouth ruined by drooping at the corners. Adeline was a healthy 33, a woman with an outdoor instinct that in several respects made her similar to himself. "Let's get married at once."

He gave orders for his yacht to be fitted out, and travelled to the Isle of Wight with a party of friends including some of the Pagets and Hubert de Burgh. They set off for Gibraltar, where Adeline and her brother Algernon were to join them. While anchored in Lisbon harbour for the evening a hurricane occurred that might have reminded Cardigan of the far greater storm that had ravaged the Crimea. His yacht escaped, but other vessels went down or were tossed and blown about like shells. Distress signals were heard. Crowds came down to the beach, and the master of Cardigan's yacht told him that another vessel was in danger. No Portuguese boat would venture out, so Cardigan put to sea and sighted a raft bearing the survivors of a wreck. He took the raft in tow and landed the survivors, fourteen men and a poodle, while crowds cheered the Englishman and his crew for braving a gale that daunted their own seamen.

The couple were married by special licence in the Garrison Chapel, Gibraltar, by the Assistant Chaplain to the Forces, Charles Moore. There were doubtless those, in England, who smiled when they read of Adeline wearing a white silk gown, draped with a blue scarf, and a large hat adorned with feathers. The reception was at the British Embassy, where a ball was held in the evening. They lived for a week of dances and dinners on the yacht, which then followed the coast round to Barcelona, while Cardigan went by rail to Madrid.

He arrived there on 16th October, in time to witness a review of 60,000 troops in honour of the birthday of Queen Isabella II. Knowing Cardigan, it is safe to assume that he registered disapproval of troops descended from those whom Wellington had found such doubtful allies—and had not the Duke's brother said that he wouldn't trust the protection of a favourite dog to the whole Spanish Army?

From Barcelona the party went on to Leghorn. The long crossing of 500 miles across the Ligurian Sea was rough and stormy. Lady Cardigan was the only one not to fall sick, and since the cook was prostrate for most of the time Cardigan's table, for once, lacked not only luxuries but necessities. They went ashore at Elba, and stood on the spot from where a shortish figure, in legendary grey coat and cocked hat, had boarded the brig that took him to his last adventure at Waterloo.

Then came a six-hour carriage journey to Rome, where they were met by a company of Papal Guards, sent by Pope Pius IX, to escort them to the Vatican. The Pope who, but for poor health, might have followed the same profession as Cardigan, gave them his blessing. The Cardigans had many friends in Rome where Adeline, besides making "a delightful sojourn", saw "everything worth seeing"—before going on to Genoa, again by sea, and travelling from there by rail to Paris.

All the civilized world seemed to be centred upon that delectable era of the Second Empire: and Adeline found Paris, with its round of dances and concerts, where a box at the Opera afforded sights of everyone who had made their name in the world of art, or of scandal, "a city of delight". And if sometimes the violins took on a plaintive note, and the wistful face of Elizabeth (but not with drooping mouth) looked out from fashionable parades at the Palais Royal or the Tuileries, one of the last to notice would have been Cardigan, who was playing the role of a mature husband, renovated by the novelty of a honeymoon, to perfection.

Back in England, they spent a few days at the Cardigan mansion in Portman Square. The year had been a remarkable one for London in many ways. There had been storms that shattered the roofs and ceilings, then a period of intense heat that made the Thames, poisoned by "the rejectamenta from over two and a half million people", stink like a sewer, until even the Commons, used as they were to stenches, found it intolerable; and at the height of summer, in daytime, a strange darkness, not caused by fog, spread over the city where people moved and went about their business by candlelight.

It was mid-December when Lord and Lady Cardigan moved into their regular family residence. The gossip that was started in some exalted quarters by the appearance of Adeline, who, from being a distant shadowy figure, was now securely and legally a part of the glory reflected by the Balaclava hero, was not current in the Midland villages: and six hundred tenants from the Cardigan estates, mounted on horseback in the medieval style, met and escorted the Earl's carriage to Deene Park.

There was still, however, a minor point concerning his marriage that Cardigan's tidy mind determined to settle. It was discovered that, in making out the licence, Adeline's surname had been spelt as "Horsay". Under that spelling, instead of Horsey, it had been copied into the register. Cardigan engaged a Q.C., Doctor Phillimore, to investigate the matter, and a ruling was finally given that the marriage was perfectly valid. One may safely assume that Cardigan, in requiring this, was actuated by legal rather than by strictly moral considerations.

Cardigan was now 60. He was the type of man whom some much younger women (and Adeline was 33), often those with artistic interests or pretensions, find attractive: tall in figure (he never gained noticeable weight) and erect as a ramrod; with a thinnish face, a high-bridged nose, and keen blue eyes that gathered up all within reach; independent to the point of being careless of praise or blame, but ready to accept praise as his due; always courteous to women, a quality bred in him by the bevy of handsome young females with whom he grew up; his general air of self-contained pride completed by a well-trained growth of whisker and moustache proper to a cavalry 'swell' who had spurred his way through an ordeal unique in the annals of war.

It might have been supposed that a period untroubled by controversy was ahead of him. As Inspector-General of Cavalry, he was remote from the day-to-day stresses of regimental existence. Always a fearless rider, the excitement of the hunting field could now be shared with his wife, for Adeline, unlike the first Lady Cardigan, was an expert at home in the saddle. There were structural improvements and lavish entertainments to plan at Deene Park, with visits to London and the Isle of Wight at appropriate seasons.

But the promised calm was short-lived. His life had been such that the eddies formed by his legacy of trouble were long in dying down: and circles that remained implacably opposed to the 'conquering hero' were now spreading a story, by means of hints in the Press and whispers in the clubs, that he had never ridden at the head of his brigade through the valley of death.

7

The story started with a book that was published in December

1856. It was entitled *Letters from Head-Quarters, or the Realities of War in the Crimea,* by an Officer on the Staff. The identity of that officer was not at once revealed: but it soon became known that he was the Hon. Somerset Gough Calthorpe, a lieutenant in the 8th Hussars at the time of writing the book. He was Lord Raglan's nephew and he had served on the Staff during the war. The book was based on letters he had written and on information gained while acting as Raglan's aide-de-camp.

One of the stories covered was naturally the charge of the Light Brigade, and Calthorpe treated this in a manner that was highly offensive to the man who had led it. Calthorpe maintained that Cardigan, after riding at the head of his regiments for most of the way, never entered the Russian battery. Instead he reined back, and made a premature retirement while the rest of his brigade swept on. The offending passage dealt with the climax of the charge, when the front line was about to clash with the Russian gunners. The passage ran: "This was the moment when a general was most required, but unfortunately Lord Cardigan was not present. On coming up to the battery (as he afterwards described it) a gun was fired close to him, and for a moment he thought his leg was gone. Such was not the case as he remained unhurt: however, his horse took fright—swerved round—and galloped off with him to the rear, passing on the way by the 4th Light Dragoons and 8th Hussars, before those regiments got up to the battery."

Those words cast a double reflection on Cardigan—that he never actually entered the battery, and that he was carried back by the bolting of his frightened horse. But neither event, as most people knew, was in keeping with his character. His dash and courage in the field, with a readiness to err on the side of recklessness, had never been doubted; his many opponents had always been silent on that score; and he was easily the master of every horse he encountered.

But however much it lacked foundation, Calthorpe's attack was welcomed by those who were ever ready to strike at Cardigan. There were hints in the Press to give it substance; gossip provided the usual spate of variations: the 'conquering hero' might well be veering towards a topple.

Cardigan, who resented the slight on his horsemanship almost as much as the slur upon his courage, experienced a natural and growing resentment. Then he became enraged. He communicated with Calthorpe and demanded a modification of his statements. When this was refused, he sent an army colleague and his friend de Burgh to remonstrate with Calthorpe, who still remained obdurate: and when it became clear that there would be no withdrawal, Cardigan set out to damage Calthorpe.

The latter, who was now a major, was on the point of transferring from the 8th Hussars to the 5th Dragoon Guards: and when the change had been effected he was appointed A.D.C. to the Earl of Carlisle, Lord Lieutenant of Ireland. Cardigan first tried to prevent the transfer, and begged the help of the Prince Consort, who, as he usually did in such cases, declined to intervene. Cardigan then applied to the Earl of Carlisle, pressing for Calthorpe's dismissal from his Staff appointment in Dublin.

But Carlisle replied that "while Major Calthorpe is thought worthy to continue in the Queen's service, I cannot dismiss a friend, a relative, and a young officer". There still remained a court martial as a possible means of redress; but the Duke of Cambridge, who was Commander-in-Chief, refused such a procedure by saying that it was not within his military capacity to notice *anonymous* publications—though by then it was well known that Major Calthorpe was the author.

The controversy stretched over months. During that time Calthorpe, far from consolidating his ground, failed to hold it. "That I may have been in error in certain instances," he wrote, "I am ready to admit"; while the following letter, supporting Cardigan, appeared in *The Times* on 10th February 1857. It came from William Cory, who had served with the 11th Hussars in the Crimea.

"I was in the Light Brigade charge at Balaclava. The assertion that Lord Cardigan retired between the advancing squadrons of the 8th Hussars and the 4th Light Dragoons is palpably untrue— and for this reason. His Lordship was in front of the whole Brigade leading, and these two regiments, forming the second line, passed the guns almost simultaneously with the first, and, becoming instantly engaged in hand-to-hand conflict, could not preserve the compact order of their advance for him to retire between them, had it been possible for him to extricate himself so easily."

In the same month Cardigan, still on the offensive, spoke of the matter before the House of Lords. Some years earlier, he said, when a man's character had been maligned, he could uphold himself by appealing to the laws of honour. But duelling was no longer practised. "If it were merely a question of the present, these allegations might have been passed over on account of the insignificance of the officer by whom they have been brought forward." But to be published in a book made them matter of history.

He asked Lord Panmure, Secretary for War, if he deemed it right that a junior officer should be permitted to malign his superior officer, and continue to hold an honourable Staff appointment in Ireland. He requested that all future editions of the book be stopped.

In his reply, Lord Panmure said that he would "strongly recommend the noble Earl to rest upon the high testimonials which he has in his possession to refute the injustice to which he has been subjected". He reminded Cardigan that he had a course open to him in an appeal to civil tribunals.

It is unlikely that Cardigan would have been content to rest upon the subdued satisfaction of testimonials. But in any case he awaited the appearance of a third edition of Calthorpe's book in the following year. When he saw it, he took on a new lease of indignation. Calthorpe put forward two different reasons for not withdrawing any of his former statements: one, that it would have been inconvenient to the publishers and to himself; the other that it was "too late"—though the controversy had started in 1856.

But apart from these evasions, Calthorpe added a footnote that repeated the slighting references to Cardigan's conduct at Balaclava. The footnote ran:

The Earl of Cardigan has stated, since the publication of the first edition of this book, that he considers the account given of the part taken by him in the Light Brigade charge "unworthy of any reply, as it is well known" that he led the Light Brigade up to the Russian cavalry in rear of the battery, and "that the 8th Hussars did not advance as far as the battery, but became engaged with the Russian cavalry short of it". The author could only rely on statements furnished him by officers engaged in the charge: but as the excellence of Lord Cardigan's horsemanship is unquestionable, the idea that his horse ran away with him is no doubt erroneous! Several officers of the 4th Light Dragoons and 8th Hussars bear witness to the fact that his Lordship retired between these regiments as they were advancing, and it has been confidently asserted to the author, by two senior officers of the 8th Hussars who were present, that their regiment was not halted until it had gone 300 yards beyond the Russian battery, when it was wheeled about for the purpose of attacking the enemy's cavalry, which had assembled in its rear.

The implication that he had galloped from the field so angered Cardigan that he applied to the Court of the Queen's Bench, for a rule calling upon Calthorpe to show cause why a criminal information should not be exhibited against him for libel. The court at first objected, saying that Cardigan had allowed two editions of the book to appear without applying for such a rule, and that his complaint followed upon the publication of a third edition some years later.

But the rule was finally granted, and the case came up for judgment on 10th June in Westminster Hall. Lord Chief Justice Cockburn, assisted by three other judges, presided. Mr. Bovill, Q.C., and Mr. Garth, a junior counsel, appeared for Cardigan. Calthorpe was represented by Mr. Coleridge, Q.C., and Mr. Serjeant Shee.

The hearing opened with the reading of affidavits from survivors of the 17th Lancers, who had ridden in the front line at Balaclava. These declared that Cardigan, after entering the Russian battery, had penetrated some way beyond it—and this testimony, by men who had been in the charge, was in marked contrast to the weak counter-declarations advanced by Calthorpe.

He admitted that he had only *watched* the Light Brigade advance, and that its movements were soon hidden by smoke. "I cannot, therefore, of my own knowledge, say anything respecting the conduct of Lieutenant-General the Earl of Cardigan on that occasion."

From that it needed but a few steps of legal argument before Calthorpe's counsel agreed that his client's original contention had rested upon a mistake. But while agreeing that Cardigan had indeed entered the Russian battery, Calthorpe now insisted that Cardigan had ridden away from the guns as quickly as he could.

To support this, Calthorpe claimed that several officers and men of the 8th Hussars and 4th Light Dragoons had declared on oath that Cardigan was making for the rear while their regiments (neither of which had been in the front line) were approaching the battery.

This shifting of ground, this "substituting of one libel by another", as the Lord Chief Justice called it, was immediately seized on by Cardigan's counsel; and in attempting to make light of this, it was pleaded that the different statements advanced by Calthorpe were due to "a very natural mistake". Mr. Coleridge now went so far as to say it was "utterly immaterial" whether Lord Cardigan rode into the midst of the enemy guns or not; while Mr. Garth added to Calthorpe's discomfiture by quoting him as saying, "I cheerfully declare myself satisfied that the Earl entered the Russian batteries."

Mr. Garth pointed out that "regretfully", or some other expression of apology, might well have replaced the word "cheerfully" when applied to the case in hand. "But", he went on, "such was the spirit in which this young officer thought it becoming to deal with the military reputation and personal character of a general officer of such high standing in the army."

Without calling on Cardigan to refute the evidence advanced against him, the Lord Chief Justice, in his summing up, said that the charge went "to the root of that which is the very foundation of the soldier's character, which is courage". Major Calthorpe's book contained a most serious libel on the Earl of Cardigan by implying that he lacked personal courage in discharging his military duty. The later imputation made by Calthorpe was totally different from the one he originally preferred: and the Lord Chief Justice agreed with Mr. Garth that Calthorpe's admission of having brought an unfounded charge "might have been made in a more generous spirit than it was". His closing statement, that "those who criticize the conduct of men placed in such trying circumstances would do well to ask themselves how they would have acted in a similar state of things", was greeted with applause.

But while recognizing the essential fairness of the summing up, it must still be asked how certain soldiers testified on oath to having seen Cardigan retiring from the battery as the 8th Hussars and 4th Light Dragoons were sweeping on. Not all those witnesses agreed with Calthorpe's contention that Cardigan had passed between those regiments, which formed the third line of the Light Brigade. Some declared that Cardigan had ridden past the left, or outer flank of the 4th Light Dragoons, who, as well as being on the left of the line, veered further to the left in order to avoid the limber carriages as soon as they entered the battery, while the 8th Hussars swerved to the right.

For Cardigan to have been well on the left, it would have been necessary for him to have cut his way, single-handed, through the Russian gunners, and then have diverged to the right in order to come out between the two regiments of the advancing third line. Such a feat would have been impossible, and it certainly never figured even among the most extravagant claims made by Cardigan.

But those who declared they had seen Cardigan emerge in that way did so in perfect good faith. For the figure they saw was that of Lieutenant Houghton of the 11th Hussars, who, apart from being in uniform similar to that worn by Cardigan, had been mounted on a chestnut charger that closely resembled Ronald. Houghton was mortally wounded early in the charge, and when seen by witnesses, amid the smoke and confusion, he was riding alone and at slow pace up the north side of the valley. Lieutenant Hunt, of the 4th Light Dragoons, shared the experience of those who were deceived by noting the likeness between the two chargers.

This case, the last of several in which he was involved, had not been of Cardigan's seeking. The Press, for once, endorsed a result that vindicated Cardigan, together with the favourable comments voiced by the Lord Chief Justice: though Greville wrote in his diary that "the world is weary of Cardigan and his fanfaronades, and of Crimean accusations and recriminations, and it is time that the subject should be allowed to drop".

But the army, as well as the Press, hailed Cardigan as the gainer, knowing full well the difference in proven calibre between a young aide who, in absolute safety, watched (and who was later to criticize) and the man who maintained parade ground order while leading his troops on their last heroic ride.

8

Whilst allowing for the effusiveness of her nature, there is no reason to doubt Lady Cardigan's description of her marriage as "a veritable romance". "No two people", she went on to say, "could be better suited." Both had tolerance and understanding—qualities that count for more in human relationship than any gifts of intellect. For while it is true that Cardigan had a jealous instinct that made him inordinately proud of his possessions (and he regarded his wife as one of these) his jealousy was not of the deadly kind that ruins normal life. It found expression in little things, such as putting aside guests and always giving his arm to his wife when dinner was announced. For some time this noticeable habit flattered her, but later she found it an embarrassment and asked that she might be 'taken in' by someone else.

Cardigan's feeling of pride extended over Deene Park and everything connected with it. For years the Brudenell estates had been noted for the venison they provided; and when, during dinner one night, Lady Cardigan ventured to criticize the course, Cardigan's ancestral instincts were deeply wounded. He ordered the servants out of the room, and during their absence he forbade Lady Cardigan ever to make disparaging remarks about the Deene venison again.

But neither she, nor the servants, were greatly perturbed by the frequent outbursts of Cardigan's fiery nature. They knew that his temper was not only short, but short-lived; and his servants regarded him with the same mingled feelings of respect, admiration, and near devotion that he inspired in most of the private soldiers (those infallible judges of character!) whom he had commanded.

Lady Cardigan was well fitted to look after herself; and when her husband's temper threatened to exceed its usual bounds she bombarded him with crockery that she snatched from the table, and so cooled him down. But there was one feature of Cardigan's early life that never ceased to rankle in her mind, and that even the luxury of breaking plates was powerless to relieve. She could not endure any mention or reminder of the first Lady Cardigan; and when she discovered that an attractive miniature, standing on a table to which it had been relegated some years before, was of her predecessor, this memento was promptly hurled on the floor and crushed into fragments by Adeline's heel.

But while repeating that tolerance and understanding counted for much in their marriage, it is possible to suspect that both tended to exaggerate its almost idyllic nature. Lady Cardigan's expressed belief that no one "could be a more devoted husband

than Lord Cardigan" was matched by his assertion that they were
never apart for one hour out of the twenty-four. Yet he not
infrequently took 'mysterious ladies of the half-world' (as they
were then called) to a little tower that stood in the grounds. These
incidents were never mentioned between them, though Lady
Cardigan confided to her agent that he (Lord Cardigan) "thought
I didn't know, but I never interfered with him".

If Cardigan bore any recurring grudge against his second wife
it was probably because she followed the fashion of the first Lady
Cardigan in failing to bear him children. His illegitimate brood
could not overcome the chagrin he felt in knowing that he
would indeed go down as "the last of the Brudenells", a fact that
weighed but lightly upon his wife, who, while being as great an
egoist as himself, could hardly endorse his feeling of family pride.

But it was part of his nature to believe that Lady Cardigan
shared his regret at their childless state, as was made clear one
Christmas Eve when he found the villagers decorating the nearby
church. On one of the walls was an illuminated text with the
quotation from Isaiah, "Unto us a child is born, unto us a son is
given." Cardigan told them to take it down as the words
"reflected on her Ladyship".

Always a music lover, Cardigan, engaged a Monsieur Holstein
to act as Master of the Chapel Music at Deene Park, to which
somewhat grandiloquent title was added a salary of £100 for one
year. A village band was also formed, and enthusiastic local
players met twice weekly for practice in the musicians' gallery
of the Cardigan's ballroom. On Adeline's birthday she was
roused at seven o'clock in the morning by the strains of the
band playing beneath her bedroom window. The bandsmen were
given breakfast, after which they paraded through the village
while the church bells rang to rival their music.

On Sundays the full rigour of Victorian religious observance
permeated the atmosphere of the Cardigan household. The servants, all in black with the women wearing soberly trimmed
bonnets, were drawn up in line to undergo inspection by the
military eye of their master. Every man and maid who could be
spared from duty was expected to be present, and those who
defaulted, without valid excuse, felt the rough edge of a tongue
that had long since known how to castigate.

Then came the measured silent walk to the parish church of St.

Peter, where the Earl, in his frock coat and with his silk top hat resting beside him in the family pew, was united in simple faith with the farmers and tenants in their solemn broadcloth. His military fame had made Cardigan a tradition, a human landmark: and thirty years after his death the villagers still spoke of him in a friendly, familiar way, as though his tall figure might at any moment enter into their circle.

According to Lady Cardigan, her husband "never seemed to attach any importance" to the part he played in the war. But such reticence is not in keeping with what we know of his character, while it is contradicted by the many large pictures he commissioned and that now dominate the walls at Deene Park: each one commemorating the exploits of the immortal Hussar riding at the head of his squadrons, leading them into the fury of massed guns, or repelling the thrust of Cossack lances. He also commissioned two silver statuettes of himself mounted on Ronald.

On one occasion, when discussing Crimean memories, Lady Cardigan asked what he was thinking as he rode into the valley of death. "Of what was I thinking? Why,"—there was no hesitation, the answer was always seething in his mind—"what that damned fellow Nolan meant by asking if the Light Brigade was afraid."

Cardigan was a life-long sufferer from the cold, and Deene Park, like most other residences of its kind, was plagued by draughts. The prevailing low temperature, though sixteen men were employed to tend the fires, drew as many complaints from Cardigan as had the Russian winter, and he eventually had some early kind of heating apparatus installed to take the chill from the air.

Another improvement was an immense bath sunk in the floor of one of the turrets. It was lined with marble and approached by marble steps. Cardigan fairly exerted himself to make the house remarkable for comfort and hospitality: a score of men were busy throughout the winter preserving ice for use in summer. But touching his own peace of mind, there was a positive ban, imposed by a section of society, that he never overcame, and that preyed upon his mind perhaps more persistently than the grievance he felt over having no legitimate offspring.

It was levelled against his wife, who, by the circumstances of her elopement and subsequent alliance with Cardigan, and also because of the questionable company to be found at Deene, at

Portman Square, or at Cowes, was judged to have offended against the strict moral code that applied, in tacit principle at least, to the ladies of her day. An element of jealousy no doubt entered into the stricture; for the vivacious Adeline outshone many of her critics in personal attainments and appearance.That Cardigan's repeated praise of her "graceful carriage" and "fine horsemanship" was well deserved was apparent to every rider in the Row. But the presence of the couple, as it had earlier done, still caused a contour of isolation to be drawn about them: and Lady Cardigan, who cared nothing for reputation, continued by her free and easy manners to justify the scandal that caused many London and some of the great provincial houses to be closed against her.

This social ostracism weighed more heavily upon Cardigan, who tried in vain to overcome it. He told his relatives that to acknowledge Lady Cardigan, even by a formal call, would be better than nothing. He went out of his way to renew or continue friendships, with the hope of bringing her into line with them. But as soon as this was detected he countered a polite but none the less cold shoulder. One of his sisters, egged on by her husband, declared that she would never enter Deene Park, which was "an infamous house"; and in course of time Cardigan, with a consistent loyalty that does him credit, deliberately refused to enter circles, or to accept invitations, that excluded Adeline.

The known attitude of the Queen towards Cardigan and his wife set the pattern for many. The brief period during which she had been more woman than Queen in surrendering to the current hero-worship of Cardigan was now part of a conveniently forgotten past. She gathered her ample skirts about her thick ankles and decided to eradicate the pictorial reminder of that time conveyed by Sant's painting of Cardigan with herself, and the royal children, in the Great Gallery of Windsor Castle. She was there shown standing a little behind the Prince of Wales: but now she gave instructions for her portrait to be painted over and blotted out. For some years, in a certain light, her outline could still be traced. Later it vanished, and with its disappearance the peace of a virtue well satisfied with itself descended over the mausoleum at Frogmore.

The Queen's repudiation of Cardigan was again reflected when

15

his claim to be nominated as colonel of one of the Household Cavalry regiments was put forward. Such an appointment, she objected, would bring him into contact with the Court: and for the sake of her ladies the Queen returned a firm "No!"

But it needed more than a series of bans and refusals to take the heart out of Cardigan when it came to crying up his own deserts. Most men carry a dream of their past into later life, and Cardigan had long since cherished the hope of becoming Lord Lieutenant of Northamptonshire.

When Lord Exeter, who had held the post, died in 1867, Cardigan repeated his application; and once again the Prime Minister, who was now Lord Derby, regretted that he was unable to submit the name of Cardigan to the Queen.

This final disappointment, together with the resentment caused by society's rejection of his wife, made Cardigan reflect, with the bitterness of a cynic, on the many intrigues that went unnoticed and unpunished merely because the actors involved kept out of the limelight.

9

In Cardigan's time the landed gentry were still regarded as 'givers of bread'. Whatever their personal failings, custom and tradition had formed in most of them the knowledge that privilege could best be justified by observing a sense of responsibility towards their tenants and other dependants: and there is ample evidence, provided by local papers and by his correspondence, that Cardigan never fell short in fulfilling the duties that were part of his social position.

Even so, a great part of that evidence has been lost since Cardigan refused to let his name be published in connection with any charity. The stipulation, "You must not put my name in a subscription list," accompanied many a donation sent to secretaries who appealed to him for help. A journalist of the day said that Lord Cardigan's "good deeds have had no public setting"; and these extended to movements that differed from his own Tory and Protestant principles.

The organizers of a Roman Catholic fund for an orphans' home were astonished by the "princely amount of his subscription":

he gave a plot of land as site for a Wesleyan chapel, and he helped to build several churches and to establish institutions that were part of the national faith.

He maintained a village school, and sent his own vehicles to convey children from outlying farms and hamlets. Soup and food were distributed weekly at Deene Park to those who applied for it. At Christmas time he and his wife undertook the clothing of seventy-five boys and girls from various parishes. A Leicester journal of January 1840 records that "Lord Cardigan, with the liberal zeal of his station, caused to be delivered through the clergymen of the following parishes, of which he is nearly the sole proprietor, at Corby two fine fat beasts, and one each to the parishes of Deene, Deenethorpe, Stanion, and Glapthorn, with a quantity of bread, coals, and a quart of ale to each man, a pint to his wife, and half a pint to each of his children."

The harsh judgments of Cardigan formed by newspapermen and (mostly) anonymous correspondents were seldom echoed by the private soldiers who served under him. Early in his career Cardigan was responsible for raising a private to commissioned rank, and then, to consolidate his advancement, Cardigan provided him with £2,000, to be repaid if and when it was convenient. When Major Jenkins, of the 11th Hussars, died at Brighton, the future of his son, a theological student at Oxford, was left doubtful. Cardigan came to the rescue with the necessary sum, asking no more of the young man than that he should pay it back when he was a bishop, "but not before".

With the outbreak of war, Cardigan gave £500 to help maintain the wives and children of the regiment; further help was given to married soldiers, while care was taken to provide the men "with everything calculated to tend to their comfort in an Eastern clime". On leaving the Crimea, Cardigan gave £100 to be laid out for the benefit of sick and wounded in Florence Nightingale's hospital at Scutari.

Scattered through Cardigan's correspondence are several appeals, pages of abuse, and tokens of respect. One of the latter, addressed from Wycliffe Cottage, The Green, Tottenham, is dated September 1866, and must have followed one of Cardigan's visits to his yacht.

"If you were the gentleman [it runs] who last Monday week, in the Isle of Wight, near Ventnor, inquired of me the way to

East Dean, I shall be highly gratified to find that I had the privilege of exchanging words with the leader of the heroes of the
Balaclava charge, however much I may differ from you on some
matters. . . . My father, Captain Mark Johnson, used to speak of
you as a gallant officer, very impartial, and liked on that account,
though a martinet. Excuse my freshness, it is a proof of non-
sycophancy."

A straightforward and dignified request for help came from
a former soldier of Crimean days, George D. Beresford, of
Edinburgh, late 7th Royal Fusiliers. It is dated 22nd October 1865.
"So many years have elapsed since I had the pleasure of seeing you
that it is probable you have forgotten my very existence. Still
remembering you were very kind and good natured to me in
former days, I am encouraged to take a great liberty with you
and ask you to do me a kindness. For nearly four years I have been
laid up with paralysis and injury to the spine which has nearly
deprived me of the use of my left side, and the expenses of so long
and severe an illness have been and are more than my very
moderate finances can bear. Under these painful circumstances I
venture to ask you to lend me £50 for the space of twelve months
to assist me to pursue a course of treatment which has been most
beneficial to me."

Cardigan followed this letter up, as he also did another from
Captain Johnston, of Hampton Court, who had formerly served
with the 13th Light Dragoons in the Crimea. Johnston had been
acting as musketry inspector in the cavalry, but since that post had
recently been abolished his income had been cut down by £50 a
year. He approached Cardigan with "extreme delicacy", pointing out that "to one who had nothing but his pay with which to
support himself in a cavalry regiment this is a most serious loss,
and under the circumstances I am obliged to ask your Lordship
to use your powerful influence with such of your Lordship's
friends as may be in command of Yeomanry regiments so
that I may obtain an Adjutancy in one of them when a vacancy
occurs".

Cardigan's influence was obviously successfully applied, for a
grateful Johnston wrote a few weeks later saying it was "univer-
sally acknowledged that a soldier seldom asks your Lordship's
assistance in vain, especially one who followed and shared your
Lordship's dangers on the memorable 25th October 1854".

But the mere appearance of Cardigan's name in print was still capable of making his enemies rush to the attack. One of the most persistent of these signed himself "A Civilian", and excused himself for using the shelter of a pseudonym by saying that "Lord Cardigan uses such very spirited language that it is by no means tempting to enter into controversy with him."

The fact that Cardigan had lived on his yacht for part of the time in the Crimea came in for constant criticism—though as well as neglecting to mention his illness, some of his critics were surprisingly ignorant of certain details. The *Dryad* is sometimes referred to as the *Enchantress*, while another writer called the vessel *De Burgh*, not knowing that Hubert de Burgh was the name of Cardigan's friend.

At a banquet he attended at Southampton in the summer of 1866, Cardigan spoke on the duties of the army, which were to fight the enemy on the battlefield and to quell civil disturbances at home. This was immediately answered, by one of his political opponents, in the following strain:

We know from sad experience in this country how you proud empty-headed aristocrats will call a peaceable open-air meeting an attempt to overcome the Government, an attempt to break the peace, and then make it a pretext for employing your armed policemen and soldiers. Now I would like to ask you what glory is attached to attacking unarmed men—almost as much as attached to yourself when you lost your head in the Crimea. Real thorough soldiers would shrink from and scorn such dastardly work, they would like to be pitted against something worthy of their steel. Such infamous warfare is only fit for dandy officers, fellows who cock a glass in their eye and stare women out of countenance, talk rubbish in Rotten Row, run long bills with tradesmen, some of which they altogether forget to pay, seduce virtuous girls and turn them on the town, and then have the impertinence to call these doings "fun".

Oh heavens, what soldiers! Why, they are an eternal disgrace to the glorious uniform they wear. Real soldiers only can describe what real soldiers are. Let me name a few real ones—Clive, Wellington, Napier, Havelock, Colin Campbell, Wolfe. I think I will mention another though it is some time since he lived. I mean Oliver Cromwell. You have no doubt read of him and how he drubbed your dandy cavaliers. How about his Ironsides, eh? How the gallant Cardigan would like to meet such a regiment under such a leader! Here would be honour for you, not to ride at and cut down unarmed men.

I would like to give you and your brother aristocrats a little wholesome advice. Don't be continually insulting the people, don't be always found with their enemies. Don't be always talking of putting them down, for be assured that the day is approaching when the real people will have their rights despite your order.

It's quite a treat to go into the Park now it is cleared of your scented up dandies, and your equally scented prostitutes. The air smells wholesome and does one good, but it is thoroughly poisoned in what you are pleased to call "the season".

I see by the papers that one of your brother idlers got drunk last week while out with his woman, fell into the sea at Ryde and was drowned. What a pity all the rest of you had not been tied to him and shared the same fate, what a godsend for the democracy of England!

This heart-felt remonstrance, signed "A working man", was written in a fine near-copperplate hand which makes nonsense of some of the claims advanced on behalf of "modern education" today.

A typical request for assistance was made by the neighbour of a certain Mr. Thomas Payne of Halsey Street, near Sloane Square, who had contracted a debt of £33 with his landlord. "If Mr. Payne cannot at once satisfy this demand," wrote the neighbour, "all his furniture and every article belonging to him will be sacrificed immediately."

A widow Ann Jones who described herself as "a poor woman from Deene", but who was then the tenant of Parke Farm, Brighton, had lost four cows with the plague; she was behind with her rent to the extent of £3 10s. "My cruel landlord has put the bailiff in my house, and if my goods are sold it will be the end of me and my poor fatherless children." This appeal, which contains some of the elements of Victorian melodrama, was sent to Cardigan (who was then staying at the Bedford Hotel, Brighton) because the writer had spent her childhood on the Deene estates, and also because "your Lordship's kindness to poor ones in distress" was well known.

10

At the age of 70 Cardigan could still show well in front of the various hunts with which he rode—the Quorn, Fitzwilliam, Cottesmore, Woodland, Belvoir and (perhaps his favourite) the Pytchley. A well-known sporting character, 'Gumley' Wilson, described Cardigan as the hardest of hard riders, one who went straight as a bird, with head well up, easy and graceful in the saddle, and not to be stopped by any fence. With thirty-six hunters of his own, he entered into rivalry with the more determined of younger riders, while he took upon himself the task of preserving the hunting rights and traditions that had been established in the Northamptonshire and High Leicestershire country.

For instance, when it was suggested that a certain Mr. Watson, of Rockingham, should hunt the forest part of the Pytchley country during the season with a separate pack of hounds, Cardigan resisted the idea, saying that he would go to any lengths to prevent a woodland pack being kept. "I shall not allow any of my coverts to be drawn by the proposed hounds of Mr. Watson, and I shall consider all running through my woods as a trespass, and act accordingly."

The sporting novelist, G. J. Whyte-Melville, and Colonel Anstruther Thomson, a master of hounds, supported Watson, but they had to give up in the face of opposition from "our impracticable friend", who insisted that the Pytchley hounds were the only and proper ones to hunt the Pytchley country.

At one of his shooting parties (and Cardigan's prowess in the saddle was almost equalled by his excellence as a 'shot') Cardigan noticed that his keeper and the beaters avoided a patch of wood. He summoned the keeper and told him to 'brush up' the wood and to place guns all round it. When the keeper tried to speak Cardigan refused to listen, and repeated his order. As a result so many pheasants were shot that, when the party went home, Cardigan was in high good humour. "Why did you try to prevent me shooting through that covert?" he asked the keeper. "Well, my lord," came the reply, "that wood does not belong to you, and the owner is shooting there tomorrow."

Cardigan was a furious driver of his own four-in-hand, and he demanded to be driven at the same breakneck speed that he always maintained as 'a whip'. For ten years from 1858 his most constant post-boy was Old Bob, a bow-legged and weather-beaten product of the Midlands. A close and sympathetic under-standing existed between the two, Old Bob making light of the abuse that was hurled at him as they bowled and jolted along the roads, and Cardigan excelling himself in inventing terms that were used to express his temper.

One of their regular excursions was when Cardigan, bound for London, set out to catch the night mail-train from Leicester. He delayed starting on the 25-mile journey until the last minute, and as soon as they started Bob, mounted on the near horse, was urged to drive faster. The pace was soon killing enough for Bob, who somehow managed to keep the carriage upright as it plunged from side to side, with strong military oaths issuing from Cardigan as he was hurled from window to window.

The first stop was at the 'Falcon', Uppingham, where horses were changed, and where the landlord, who knew that Cardigan allowed only two minutes for the operation, had the horses harnessed in advance and the traces ready to be hitched on to the carriage.

A mile further on was a well-known danger spot, Wardley Hill, that postilions, aware of a sharp curve and a stream that ran half-way down, treated with respect. At this point Bob, hoping that he might be allowed to apply the brake, invariably called out, "What about Wardley Hill, my Lord?" And back would come the shouted reply, "Gallop down it, you fool! If I'm not afraid to risk my neck, you needn't mind breaking your bloody thing!"

Beyond that was a turnpike gate, and long before they reached it Bob had to "holler" at the top of his voice to warn of their approach and so prevent any delay. They arrived at Leicester station with the horses covered in a lather of sweat and panting as loudly as the engine. Cardigan dashed from the carriage, hurriedly took his ticket and threw a sovereign to Bob.

The presence of a guest, even a lady, in his carriage, did not cause Cardigan to slacken the pace of his usual mad drives. On one occasion, when Bob was ordered to prepare a carriage for Cardigan and a lady visitor, the only horses available were badly matched. One was a tall mare that stood at 16 hands, while the other was a smaller creature that, even by galloping hard, could not keep up with its companion. Bob timed their pace to suit the smaller mare, but Cardigan's head was soon popping out of the window. "Faster, Bob, faster," he urged, "or we shall get there next week."

The little mare was whipped up to do its utmost: and with its head flung back, eyes dilated and nostrils working like a bellows, it kicked up its heels so high that they kept up a lively drumming against the carriage.

Cardigan was soon at the window again. "Are you trying to smash the carriage up?" But as soon as Bob slowed down Cardigan demanded, "Are you driving two damned old cows? Faster, faster!" Their speed increased. A pile of stones stood in the road and could not be avoided; the carriage rocked over it on two wheels. As soon as he had breath enough to shout, and when he had settled his badly ruffled guest, Cardigan wanted to know where they were going. "To hell, my lord," responded the now reckless post-boy, "as hard as I can."

Cardigan might have taken a warning some years earlier, when he had a fall in the field that led to the formation of a clot of blood in the brain. He kept it a secret from his wife, though at times he suffered from a dizzy fit that resembled a kind of seizure. But although insensible of danger to himself when riding or driving, he was well aware of the risks to which others were exposed. He voiced these fears to Lady Evelyn Bruce when she proposed riding in a hunt, and offered to lend her a carriage from which she might see a great deal of the hounds in safety.

He was often preoccupied with thoughts of death—the "great change", as he called it, to which everyone is subject—and although he had seen active service, the presence of death inspired in him a profound morbid interest. An occasion of this occurred when Cardigan was riding with his wife and a friend, Henry Blackmore, to Newmarket. At one stage of the journey Blackmore, who was slightly ahead, went full tilt into a rope that, for some unexplained reason, had been stretched across the roadway. A fall on his head left him unconscious for three days, after which he died; and to Cardigan's sobering reflections was added the strange kind of fascination he felt at the sight of a dead body.

He made and destroyed several wills. His life-long habit of being careless with money, together with the extravagance of the second Lady Cardigan, had caused his estates to be heavily mortgaged, and he sometimes tried to make his wife aware of the problems likely to face her. He would ask her to be present when his agent called to discuss business, telling her, "You will have to do this by yourself some day."

But Adeline, like so many people and features of the age, was changing, developing a strongly eccentric vein that, within a few years, was to make her at first an amusing, then a ridiculous figure, a 'sight' to be wondered at by visitors to the Cardigan home. And with the passing of many characters of Cardigan's world—the Prince Consort died in 1861—it seemed that life itself, and the activities by which people live, were emerging from a crucible of unwelcome change.

At the theatre, for instance, leaders of fashion, including dukes and duchesses, no longer made a point of appearing exclusively in a box—they were frequently seen in the stalls; while once fashionable races, according to the diarist Greville, were becoming "a sort of pandemonium", where filthy and offensive tipsters bawled their offers of bets and puffed tobacco in the faces of gorgeously attired ladies.

But Cardigan, secure in a consistency that left him unafraid of being on the losing side, had the satisfaction of knowing that, as a political and a social symbol, he had at least served his caste by making a determined gesture.

II

According to Cardigan, his most valued military distinction was not the leadership of the Light Brigade at Balaclava, but his appointment to the Colonelcy of the 11th Hussars. He had formerly been Colonel of the 5th Dragoon Guards, but when the opportunity came of transferring to his old regiment it found him more than ready.

In the same year, 1860, his post as Inspector-General of Cavalry came to an end. Twelve months later he was promoted lieutenant-general, and soon afterwards he published a small volume, *Cavalry Brigade Movements*, which, as he explained in a preface, had been compiled "in consequence of the want of system and uniformity which at present exists in the Cavalry". In it he gave directions for the changing of front and positions by mounted troops, with explanations of the various signs and figures by which such changes were made—complicated manœuvres which would probably addle the brains of some who disparage Cardigan as a blockhead.

But although he had reached the age when the storms of life are generally held to be over, and with a military standing that raised him above the level of regimental rivalries, Cardigan's utter disregard of opinion, and the indifference with which he displayed it, could still make him the centre of trouble. An instance of this occurred when he was among those who attended the Prussian Army manœuvres, held on the Rhine near Düsseldorf, in September 1861.

The British party included the Prince of Wales (the future Edward VII), who was attended by General Bruce and Captain Teesdale. The behaviour of the British Staff was closely observed by a German officer, Prince Kraft zu Hohenlohe-Ingelfingen. He noted their avoidance of popular applause, their way of keeping to the back of the carriage in which they travelled. But when Cardigan arrived on the scene, the hitherto amiable relations between British and Prussian became increasingly strained.

Cardigan made it clear that he was not impressed by the Prussian Army—an army that, within a few short years, was to wrest territory from Denmark, defeat Austria, and totally humiliate France—while his bearing towards Prussian officers was judged to be so arrogant that several issued challenges and called him out.

It might have been argued that their willingness to fight a much older man made their conduct no less reprehensible than Cardigan's. But General Bruce prevented more serious embarrassment by instigating a move that, together with a little diplomatic pressure, led to Cardigan's somewhat hurried departure for home.

With the passage of time Cardigan's connection with the 11th Hussars became practically restricted to regimental dinners. At each of these occasions he and another old officer carefully avoided each other and never exchanged a word. The rest of the company understood, without always sympathizing with, that spectacle of estrangement, since the other officer was John William Reynolds, of 'black bottle' notoriety; but prior to one of these dinners (the last, in fact, that Cardigan attended) various members of the regiment decided to attempt a reconciliation between the two.

A former surgeon, who was also the senior member of the regiment as regards age, was chosen as intermediary, and he entered upon the task with a feeling of nervousness. Having established that Reynolds was in favour of the move, the ex-surgeon approached Cardigan and requested "a great favour". He then went on to explain that he had been elected, by the regiment, to ask that Cardigan might overlook old grievances and shake hands with Captain Reynolds.

Cardigan's immediate reaction was an angry one. "Quite impossible," he affirmed.

The ex-surgeon reminded Cardigan that they were no longer young. "Why carry this miserable quarrel to the grave?"

Cardigan's mood—perhaps it was influenced by mention of the grave—seemed to soften. He asked if Reynolds was ready to meet him half-way; and when he was assured that he was "only too anxious" a sign was made for Reynolds to approach.

He came forward quickly. The two men grasped hands; neither spoke.

At that moment dinner was announced, and still holding hands Reynolds and Cardigan walked into the dining-room and sat down side by side. As they did so they were back at another Mess table, where conversation reflected the pride of serving in a crack regiment, where silver and glass gave back the broken light of chandeliers, and where the shadows of a May evening, of twenty-five years ago, lengthened over the Canterbury fields and waters of the Stour.

And now Cardigan's old regiment was added to the departing embodiments of his age. He inspected the 11th Hussars, for the last time, on 5th May 1866, on the eve of their sailing for India; and this time (was his sight less keen, more mellow, or had all ranks taken the lessons of his discipline to heart?) he had only praise for the riding, the manœuvring, and the state of the horses.

"Eleventh Hussars," he said, as he faced their extended lines, "I assumed the command of you many years ago, at Cawnpore. You are now returning to that distant land. You are sure, if the occasion offers, to distinguish yourself in the field. You have my hearty good wishes. I bid you farewell, and assure you that I am proud of the honour of being your Colonel." The riders in their hussar blue, cherry-coloured overalls, and with nodding plume, receded into the distance. . . .

12

On a day in March 1868 the Pytchley hunt held one of its frequent meetings at Rockingham Castle. Cardigan was present, as usual, but he did not follow the hounds. Instead he started to return home, and on the way he met Colonel Anstruther Thomson. The Colonel was somewhat surprised when Cardigan said, "You have known me for many years"; and when the Colonel assented, Cardigan went on, "I have always been a very healthy man." He then continued, "Just now I had a fit of giddiness. I'm not well." But the failing was short-lived, and about an hour later he was back in the saddle.

On the 26th Lord and Lady Cardigan went riding with a guest, Sir Henry Edwards. Cardigan was mounted on a young restive colt, and the groom pointed out that the colt, when not with other horses, was inclined to be difficult. Cardigan, who was always ready to parry any remark that might have bearing on his horsemanship, at once said, "I suppose you think I'm too old to ride?"

But that was not in the groom's mind. Something had occurred that made him, perhaps, doubly apprehensive that morning. One of Cardigan's keepers, a young man named Bell, had been killed by the accidental explosion of a gun. On hearing this Cardigan at once postponed his ride in order to see the dead man's sister, who lived in a lodge at the head of an avenue leading to Deene.

He stayed with the dead man's sister for some time, talking to her, as she later said, with great kindness, and while there the morbid fascination inspired in him by the sight of a corpse was most marked. He moved the body and arranged the limbs to satisfy himself that the fatal shot must have been accidental. The girl watched with no little feeling of astonishment, and heard him say that he had seen many gunshot wounds, of a more ghastly kind, in the Crimea. After leaving he returned to the lodge, and had the body moved to what he considered was an appropriate position for a final inspection.

He then set off, at an easy trot, in the direction of Deene. Just before entering the village he met the local surveyor, and Cardigan complimented him on the state of the roads, saying that carriage travel was now much smoother than in the past. This must have been the very last occasion on which Cardigan spoke, for a few minutes later the surveyor, who was on foot, encountered a child coming from the direction of Deene Park.

The child caused the surveyor to stop by exclaiming, "He's

fallen from his horse." After running some way down the road the surveyor caught sight of Cardigan's horse, now riderless, making its way home; and near a pile of stones Cardigan was lying, with an arm covering his head that was bent in such a way as to be partly under his chest. He was foaming at the mouth, and his face was a bluish-leaden colour.

The surveyor hastily removed his neckerchief and tried to restore feeling by chafing hands and forehead. Meanwhile people were emerging from their nearby cottages. One went to summon a carriage. By the time it arrived the surveyor had managed to bring Cardigan to his feet and, perhaps unwisely, to support him for some hundred yards along the roadway.

But no word came from Cardigan as he was carried to his room; neither did it over the two days that he lingered, with doctors from Stamford, Weldon, King's Cliffe and even London in attendance. He died on Friday 28th March 1868, in his seventy-first year. It was generally agreed that death was caused by congestion of the brain, while it was also asked whether his horse had shied away at the heap of stones or whether the effort of bringing it under control had been responsible for the seizure.

With the mask of death settled over the "gallant handsome face" (to quote from a tribute by Whyte-Melville) the face of "a stern commander who never failed a friend", "that never hardened towards a suppliant as it never blanched before a foe", his body lay in state in the Deene ballroom.

The coffin stood on a dais, approached by two steps, in the centre. The shutters were closed, and blinds covered every window along the length of the house. The walls of the room were hung with black. Its only light came from one or two oil lamps whose dimness mingled with the flames of candles that flickered in massive candlesticks standing at each of the corners of the richly draped coffin. His peer's robes, and the regalia of his orders of knighthood, were placed upon the coffin. Also displayed on the pall were the uniform and the busby he had worn, and the sword he had carried, at Balaclava. His coronet and crest, embroidered in gold and silver thread, were shown on silken banners.

For part of those two days people to the number of two thousand passed through the room, attracted by curiosity, a liking for the trappings of death or by a genuine wish to pay respect to a hero who, mounted and riding straight in the manner of a knight, had imparted a touch of romantic fire to the popular mind.

Cardigan died at precisely 9.50 p.m. The normal hour for the sounding of the "Last Post" in regimental quarters is ten o'clock. But from then on the 11th Hussars changed the time of sounding to coincide with the moment of his death. . . . The regiment, however, together with most others of its kind, has now vanished. In 1969 it was amalgamated with the 10th Hussars, so that only a tenuous thread of survival, and that in record only, may be said to exist. Even so, the new regiment of Royal Hussars (Prince of Wales's Own) still continues the custom of sounding the "Last Post" at ten minutes before the usual hour in memory of the colonel who, many years ago, made the 11th into so perfectly disciplined and notable a body of cavalry.

13

Lady Cardigan survived her husband by a good many years, dying in May 1915 at the age of 91. There had always been an eccentric side to her character; and with his death, and as she grew older, all vestiges of restraint were cast aside. Her vanity and extravagance had increased with his notoriety, and a visit to Deene Park became as worthwhile, on account of her presence, as it was by the reputation accorded to the place by the seventh earl.

The ban imposed upon her by society had never been lifted, and she did her best to soothe her injured feelings by toying with various real or imaginary offers of marriage. According to her, she received twelve offers for her hand within five years of Cardigan's death: and her widely ranged sight eventually settled on a Portuguese, Don Antonio Manuelo, sometimes called Count de Lancastre on account of a shadowy descent he claimed from John of Gaunt, son of Edward III. She had considered an alliance with Disraeli, who was then a widower; but although such a match might have caused some of the people who turned their backs upon her to offer a smiling front, she was, on her own witness, finally 'put off' by Dizzy's putrid breath.

She kept up a kind of seedy state at Deene Park (which was once invaded by bailiffs who forced a sale of horses, carriages and clothes), at the family house in Portman Square, and at Cowes,

where, at regatta time, as evening settled down on the summer
sea, yachting parties became accustomed to the sight of a row-
ing boat in which Lady Cardigan reclined, strumming a guitar
and singing in her always musical voice.

Visitors to Deene, who were mostly hunting or racing
enthusiasts, were sometimes startled to encounter a coffin in the
ballroom. It was made for Adeline, and after the butler had
lifted and helped her into it, to make sure she would one day rest
there in comfort, the servants were summoned to see how well
she would look even when canopied by the darkness of death.

The ghostly figure of a grey nun was said to haunt Deene, and
Lady Cardigan delighted to put on the garb of the cloister and to
walk, silently and with appropriate 'floating' gestures, in and out
of a room full of guests who obliged by simulating terror and
diving under tables or behind chairs.

Sometimes she greeted visitors with her face made up like that
of an ageing demi-rep, and wearing a wig of heavy blonde curls
with a scarlet geranium behind one ear; at others she appeared in
what she called her "bicycling costume", which consisted of her
late husband's cherry-coloured overalls and blue tunic, with a
leopard skin over her shoulders. But enough of such female
vagaries. . . .

14

It was a chilly April day when the Earl's funeral procession
formed in the courtyard of Deene Park. At its head came the
valet, Matthews, whose service with Cardigan dated from the
time of Adeline's elopement and who now carried on his out-
stretched arms a crimson cushion bearing his dead master's
coronet. The band of local players dictated a solemn pace, and
black plumes waved about the coffin that was covered with
crimson velvet, on which were placed the Earl's decorations
including the insignia of the Legion of Honour.

They moved away from the great oak entrance door over
which the hatchment was hung, towards the church of St. Peter.
The pall-bearers were former officers of the 11th Hussars, one of
whom, Colonel Douglas, an old friend of Cardigan, had led the
regiment at Balaclava.

For him, time must have flowed backwards with the sense of a dead past pressing on his mind, like the weight of dead clay pressing upon his shoulder. The gentle swells of English land, rising out of the flatness, became the steeps and ridges of the implacable Crimean landscape where the ghosts of men waited, in unconquerable ranks, for the remonstrance that prophesied their doom.

Allow me to point out that the Russians have a battery in the valley on our front, and riflemen and batteries on both flanks.

All roads leading to the church were packed with people and vehicles: dog and pony carts, wagonettes, post-chaises and gigs. Many had ridden. Others had come on foot some 10 or 12 miles from outlying villages: sober countrymen and women in their Sunday black, children clutching flowers from the cottage gardens, ploughboys who had left their teams—all quiet now, their slow talk hushed, heads craning as two grooms appeared leading Ronald, richly caparisoned and moving with slow majestic steps as though fully conscious of the dignity proper to a dumb beast who had charged into the smoke of enemy guns.

Away from the Willow Brook and the beds of newly green reeds fronting the long line of the house, away from the little tower where the ever-youthful Earl had laughed with his lady loves. The bandsmen puffed their cheeks. The strains of Handel's "Dead March" mingled with the church bell and floated away over the park trees, where rooks circled protestingly about the steeple. The very grass was peopled with ghosts, line after line of dead men spurring forward, riding into a moment of time that they made immortal.

The Brigade will advance.

They were passing the coppice, where the matted branches of oak, elm and chestnut were riddled by the fresh green of opening leaves. Pigeon and blackbird soared away from the ground ivy and took refuge in the lightly stirring beech boughs. The head of the procession entered the church as the thick wedge of countryfolk wavered to a halt between the tombs and the green mounds of those who had known and served 'the family' over the years. The emblazoned escutcheon of the dead peer hung in front of the pulpit. The Bible was open at the words of St. Paul to the Corinthians, touching the change wrought by death and the transformation of the natural body into the spiritual.

16

Here goes the last of the Brudenells.

The soldiers of the 11th resigned their burden, with its past volume of vanity and irritations, peccadilloes, iron discipline, and valour that never reached breaking point. All was muffled now. The bandsmen put down their instruments. The people stood motionless, as once the Light Cavalry had stood to their horses in the growing light of a bleak October dawn. The bell was silent; the sound of footsteps on the stone floor died away.

Bibliography

Manuscripts

The Brudenell Papers

Files of the following publications between the years 1824–68:

Alligator
Brighton Gazette
Canterbury Weekly
Cork Evening Herald
Court Journal
Daily News
Dublin Evening Mail
Dublin Evening Post
Examiner
Globe
Hansard
John Bull
Kent Herald
Kentish Gazette

Limerick Chronicle
Lincoln, Rutland and
    Stamford Mercury
Morning Chronicle
Morning Post
New Weekly Dispatch
Northamptonshire Herald
Northamptonshire Mercury
Punch
Satirist
Southern Reporter
Spectator
Sussex Advertiser
The Times

Cavalry Journal, October 1939
United Services Magazine

General

Adye, Lieutenant-Colonel John, *A Review of the Crimean War* (Hurst and Blackett, 1860).

Airey, Major-General Sir Richard, *Opening Address before the Board of General Officers at Chelsea* (Murray, 1856).

Airlie, Mabel Countess of, *With the Guards We Shall Go. A Guardsman's Letters in the Crimea, 1854–5* (Hodder and Stoughton, 1933).

A Subaltern Officer, *Letters from the Crimea* (Sotheran, 1873).

Baker, B. Granville, *Old Cavalry Stations* (Heath Cranton, 1934).

Barrett, C. R. B., *History of the 13th Hussars* (2 vols., Blackwood, 1911).

Bell, Major-General Sir George, *Soldier's Glory, being Rough Notes of an Old Soldier* (2 vols., Bell, 1867).

Blake, R. L. V. ffrench, *The 17th/21st Lancers* (Hamish Hamilton, 1968).

Brakenbury, George, *The Campaign in the Crimea* (Colnaghi, 1856).

Brett-Smith, Richard, *The 11th Hussars* (Leo Cooper, 1969).

Buchanan, George, *Camp Life as seen by a Civilian* (Maclehose, 1871).

Calthorpe, Major the Hon. Somerset J. G., *Letters from Headquarters* (Murray, 1856 and 1858).

Cannon, Richard, *The 15th Hussars* (1847).

Cardigan, Lady, *My Recollections* (Eveleigh Nash, 1909).

Cardigan, Lord, *Eight Months on Active Service* (Clowes, 1855); *The Cavalry Brigade Movements* (Clowes, 1861).

Carew, Peter, *Combat and Carnival* (Constable, 1954).

Chesney, Kellow, *Crimean War Reader* (Muller, 1960).

Clifford, Henry, *Letters and Sketches from the Crimea* (Michael Joseph, 1956).

Cook, Sir Edward, *Delane of "The Times"* (Constable, 1915).

Cooper, Leonard, *British Regular Cavalry, 1644–1914* (Chapman and Hall, 1965).

Creevey, Thomas, *Papers, edited by Sir Herbert Maxwell* (Murray, 1904).

Croker, J. W., *Papers, edited by Louis J. Jennings* (Murray, 1884).

Dale, Antony, *Fashionable Brighton* (Country Life, 1947).

Danby, Paul, *The Red Army Book* (Blackie, 1904).

Daniell, David S., *The Story of the 4th Queen's Own Hussars* (Gale and Polden, 1959).

Dodd, George, *Pictorial History of the Russian War* (Chambers, 1856).

Duberly, Mrs. Henry, *Journal kept during the Russian War* (Longmans, Brown, Green and Longman, 1855); *Letters*.

Evelyn, George P., *A Diary of the Crimea* (Duckworth, 1954).

Fane, Lady Augusta, *Chit Chat* (Thornton Butterworth, 1926).

Fortescue, Sir John W., *A History of the 17th Lancers* (Macmillan, 1895); *A History of the British Army, Vol. 13* (Macmillan, 1930).

French, Lieutenant-Colonel the Hon. E. G., *Goodbye to Boot and Saddle* (Hutchinson, 1951).

Gibbs, Peter, *Crimean Blunder* (Muller, 1960); *The Battle of the Alma* (Weidenfeld and Nicolson, 1963).

Gotch, J. A., *The Old Halls and Manor Homes of Northamptonshire* (Batsford, 1936); *Squires' Homes and other old Buildings of Northamptonshire* (Batsford, 1939).

Granville, Harriet Countess of, *Letters, edited by the Hon. F. Leveson Gower, Vol. 2* (Longmans, Green, 1894).

Greville, Charles, *Memoirs, 1840-1860, edited by Lytton Strachey and Roger Fulford*, (8 vols., Macmillan, 1938).

Hamley, General Sir Edward, *The War in the Crimea* (Seeley, 1891).

Harris, John, *The Charge of the Light Brigade* (Parrish, 1965).

Hibbert, Christopher, *The Destruction of Lord Raglan* (Longmans, Green, 1961).

Higginson, General Sir George, *Seventy-One Years of a Guardsman's Life* (Murray, 1916).

Hitchcock, Lieutenant-Colonel F. C., *Nolan and Balaclava* (Cavalry Journal, 1941); "The Light Brigade at Balaclava" (*Army Quarterly*, July, 1949).

Hohenlohe-Ingelfingen, Prince Kraft zu, *Aus Meinem Leben* (Mittler, Berlin, 1905).

Humbley, W. W. W., *Journal of a Cavalry Officer including the memorable Sikh Campaign of 1845-46* (Longmans, Brown, Green and Longmans, 1854).

Jowett, Sergeant W., *Diary* (Porter, 1856).

Kelly, Mrs. T., *From the Fleet in the Fifties* (Hurst and Blackett, 1902).

Kinglake, Alexander W., *The Invasion of the Crimea* (9 vols., Blackwood, 1877–88).

Lysons, General Sir D., *The Crimean War from First to Last* (Murray, 1895).

MacMunn, Lieutenant-General Sir George, *The Crimea in Perspective* (Bell, 1935).

Mallet, Charles E., *A History of the University of Oxford, Vol. 3* (Methuen, 1927).

Mitchell, Sergeant A., *Recollections of One of the Light Brigade* (Ginder, 1885).

Murray, Major J. S. F., *A Short History of the 15th/19th Hussars* (Gale and Polden, 1935).

Murray, Reverend Robert H., *A History of the 8th King's Royal Irish Hussars* (2 vols., Heffer, 1928).

Nevill, Lady Dorothy, *Under Five Reigns* (Methuen, 1910).

Nolan, E. H., *The Illustrated History of the War against Russia* (2 vols, Virtue, 1857).

Paget, General Lord George, *The Light Cavalry Brigade in the Crimea* (Murray, 1881).

Parry, D. H., *The Death or Glory Boys* (Cassell, 1899).

Peard, Lieutenant G. S., *Narrative of a Campaign in the Crimea* (Bentley, 1855).

Pemberton, W. Baring, *Battles of the Crimean War* (Batsford, 1962).

Robinson, Assistant-Surgeon F., *Diary of the Crimean War* (Bentley, 1856).

Rogers, Colonel H. C. B., *The Mounted Troops of the British Army, 1066–1945* (Seeley Service, 1959).

'Roving Englishman', *Pictures from the Battlefields* (Routledge, 1855).

Russell, Sir William Howard, *The War in the Crimea* (Routledge, 1855); *The British Expedition to the Crimea* (Routledge, 1858); *The Great War with Russia* (Routledge, 1895).

Ryan, George, *Our Heroes of the Crimea* (Routledge, 1855); *Was Lord Cardigan a Hero at Balaclava?* (Field, 1855).

Ryder, Corporal, *Four Years' Service in India* (Burton, 1853).

Sayer, Captain, *Despatches and Papers Relative to the Campaign in the Crimea* (Harrison, 1857).

Stanton, A. H., *On Chiltern Slopes* (Blackwell, 1927).

Sterling, Lieutenant-Colonel Sir Anthony, *The Highland Brigade in the Crimea. Letters written 1854-55* (Macqueen, 1897).

Stirling, A. M. W., *William de Morgan and His Wife* (Thornton Butterworth, 1922).

Stocqueler, J. H., *A Familiar History of the British Army* (Stanford, 1871); *A Personal History of the Horse Guards* (Hurst and Blackett, 1873).

Thomson, Colonel J. Anstruther, *Eighty Years' Reminiscences, Vol. 1* (Longmans, Green, 1904).

'Thormanby', *Kings of the Hunting Field* (Hutchinson, 1899).

Tollemache, Major-General E. D. H., *The Tollemaches of Helmingham and Ham* (Cowell, 1949).

Townsend, William C., *Modern State Trials, Vol. 1* (Longmans, Brown, Green and Longmans, 1850).

Trevelyan, Sir George, *The Life and Letters of Lord Macauley* (Longmans, Green, 1881).

Tulloch, Colonel Alexander M., *The Crimean Commission and the Chelsea Board* (Harrison, 1857).

Victoria, Queen, *Letters, edited by A. C. Benson and Viscount Esher* (3 vols., Murray, 1908).

Vieth, F. H. D., *Recollections of the Crimean Campaign* (Lovell, 1907).

Vulliamy, C. E., *Crimea* (Cape, 1939).

Wake, Joan, *The Brudenells of Deene* (Cassell, 1953).

Waterfield, Private, *Memoirs, edited by Arthur Swinson and Donald Scott* (Cassell, 1968).

Watteville, Colonel H. de, *The British Soldier* (Dent, 1954).

Whitton, Lieutenant-Colonel F. E., *Service Trials and Tragedies* (Hutchinson, 1930).

Wightman, J. W., "One of the Six Hundred on the Balaclava Charge" (*Nineteenth Century*, May 1892).

Williams, Captain G. T., *Historical Records of the 11th Hussars* (Newnes, 1908).

Wilson, Colonel Townshend, *Our Veterans of 1854* (Skeet, 1859).

Windham, Lieutenant-General Sir Charles A., *Crimean Diary and Letters* (Kegan, Paul, Trench, Trubner, 1897).

Wood, General Sir Evelyn, *The Crimea in 1854 and 1894* (Chapman and Hall, 1895).

Woodham-Smith, Cecil, *The Reason Why* (Constable, 1956).

Yates, Edmund, *Recollections and Experiences* (Bentley, 1885).

Young, Brigadier Peter, *The British Army* (Kimber, 1867).

Index

249

250 **INDEX**

Brown, Lieutenant-General Sir George, 129, 189
—— Sergeant Richard, 130
Browne, Mrs., 105
Bruce, Lady Evelyn, 233
—— General, 235
Brudenell, Ann (later Lady Lucan), 18, 128
—— Sir Edmund, 15, 16
—— George, third Earl of Cardigan, 17
—— George, fourth Earl of Cardigan, 17
—— Harriet Georgina (later Lady Howe), 18, 54, 83
—— James, fifth Earl of Cardigan, 17
—— James Thomas, seventh Earl of Cardigan; ancestry, 15, 16, 17; birth, 18; at Harrow, 19, 20; as huntsman and rider, 21, 38, 231; at Christ Church, Oxford, 23, 24, 25; enters Parliament, 26, 27; European tour, 27; joins the Yeomanry, 28, 29; enters 8th Hussars, 31; discipline, 33, 45, 62, 67, 137; affair with Elizabeth Johnstone, 36; figures in Johnstone divorce case, 36; marries Elizabeth Johnstone, 37; attitude to Catholic emancipation, 39, 40; opposition to Reform Bill, 40, 41, 42; election campaign, 42, 43, 44; transfers to 15th Hussars, 45; dispute with Captain Wathen, 47, 48; at Wathen court-martial, 48, 52; relieved of command, 53; agitates for reinstatement, 53; appointed to 11th Light Dragoons, 55; controversy over his appointment, 56, 57; journey to India, 57; Indian tour, 58, 59, 60; returns to Canterbury, 60; escorts Prince Albert, 63; "Mr. Snooks" affair, 65, 66; attacked in Press, 66, 69, 76, 77, 86, 88, 101, 114, 125, 126, 197, 204, 210; "black bottle" affair, 67, 68, 69, 70; attitude to "Indian officers", 70, 71, 84, 85; dispute following Brighton party, 74, 76; duel with Captain Tuckett, 77, 78, 79; arrest after duel, 79; dispute with Lieutenant Forrest, 80, 81; appears before magistrates, 81, 82, 83; at Brighton court-martial, 83, 84, 85; reprimanded by Commander-in-Chief, 85, 113; opposition following court-martial, 86; in Drury Lane scene, 88, 89; support in Press, 90, 91, 92, 115, 126; dispute with Doctor Sandham, 92, 93, 94; trial in House of Lords, 94, 98; Sunday flogging controversy, 99; official reaction to flogging, 101; seeks Lord-Lieutenancy, 103, 226; applies for Order of the Garter, 103, 104; at Isle of Wight, 105; meets Adeline de Horsey, 105, 107; joins her in London, 107, 110; breaks with first Lady Cardigan, 110; military

duties, 110, 111, 112, 113, 120; further difference with Forrest, 113; action brought by Lord William Paget, 116, 117, 118, 119, 120; defends action of troops in Ireland, 121; on Lord-Lieutenancy of Ireland, 121, 122; prepares for active service, 124, 125; appointed to Light Brigade, 127; leaves England, 130; journey to Constantinople, 132; sails to Varna, 133; assumes independent command, 133, 137; meets Fanny Duberly, 134; entertained by Bashi-Bazouks, 134, 135; at Devna, 135; quarrels with Lucan, 138, 144, 146, 149, 151, 156, 157, 159, 168, 199; "sore-back" reconnaissance, 139, 140; opinions of, 141; at Isyteppe, 141, 142, 143; sails to the Crimea, 145; lands in the Crimea, 147; carries out reconnaissance, 148, 149; marches to the Alma, 150; skirmish at the Bulganak, 150, 151, 152; at battle of the Alma, 153; recalled from pursuit, 154; at Mackenzie's Farm, 155, 156; encamps near Balaclava, 156; quarrels with Lord George Paget, 158; indispositions, 160, 186, 188; on siege of Sebastopol, 161, 162; watches charge of Heavy Brigade, 165; difference with Captain Morris, 169; questions order to charge, 179, 171; leads charge of Light Brigade, 173, 174, 175, 176; in the Russian battery, 176; rides back from the valley, 177, 178, 179, 180; disclaims responsibility for charge, 181, 183; on field after the charge, 182; overruled on position of cavalry, 185; at Inkerman, 187; aids survivors of charge, 185, 188; applies to go home, 190; leaves the Crimea, 190; at Constantinople ball, 190; reception in England, 194, 195; at Windsor Castle, 195, 196; at Mansion House banquet, 197; appointed Inspector-General of Cavalry, 198; at Northampton reception, 199; decorations, 201; at the Crimean inquiry, 205, 206, 207; at Captain Portal's wedding, 207, 208; on duties of a cavalry general, 209, 210; dispute with Colonel Buck, 210, 211; first wife's death, 212; marriage to second Lady Cardigan, 213; continental travels, 213; confirms validity of second marriage, 215; controversy with Major Calthorpe, 216, 217, 218, 219; exonerated after action, 219, 220, 221; later life at Deene, 222, 223, 224, 225; resents ostracism of wife, 225; Queen's disapproval, 225; appeals made to him, 226, 227, 228; continued abuse, 229; method of travelling, 232, 233;